A BRIEF HISTOR ROCK

Publisher and Creative Director: Nick Wells
Commissioning Editor: Polly Prior
Art Director: Mike Spender
Layout Design: Jane Ashley
Digital Design and Production: Chris Herbert
Text Updates: Hugh Fielder

Special thanks to: Sara Robson, Jason Draper, Chelsea Edwards, Karen Fitzpatrick, Anna Groves, Jake Jackson,
Dawn Laker, Rosanna Singler, Digby Smith, Catherine Taylor and Gemma Walters

This edition is an updated version of Flame Tree Music Guides: *Rock* (2011)
FLAME TREE PUBLISHING
6 Melbray Mews, Fulham
London SW6 3NS, United Kingdom
www.flametreepublishing.com

Further information on the artists and bands in this book can be found in the curated
online music database FLAME TREE PRO at **flametreepro.com**, with comprehensive
coverage of rock, pop, jazz, blues, country, classical and opera.

This edition first published 2019

19 21 23 22 20

1 3 5 7 9 10 8 6 4 2

The CIP record for this book is available from the British Library.

ISBN: 978-1-78755-283-8

Printed in China

A BRIEF HISTORY OF ROCK

Richard Buskin, Alan Clayson, Joe Cushley, Rusty Cutchin,
Hugh Fielder, Mike Gent, Drew Heatley, Jake Kennedy, Colin Salter,
Ian Shirley and John Tobler

General Editor: Michael Heatley

FLAME TREE
PUBLISHING

CONTENTS

THE EIGHTIES

THE NINETIES

THE 21ST CENTURY

INTRODUCTION

Perhaps this introduction should start with a disclaimer. Though you are holding a guide to rock music in your hands, this book includes artists who would never use that four-letter term to identify themselves. So if you are offended by the idea of reading about Eminem as well as Pink Floyd, then please return the book to the shelf!

Music may not have changed the world in the way the peace-loving hippies of the 1960s hoped, but has certainly exerted an influence. Its multicultural, multiracial roots have encouraged acceptance of people's differences. Those differences have in turn helped make some distinctive music, and that is fully reflected in these pages.

The roots of rock music lie in black music. Just as rap has transcended the colour barrier, so it is harder than ever in the twenty-first century to place artists and their music in boxes or categories. When Run DMC and Aerosmith brought rock and rap together back in 1986 their rock-rap fusion was considered unusual; since then, careers have been built on such cross-fertilization.

Samplers also mix and match by extracting musical phrases from well-known songs and building others around them, with the result that classics have enjoyed a new life and reached a new audience. All this makes the imposition of genres more and more difficult, if not futile – hence our reliance on decades to split up the artists in these pages.

The history of popular music has been one of innovation followed by imitation – critics would say there is more of the latter than the former. Just as a guitarist will learn their instrument through playing existing songs, so these will come out sounding different to the original and perhaps suggest a new avenue of exploration.

Our Sounds & Sources articles at the beginning of each chapter are intended to join up some of the dots and suggest strands that have continued, mutated and evolved through the decades. The Early Years chapter reflects the country and blues musics that came together to form Elvis Presley's brand of rock'n'roll in the 1950s – the spark that lit the fuse for the musical and cultural explosion that followed.

The relation between black and white music gradually disappeared – disco was perhaps the first sub-genre where the identity of the artist involved was irrelevant, and that has now been followed by rave, trance and other dancefloor-aimed classifications. Rock and dance first mixed in the 1960s and the inter-relation has become more intimate in subsequent years.

The choice of Key Artists is, inevitably, a subjective one and will stir most controversy. Indeed, only the likes of The Beatles and The Rolling Stones are likely to poll unanimous approval. In an era of text-message voting and internet discussion, you will unfortunately have to live with our choices. The death of Michael Jackson in 2009 was greeted not only by grief but also by a recognition that worldwide superstars of his stature are fewer and further between these days than ever before, such is the fragmentation of the music scene. Reality television and the mad dash for fame seem to have taken over from true star quality.

Jackson's death was surrounded by mystery, and he joins a roll call of stars who died too young – one that began with Buddy Holly and continued with Hendrix and Kurt Cobain. Part of the public's fascination with the likes of Eminem and Babyshambles' Pete Doherty lies in what might be considered their seemingly self-destructive urges.

Music has always had a bearing on fashion, cinema and other aspects of popular culture. That ongoing process continues today, and has been accelerated – if not exaggerated – by the 24-hour availability of music television. Once upon a time, record purchasers might not have been certain even what race the recording artist was – now they will not only have seen them perform on the small screen but may also have digested every possible piece of personal information via the internet. The demise of Britain's TV music showcase *Top Of The Pops* in 2006 showed an era had ended: the future is still unfolding.

Ten years ago, you would have bought this book in a bookshop. Now you may have purchased it through an internet bookseller. In the same way, the means by which music is purchased has changed with the advent of the World Wide Web.

The way we listen to music has also changed. Today's consumers are as likely to listen through a computer or, if on the move, MP3 player as a stereo system, making this perhaps more of a solitary experience. Similarly, festivals seem to be ways of big acts reaching the maximum number of people through the least effort expended rather than the sense of community such efforts used to engender.

But rock music, like the world at large, is ever changing. This book's carefully researched illustrations add the all-important visual dimension, leaving you to supply your record/CD/MP3 collection to complete the total picture. With that in mind, read and enjoy!

Michael Heatley

Rock'n'roll did not spring fully formed from Memphis in the shape of Elvis Presley but was the coming together of several different roots musics. Country, jazz, doo-wop and the blues had all enjoyed significant audiences in their own right, and all would have a bearing on the sounds to come.

The music scenes across America had been local or, at best, regional. But just as the advance of radio beamed entertainment to new audiences, the migratory nature of life made American cities centres of musical change. As wartime industries demanded labour, so rural workers would bring themselves and their tastes to town. Clubs were opened to serve their leisure needs, and record labels surely followed.

The 1950s was the decade when the straitjacket imposed by the recent world war was loosened a little – and rock took full advantage. The Sun studios in Memphis and Chess Records in Chicago were the places to be as the likes of Elvis, Jerry Lee Lewis and Chuck Berry turned the existing generation gap into a chasm.

With the music publishers of Tin Pan Alley no longer controlling the writing and recording of music, teenage subjects were addressed in lyrics for the first time by rock's new songwriters. Meanwhile Britain began its rock'n'roll odyssey via skiffle, using acoustic and/or home-made instruments.

THE EARLY YEARS

THE EARLY YEARS: SOUNDS + SOURCES

The creation of rock'n'roll changed youth culture as we know it. But whether you consider the era began with Bill Haley's 'Rock Around The Clock', which reached No. 1 in the US charts in May 1955, Elvis Presley's bursting out of Sun Studios in Memphis with 'That's All Right' the previous year or his hip-swivelling to a national US audience a couple of years later, there is little doubt that when the genie came out of the bottle it would not be put back in.

MIXING IT UP

The twin musical ingredients that led to the explosion that was rock'n'roll were blues and country. The former was an urban phenomenon, or certainly became one as the black migration from the southern states to the cities grew in number. Country and western also grew in popularity to transcend its regional beginnings. A music that had been hitherto passed down the generations through the folk tradition was now reaching new audiences with the help of radio. It created national celebrities in cowboy singers like Gene Autry and Roy Rogers.

The divide between the musics was, quite simply, the colour bar. It was not usual for white youth to listen to and enjoy black or black-influenced music, nor for blacks to listen to country. Radio stations, likewise, remained exclusive, but performers like Bill Haley, with his country-music background, helped smudge the line. His inspiration was bluesman Joe Turner, who had relocated from Kansas to New York in 1939 and helped spark a boogie-woogie craze. His 'Shake, Rattle And Roll' became an early rock'n'roll anthem in Haley's hands in 1954 – Elvis Presley would succeed with Big Mama Thornton's 'Hound Dog' in 1956. Rhythm and blues had started life in the worksongs of the oppressed blacks, been refined into rural blues and then

Big Joe Turner's version of 'Shake, Rattle And Roll' was the one cleaned up to become Bill Haley and The Comets' 1950s hit.

exported to the great industrial cities of the north and west. The war effort sped up that process. The music of such now-legendary guitar and vocal performers as Big Bill Broonzy would become more widely appreciated, and the likes of the much-travelled John Lee Hooker would make a bigger mark in Detroit than in his native Mississippi. With his cherry red Gibson electric guitar, he was the archetypal urban bluesman.

BREAKING THROUGH

The blues phenomenon had largely been ignored by the major labels, so a string of independents sprung up to fill the gap: King, Chess, Aladdin, Specialty and Modern just a handful. Chess would afford Jackie Brenston the opportunity to record what was arguably the first rock'n'roll record, 'Rocket 88', in 1951. The crucial early breakthrough to the white mainstream was made by black vocal groups like The Dominoes and The Orioles, whose harmony-coated hits 'Sixty Minute Man' (1951) and 'Crying In The Chapel' (1953) appealed to a white audience. Interestingly, Bill Haley covered some of the black blues artists like Ruth Brown, whose music was initially considered too hard-edged to 'cross over'.

Louis Jordan was the James Brown of his day, the figurehead of raucous black music whose innovations included adding an electric guitar to his line-up in the mid-1940s. His influence was to be heard in later acts like Little Richard and Screamin' Jay Hawkins, while Milt Gabler, the man who produced him, went on to work with Bill Haley, taking Jordan's patented shuffle rhythm with him. Jordan notched up many entries on Billboard's 'race' chart (the name changed to R&B in 1949).

NASHVILLE TO CASHVILLE

Country music was firmly established on American radio by the 1930s, the Grand Ole Opry being broadcast across the nation from the music's spiritual home in Nashville. The Delmore Brothers hillbilly duo were the progenitors of

Louis Jordan was a charismatic 1940s band leader who, with his shuffling rhythms, made an impact on Little Richard and Bill Haley.

The Everly Brothers, drawing from gospel and Appalachian folk as did the Carter family, whose family tree would one day encompass Johnny Cash. The Delmores were also leaning increasingly towards uptempo material that reflected Western swing and boogie-woogie. By the end of 1947, they were using electric guitars and drums.

Electric instrumentation, in the hands of pioneers like Ernest Tubb, helped country music be heard in the noisy bars and juke joints where it was played live. Another variation that edged the music towards what we now term rock was Western swing, a genre synonymous with Bob Wills. His fusion of jazz and country found a ready audience of dancers. Dancing and movement would also be the major audience reaction to rock. Hard-living Hank Williams was country music's first superstar. It is astounding that he enjoyed so much success and influence in such a short life: he was only 29 when he died on New Year's Day, 1953. Yet even then the songs he wrote were already being covered by more mainstream acts, albeit in a far more refined way so that they were purveyed by the so-called 'hillbilly Shakespeare'.

LET THE GOOD TIMES ROLL

Chess Records was formed by Polish immigrant brothers Phil and Leonard Chess to promote the work of Muddy Waters, whose records they realized would sell to the audience that flocked to their Chicago nightclub. Using future Sun boss Sam Phillips as talent scout they found Howlin' Wolf, whose work, along with that of Little Walter, Bo Diddley and Chuck Berry, would influence a wave of 1960s rock bands like The Animals, Fleetwood Mac and The Rolling Stones.

While the 1930s had been the years of depression, there was now a new post-war generation of white youth unwilling to submit to the cultural straitjackets of its parents: films like 1953's *The Wild One* and James Dean's *Rebel Without A Cause* (1955) gave them their first role models, while it was when 'Rock Around The Clock' was included on the soundtrack to the film *The Blackboard Jungle* (1955) that it took off in a big way. Rationing, austerity and the recent strictures of

The walls of many of Nashville's bars are covered by the memorabilia of gigs and shows from previous decades, some dating back to the 1930s.

wartime life were anathema to this new generation. They were living in a free world, albeit one that would increasingly be overshadowed by the nuclear arms race. Why not live each day as if it were their last? When he founded Sun Studios and its retail arm, Sun Records, in Memphis, Sam Phillips had dreamed of finding a white singer who could sing the blues. If he could do this, he believed, he would break down the racial barriers that shackled black artists just as surely as they had been by their slave-masters. That man, of course, was Elvis Presley.

SHOCK AROUND THE CLOCK

The 1950s was the decade when rock'n'roll crossed the globe like a tidal wave. The music first hit Britain, where it inspired an enthusiastic reaction, then spread to the rest of the world. And if the language in which it was sung was universally English, the combination of minimal lyrics and driving beat swiftly made rock'n'roll universally acceptable. To the world's youth, that is. The powers that be immediately smelt trouble: Indonesia and Argentina were quick to ban the new music in 1957, while South Africa's regime employed troops with tear gas to stop rock fans rioting. The fact the music had emerged from black roots was, doubtless, coincidental. Germany proved a fertile breeding ground for rock. The nation that lost the Second World War was now occupied by American forces, and their tastes would help make the former Fatherland an early convert to the rock cause. Though Elvis Presley's arrival in the country on national service was in a strictly non-singing capacity, the less inhibited Little Richard was one of many regular Stateside visitors. And The Beatles would soon use Hamburg's clubs to work up their world-beating stage act.

SUN-RISE

But it was the Sun Records' studio in Memphis, Tennessee, that had been the real launch-pad for rock. Even though label founder Sam Phillips sold Elvis Presley's contract to RCA Victor to ease crippling debts and stave off the

Dancing, drinking and flirting in dance halls, the youth of the 1950s started to strike out from the austerity of their parents' generation.

immediate danger of bankruptcy, he knew even then that he had other irons in the fire – namely pianist Jerry Lee Lewis, Carl Perkins and Johnny Cash, all of whom would enjoy long and influential careers.

Bill Haley smudged the boundaries of the colour bar, playing country with a blues beat and covering blues songs with a down-home twang. But when it came to versatility Ray Charles was hard to beat. Bringing churchy call and response vocals to popular music, he would eventually veer off into country and western, proving that no material was off limits. Being both blind and black was no barrier to his towering talent … little wonder Stevie Wonder was among those hanging on his every note. By the late 1950s, however, rock'n'roll had already lost some of its shock value, with impresarios and theatre owners waking up to its money-making potential. In the US, Buddy Holly's ill-fated Winter Dance Party tour was drawing sizeable crowds, the 1,500 people at its last port of call, Clear Lake, Iowa, contrasting well with the town's population of 30,000.

THE TEEN REVOLUTION

While traditional composers had written about romance from an adult viewpoint, teenage emotions were now taking pride of place. Other topics included the twin teenage banes of parents and school, and these caught the ear and imagination of a new generation less inclined to knuckle under to authority as their parents had been. Buddy Holly was one of rock's first singer/songwriters, penning his own breathy paeans to teen life, while The Everly Brothers had the writing team of Felice and Boudleaux Bryant to lean on. Don and Phil's charming harmonies were crucial in shaping the 1960s sounds of The Beatles and Hollies, to name just two of many groups. A series of attractive US male singers emerged to service the new audience, such as Paul Anka, Ricky Nelson and Pat Boone. Television helped promote Nelson as a 'safer' version of Elvis, while Boone, the clean-cut, God-fearing boy-next-door, also starred in several teen-orientated films. Not to be outdone, Connie Francis and Brenda Lee told of romance from a female perspective.

As well as R&B, Ray Charles successfully turned his hand to a number of musical styles, including gospel, pop, country and early rock'n'roll.

THE ROCK'N'ROLL GOSPEL

Girl groups would not emerge until the following decade, but there were many doo-wop-influenced male vocal combos already out there like Dion and The Belmonts and Frankie Valli and The Four Seasons. Often drawn from immigrant Italian or Hispanic stock, they made the transition from street-corner harmonizing to the hit parade in style. Their black counterparts, like The Drifters and Coasters, successfully sanitized rhythm and blues with help from white writers Leiber and Stoller. The rock'n'roll gospel was being spread by the likes of DJ Alan Freed, instigator of a number of 'rock exploitation' movies, and Dick Clark, whose *American Bandstand* TV show, broadcast nationally from Philadelphia from 1957 onwards, was influential enough to spawn a local 'scene' from which the likes of Frankie Avalon, Fabian and Bobby Rydell sprung. All were fresh-faced Italian-American teen idols with varying degrees of natural talent. Instrumentalist Duane Eddy recorded for Philadelphia's Jamie label, proving influential with his 'twangy guitar'.

SINGLED OUT

The 78-rpm shellac record had been the standard method of sound reproduction until Columbia Records pioneered the 12-inch album, playing at 33 ⅓ rpm (revolutions per minute), in 1948. The following year, RCA offered a 45-rpm, seven-inch disc that would become known as the single. RCA also introduced the 'auto-changer', enabling several singles to be stacked over the turntable and played in succession.

Having been knocked out by Elvis Presley, Britain got off the canvas and mounted a fightback in an attempt to prove that home-grown music could stand on its own two feet. The skiffle boom, led by Lonnie Donegan, established local 'scenes' based around coffee bars. Many of Britain's most successful rock names of the late 1950s and 1960s would start their musical lives in skiffle groups, playing acoustic guitars, tea-chest bass or home-made percussion.

The flamboyant Alan Freed was the first to coin the term rock'n'roll. He championed the vital, vibrant beat of the new sound.

SINGING FOR BRITAIN

Another answer came in the shape of home-grown Elvis 'clones' like Terry Dene, Marty Wilde, Vince Eager and Dickie Pride, whose careers were launched by impresario Larry Parnes. They would enjoy brief fame before the 1960s beat boom swept everything aside. Cliff Richard was the survivor who proved the rule. Born in Lucknow, India, but raised in Britain, his 'fairy godfather' was Jack Good, a seminal figure in the development of British rock who devised the *6.5 Special* TV programme, which first aired in 1957.

Good encouraged Cliff to drop his guitar and shave off his Presley-esque sideburns, suggesting he move in a way the newspapers of the time considered 'depraved'. A slight curl of the lip proved equally popular with teens, to whom press disapproval made Cliff even more desirable. Good's new TV show, *Oh Boy!*, gave Cliff and backing group The Shadows the exposure they needed, and suddenly, after their debut in late 1958, they were on their way to stardom, courtesy of 'Move It'. But by June 1960, Cliff and The Shadows were residents at the London Palladium in an old-fashioned 'variety show', just as role model Elvis Presley would be neutered by the restrictions and conventions of Hollywood.

Billy Fury, Joe Brown and Johnny Kidd were rare examples of 'credible' British rockers. Fury and Brown (on lead guitar) combined on 'The Sound Of Fury', a fine – if belated – example of Britain trying to emulate authentic rock'n'roll. Kidd had already registered hits like 'Please Don't Touch' before 'Shakin' All Over' hit No. 1 just after the decade ended.

As far as the 1950s went, America held all the aces. But British beat, and The Beatles, would soon attempt to redress the balance.

The US led the way with the rock explosion of the 1950s but there were some notable exceptions, such as Johnny Kidd and his band in the UK.

THE EARLY YEARS: A-Z OF ARTISTS

CHUCK BERRY (GUITAR, VOCALS, 1926-2017)

Charles Edward Anderson Berry was born in St Louis, Missouri. His first hit was 'Maybellene' in 1955. 1956 saw the classic Berry composition 'Roll Over Beethoven', and 'School Day' reached No. 3 in the US and gave Berry his first UK hit. By the end of the decade his chart placings began to slip and he spent two years in jail for transporting a minor for immoral purposes. His time inside, from February 1962 to October 1963, was put to good use: studying law and writing a string of hits. In May 1964, Berry toured the UK to a tumultuous reception. In 1971, Berry released *San Francisco Dues*, his finest work for years. But Berry produced little new material in the 1970s and ended the decade in jail again on tax charges. In 1986, he was inducted into the Rock And Roll Hall Of Fame.

JOHNNY CASH (GUITAR, SINGER/SONGWRITER, 1932-2003)

Arkansas-born Cash enjoyed a 49-year-long career involving several periods of huge popularity. After USAF service, he formed a trio with Luther Perkins (guitar) and Marshall Chapman (bass). Cash played rockabilly, scoring more than 20 US country hits and several US pop hits before signing with Columbia/CBS in 1958, when he became among the biggest country music attractions, remaining with the label until 1987. Cash became an American treasure during the 1960s, particularly after recording the live albums *Folsom Prison* (1968) and *San Quentin* (1969). In 1968, he married June Carter (of The Carter Family), and they fronted a hugely popular live revue for many years. After 1976, further mainstream success seemed an impossibility, until producer Rick Rubin offered to produce him; 1994's *American Recordings* was the first of four Grammy-winning albums on Rubin's label. Cash's daughter, Rosanne, keeps the Cash name popular.

Onstage, Chuck Berry had a number of popular moves, including the famous 'duck walk'.

EDDIE COCHRAN (GUITAR, SINGER/SONGWRITER, 1938-60)

Oklahoma-born Cochran was a rising star of rock'n'roll, guest-starring in 1956's *The Girl Can't Help It*, the best ever rock movie. His lyrics spoke to teenagers, like 1958's 'Summertime Blues' (US Top 10/UK Top 20) and 1959's 'C'mon Everybody' (UK Top 10). After dying in a car crash while on tour in Britain with Gene Vincent, his UK popularity increased, with 1960's 'Three Steps To Heaven' topping the UK charts. After Presley and Holly, Cochran is probably the best-loved US rock'n'roll star in Britain. Among his other hits were 1959's 'Teenage Heaven' and 'Something Else'.

BO DIDDLEY (GUITAR, VOCALS, 1928-2008)

Born Ellas Bates in McComb, Mississippi, Bo Diddley developed his guitar skills and stage persona in Chicago. He had his first guitar by the age of 10. By 1951, at 23, he was a regular in clubs on Chicago's South Side. By 1955, he was signed to Checker, a spinoff of Chess Records. His debut single was a two-sided gem that featured his compositions 'Bo Diddley' and 'I'm A Man'. The single gave the world the 'Bo Diddley beat', a staccato rhythm that became a standard part of the rock'n'roll repertoire. Diddley's songs, like 'You Don't Love Me', 'Pretty Thing', 'Diddy Wah Diddy', 'Who Do You Love?' and 'Mona', reflect the energy and drive of early rock'n'roll.

FATS DOMINO (PIANO, SINGER/SONGWRITER, 1928-2017)

Signed to Imperial Records, New Orleans-born Antoine Domino's first million-seller, 'The Fat Man' (1949), began a run of over 60 US pop and R&B hits by 1964, many written by Domino with Dave Bartholomew. Other million-sellers included 'Ain't That A Shame' (1955), 'Bo Weevil', 'I'm In Love Again' and 'Blueberry Hill' (all 1956) and 'Whole Lotta Loving' (1958). Domino's secret appears to have been that he never changed, his smoky Louisiana accent and percussive piano-playing instantly recognizable. Twist king Ernest Evans used the name Chubby Checker in polite emulation. Domino's last US hit was a 1968 cover of 'Lady Madonna' by The Beatles, who apparently wrote the song in Domino's style. In 2005, Domino's house was destroyed by Hurricane Katrina, but he happily survived. He died of natural causes in 2017.

Influential rockabilly guitarist Eddie Cochran had a brief but prolific career.

DUANE EDDY (GUITAR, B. 1938)

With producer/co-writer Lee Hazlewood, Eddy scored 20 US hits between 1958 and 1961, showcasing his 'twangy' guitar on the Jamie label, part-owned by Hazlewood. Eddy's US Top 10 hits were 1958's 'Rebel Rouser', 1959's 'Forty Miles Of Bad Road' and 1960's 'Because They're Young'. After signing with RCA in 1962, his appeal largely left him, his biggest hit being 1962's US Top 20 '(Dance With The) Guitar Man'. After a 20-year-plus US chart absence, he returned as featured instrumentalist on a revival of his 1960 'Peter Gunn' hit by The Art Of Noise.

THE EVERLY BROTHERS (VOCAL/INSTRUMENTAL GROUP, 1957–73, 1983–2004)

Don and Phil's first success came in 1957 with 'Bye Bye Love' – No. 2 in the US, 6 in the UK. Hit followed hit: the mildly risqué 'Wake Up Little Susie' (1957), the heavenly ballad 'All I Have To Do Is Dream' (1958) and the first self-penned smash '('Til) I Kissed You' (1959). Further big sellers ensued: 'Lucille' (1960) and innovative pop epic 'Temptation' (1961). But troubles loomed. Don became reliant on drugs and then came the 'British Invasion'. Deciding to join rather than be beaten, in 1965 they recorded an album, *Two Yanks In England*, with The Hollies. But their run seemed to have ended and long-running grievances erupted, resulting in the brothers not playing together again for 10 years. It took their father's funeral to reconcile them. *The Everly Brothers' Reunion Concert* (1983) saw them back in the charts. They continued to tour and record, joining Simon and Garfunkel on their Old Friends tour in 2003 to 2004, until Phil fell ill with lung disease. He died in 2014.

BILL HALEY (GUITAR, VOCALS, 1925–81)

William John Clifton was blind in one eye and shy about his disability. Nevertheless he began performing in a series of bands. 'Crazy Man Crazy' (1952) by Bill Haley with Haley's Comets became the first charting rock'n'roll record in history, going to No. 15. In 1954 Haley recorded 'Rock Around The Clock'. The track hardly set the world alight, but the wheels of fate were turning. When the producer of *Blackboard Jungle* was looking for a song to capture the mood

The Everly Brothers' approach to harmony singing was to influence nearly every rock'n'roll group of the 1960s.

of disaffected youth, 'Rock Around The Clock' fitted the bill. When the movie came out in 1955, the track stormed to No. 1. Haley's last US hit came in late 1959 with 'Skokiaan (The South African Song)'. He spent the next years touring. Haley managed a final British gig at the Royal Variety Performance in late 1979, but he was not a well man. After a difficult illness he died on 9 February 1981.

BUDDY HOLLY (GUITAR, SINGER/SONGWRITER, 1936–59)

Buddy Holly was signed by Decca and was teamed up with guitarist Sonny Curtis, bassist Don Guess and drummer Jerry Allison. Early releases received a muted response. One day Buddy was talking about their future fame, and Allison, quoting from the recent film *The Searchers*, replied, 'That'll be the day'. This became the title of The Crickets' first hit and a US No. 1 in the summer of 1957. A string of singles followed, including 'Peggy Sue', and two of the finest albums of the era, *The Chirping Crickets* (1957) and *Buddy Holly* (1958). Buddy and The Crickets toured Britain in 1958. At their Liverpool gig were teenagers John Lennon and Paul McCartney, whose compositions rang with Holly's influence year's later. On 3 February 1959, after a gig at Clear Lake, Iowa, the plane Buddy had chartered crashed in snowy conditions, killing all on board.

JOHN LEE HOOKER (GUITAR, VOCALS, 1917–2001)

John Lee Hooker's 'Boogie Chillen' topped the R&B charts in 1948. Follow-ups included the hits 'Hobo Blues', 'Hoogie Boogie' and 'Crawling King Snake Blues'. Hooker had an enormous influence on British rock bands like The Yardbirds and The Animals, who covered his 'Boom Boom' in 1964. He had a major success with 1970's 'Hooker 'N' Heat', teaming with the band Canned Heat. He won a Grammy for the star-studded album *The Healer* in 1989.

JOHNNY AND THE HURRICANES (INSTRUMENTAL GROUP, 1958–61)

Formed in Ohio in 1958 by John Pocisk (aka Johnny Paris, saxophone), Paul Tesluk (organ), Dave Yorko (guitar), Lionel Mattice (bass) and Tony Kaye (drums, replaced by Don Staczek on 'Red River Rock' and by Bo Savich), the group accumulated nine

Buddy Holly with The Crickets, with whom he co-wrote several of his most memorable songs.

US hits between 1959 and 1961. The biggest of these was 1959's 'Red River Rock', a rocked-up version of 'Red River Valley'. The formula for their hits, most of which were dominated by Tesluk's organ, was to play well-known tunes in rock'n'roll style (e.g. 'Blue Tail Fly' became 1960's US Top 20 hit, 'Beatnik Fly'). The group disbanded in 1961, reputedly due to exhaustion from continual touring. John Pocisk, who performed until 2005, died in 2006.

B.B. KING (GUITAR, VOCALS, 1925–2015)

Riley B. King was arguably the last surviving authentic blues artist. His B.B. ('Blues Boy') epithet came from his time working at a Memphis radio station. His breakthrough recording came in 1951 with 'Three O'Clock Blues'. Albums followed: *Live And Well* and *Completely Well* (both 1959), *Live In Cook County Jail* (1971) and *Together For The First Time … Live with Bobby Bland* (1974). King continued touring until 2014 and recorded with Eric Clapton and U2, among others.

JERRY LEE LEWIS (PIANO, VOCALS, B. 1935)

After signing to Sun Records in 1957, Louisiana-born rock'n'roller Lewis, noted for his percussive piano style, opened his account with two million-selling US Top 3 hits, 'Whole Lotta Shakin' Goin' On' and 'Great Balls Of Fire' (both 1957), but caused major media controversy during a 1958 UK tour, when it was discovered that his wife (also his cousin), was only 13 years old (legal in parts of the US, unacceptable in the UK). This blighted his pop career, but from the late 1960s onwards, he combined the rockabilly that made him famous with country music, becoming a major US star with over 60 US country hits, many making the Top 10, including his chart-topping 1972 revival of 'Chantilly Lace'. Despite his hell-raising lifestyle, Lewis continued to perform into his eighties.

LITTLE RICHARD (PIANO, VOCALS, B. 1932)

Georgia-born Richard Penniman, who combines frantic vocals with uninhibited pianistics, was one of 12 children. Raised in a religious family, he started recording for RCA in 1951 after winning a talent contest. Chart success followed his

Jerry Lee Lewis performs a storming rendition of the title track in the opening scenes of the 1958 film High School Confidential.

signing with Specialty Records, where Bumps Blackwell produced a series of classic rock'n'roll tracks between 1955 and 1958, including 1955's 'Tutti Frutti', 1956's million-selling 'Long Tall Sally' and 'Rip It Up', 1957's 'Lucille' and 'Keep A Knockin'' and 1958's 'Good Golly Miss Molly', among others. While touring Australia in 1957, he abandoned the music business and later decided to study to become a preacher, only recording gospel music, but returned to the fray in the mid-1960s. He continued to perform and record into the twenty-first century, although hip and leg problems have restricted his movement since 2014.

MUDDY WATERS (GUITAR, VOCALS, 1915–83)

Born McKinley Morganfield in Mississippi, Muddy Waters was first recorded by musicologist Alan Lomax. Waters' first recording for Lomax, 'I Be's Troubled', would become his first hit when he recorded it in Chicago as 'I Can't Be Satisfied' (1948). By 1951, Waters was on the R&B charts consistently with tunes like 'Louisiana Blues' and 'Long Distance Call'. In 1952, he created the smash 'She Moves Me', and later came 'I'm Your Hoochie Coochie Man' and 'I'm Ready'. Bo Diddley borrowed a Waters beat for 'I'm a Man' in 1955, and then Waters reworked the idea into 'Mannish Boy'. In 1956, Waters had three more R&B smashes, but as rock'n'roll developed he became a blues elder statesman to followers like The Rolling Stones (named after a Waters tune), Johnny Winter and Eric Clapton. Waters continued performing to acclaim and releasing albums to mixed results into the 1980s.

ROY ORBISON (SINGER/SONGWRITER, 1936–88)

Born in Texas, high-voiced Orbison first recorded with Norman Petty, but his first US chart success was 1956's rockabilly 'Ooby Dooby' on Sun Records. After writing 'Claudette' (a 1957 hit for The Everly Brothers), he became a Nashville songwriter for Acuff-Rose, and restarted his recording career with 1960's million-selling ballad, 'Only The Lonely', setting a pattern for many later woebegone hits, including 1961's US No. 1 'Running Scared', 1964's UK No. 1 'It's Over' and US and UK No. 1 'Oh Pretty Woman'. A 1965 label change and the evolution of pop music saw his US hits end in 1967,

Roy Orbison had a unique stage presence, characterized by a passive but solid beauty.

and his UK hits in 1969, while he was beset with family tragedies. In 1988, he joined The Traveling Wilburys with George Harrison, Bob Dylan, Tom Petty and Jeff Lynne, who all held him in high esteem, but he died of a heart attack before he could take real advantage of his restored popularity.

LES PAUL (GUITAR, 1915–2009)

At 13, Lester Polfus was playing country music semi-professionally and working on sound-related inventions. In the 1930s and 1940s, he worked his way from Wisconsin to New York, eventually playing for blues shouter Georgia White and bandleader Fred Waring before settling in Hollywood and working with Bing Crosby and others. Paul also developed ideas for an electric guitar design and new recording techniques like multi-tracking. Paul's interests converged when with his wife, singer Colleen Summers (whom Paul renamed Mary Ford), he recorded several albums of standards such as 'How High The Moon' and 'Vaya Con Dios'. Both became No. 1 hits and spotlighted Paul's pioneering use of overdubbing. Les Paul's namesake guitar would become synonymous with rock, and Paul would continue performing into his 90s, achieving iconic status for his contributions to the music world.

CARL PERKINS (GUITAR, VOCALS, 1932–98)

Tennessee-born Perkins was a rockabilly pioneer. Signed to Sun Records in 1955, he is most famous for 1956's US country chart-topper/US Pop Top 3/UK Top 10 'Blue Suede Shoes'. On his way to New York for a TV appearance, Perkins was involved in a serious car crash, and a 1956 Elvis Presley cover version of the song was a million-seller. Perkins was sidelined and despite continuing to record, never again reached the US Top 50. As George Harrison was a big fan, The Beatles covered the Perkins compositions 'Honey Don't', 'Matchbox' and 'Everybody's Trying To Be My Baby', but attempts to revive his career were generally fruitless, and he played in the Johnny Cash touring show for 10 years from 1965, eventually dying of throat cancer.

Guitarist Carl Perkins as part of Sun Studio's 'Million Dollar Quartet', in 1956: l–r, Jerry Lee Lewis, Carl Perkins, Elvis Presley and Johnny Cash.

ELVIS PRESLEY (GUITAR, VOCALS, 1935-77)

Elvis Aaron Presley moved to Memphis when he was 13. In 1954 he recorded 'That's All Right', which proved an instant hit. A string of No. 1s followed, including 'Love Me Tender' (1956), from the film of the same name, and '(Let Me Be Your) Teddy Bear' from *Loving You* (1957), his first two movies. When he was demobbed from the Army in 1960, Elvis seemed to have grown up, but the good tracks were outnumbered by those from the often awful films he made. His return to form was with *How Great Thou Art* (1967). But it was a TV show, known as the 1968 *Comeback Special*, which relaunched his career. His marriage ended in 1971 and his consumption of prescription drugs increased massively. He was admitted to hospital at least three times in 1975, the year that also marked his last session in a recording studio. On 16 August 1977, he died of heart failure at his Graceland home.

CLIFF RICHARD (VOCALS, B. 1940)

Born Harry Webb in India, Cliff Richard is the ultimate British pop star, with over 100 UK hit singles to his credit since 1958, when 'Move It' (widely regarded as the first credible British rock'n'roll record), reached the UK Top 3. His more than a dozen UK No. 1s include 1959's 'Living Doll' and 'Travellin' Light', 'The Young Ones' (1962) and 'Summer Holiday' (1963), the latter both title songs of movies in which Richard starred with The Shadows, his backing group until 1968. Circa 1966, he publicly proclaimed that he was a Christian. After a number of his singles failed to chart during the 1970s, he returned in 1979 with his 11th UK No. 1, 'We Don't Talk Anymore'. More recent chart-toppers include his Christmas singles: 1988's 'Mistletoe And Wine' and 1999's 'The Millennium Prayer'. His 75th Birthday Tour in 2015 included six nights at London's Royal Albert Hall.

SCREAMIN JAY HAWKINS (VOCALS, 1929-2000)

Ohio-born ex-Golden Gloves champion boxer Jalacy Hawkins evolved a stage show in which his props included a coffin and a skull, and although he never actually achieved any hit records, his larger-than-life stage show brought him great

Screamin' Jay Hawkins had intended to become an opera singer, but a lack of success led him to a career as a singer and theatrical performer.

popularity. He also co-wrote 'I Put A Spell On You', a song which was a UK hit for Nina Simone, Alan Price (ex-The Animals) and Bryan Ferry. Hawkins was surely a role model for Screaming Lord Sutch, Arthur Brown and others.

BIG JOE TURNER (VOCALS, 1911–85)

Big Joe Turner's tenure as 'Boss of the Blues' is dominated by one song, 'Shake, Rattle And Roll', which became an early rock'n'roll anthem as recorded by white artists Bill Haley and Elvis Presley. But Turner's long career and legacy of R&B hits includes boogies like 'Roll 'Em Pete', the seminal blues of 'Cherry Red', and rollicking ribald romps like 'My Gal's A Jockey' and 'Battle Of The Blues', a duet with Wynonie Harris.

GENE VINCENT (VOCALS, 1935–71)

Virginia-born Eugene Vincent Craddock, who wore a steel leg brace after a 1953 motorcycle crash and used it as a stage prop, fronted The Blue Caps: Cliff Gallup (lead guitar), Willie Williams (rhythm guitar), Jack Neal (double bass) and Dickie Harrell (drums). Gallup's lead guitar work on Vincent's early recordings has been admired by innumerable rock'n'roll players. Vincent's classic is his 1956 debut hit, 'Be-Bop-A-Lula', which he and the Blue Caps memorably performed in the 1956 rock'n'roll movie *The Girl Can't Help It*. Sadly he suffered further injury in the 1960 car crash in Britain that killed Eddie Cochran. This led to alcohol problems, and a once-great rocker turned to country music in his last decade.

HANK WILLIAMS (SINGER/SONGWRITER, 1923–52)

Insofar as rock has been shaped by country music, it has been shaped by Hank Williams. Williams, a superstar at 25 and dead at 29, set standards for popular and country music, and was a virtual hit songwriting machine. Yet, like several young rock stars who followed him, he was unable to manage the pressures that stardom brought with it and drifted into alcoholism and addiction. Williams started out performing around his native Alabama. He landed a spot on a local radio station, and was signed to MGM Records by 1947. By 1951 his songs were being covered by the biggest

Hank Williams' songs form the mainstay of country music, and have been covered by rock and pop artists.

mainstream artists, and Hank was appearing with them on stage and television to sing hits like 'Your Cheatin' Heart' and 'Hey Good Lookin''. But his life and career collapsed after his divorce from his manager/wife Audrey, and he died in the back of his car on New Year's Eve, 1952.

SONNY BOY WILLIAMSON (HARMONICA, VOCALS, 1899–1965)

The career of Mississippi's Sonny Boy Williamson began as a case of identity theft. A 1930s delta bluesman named 'Rice' Miller had landed a starring spot on the blues radio show *King Biscuit Time*. The sponsor had Miller pose as Chicago harmonica star John Lee 'Sonny Boy' Williamson. The deception worked in rural America, and, when John Lee was murdered in 1948, Miller declared himself 'the original Sonny Boy'. Sonny Boy II had his own vocal and harp style and would prove himself one of the greatest bluesmen of all. The sides he cut for Trumpet and Chess in the 1950s showcase him at full power on signature songs like 'Eyesight To The Blind', 'Don't Start Me To Talkin'' and 'Help Me'. The early 1960s folk revival and exposure in Europe made Williamson a star there and a big influence on The Yardbirds and The Animals. Williamson always returned, however, to the *King Biscuit* show.

JACKIE WILSON (SINGER/SONGWRITER 1934–84)

Detroit-born Jackie Wilson, an ex-amateur boxer, sang with gospel groups before replacing Clyde McPhatter in Billy Ward & The Dominoes in 1953. His first solo success came with 1957's UK and US hit 'Reet Petite', co-written by Berry Gordy Jr., who went on to found Motown Records. His first US Top 40 hit was 1958's 'To Be Loved', and his first US Top 10 single was 1958's 'Lonely Teardrops', also co-written by Gordy. Wilson's dynamic stage show vastly increased his popularity, and by 1972, he had accumulated over 50 US pop hits, including 1960's 'Night' and 1967's '(Your Love Keeps Lifting Me) Higher And Higher'. By 1970, the hits had diminished, and in 1972, he suffered a massive heart attack while on stage in New Jersey, and remained hospitalized in a coma for the rest of his life. The same year, Van Morrison had a minor hit single with a tribute song titled 'Jackie Wilson Said (I'm In Heaven When You Smile)'.

The blues harmonica maestro Sonny Boy Williamson would captivate audiences with his skilful, exuberant playing..

opular music's most influential decade saw British and American rock develop in parallel, the creative torch passing across the Atlantic to The Beatles, then returning as the West Coast rock boom reflected the influence of drugs on music.

In rock, guitar was now the undisputed focus of the music with 'axe heroes' like Clapton, Hendrix, Townshend and Page all inspiring a generation of followers. Meanwhile, soul music was enjoying halcyon days thanks to the twin crucibles of Motown in Detroit and Stax in Memphis both delivering dancehall-filling music.

The recording studio itself became an instrument, being used to complement the music created and add new dimensions to it. Producers like Phil Spector and George Martin became celebrities in their own right thanks to their respective work with The Beatles and West Coast girl groups.

Of the various tribes that existed, the hippies and their ethos of 'peace and love' was the most widely reflected in music. Major festivals created a sense of community: the Monterey International Pop Festival in 1967 allowed Jimi Hendrix the chance to impress his fellow Americans. Woodstock, held two years later, entered legend thanks to a feature film, but the optimism of the era was fast evaporating even then.

THE SIXTIES

THE SIXTIES: SOUNDS + SOURCES

It was the decade that began with a whimper and ended with a bang. The 1960s saw rock not only come of age but also become the pre-eminent cultural force, its impact and importance outstripping anything the worlds of fashion, film, art and literature could muster and, in turn, informing all of them.

By 1960–61, the original rock'n'roll explosion had lost its impetus. Elvis had emerged from the US Army bound for Hollywood, while the energy and excess of Little Richard and Jerry Lee Lewis had given way to softer, more harmonious sounds from industry-created stars. But the 1960s would peak in an explosion of energy, colour and creativity that has never been equalled since, as figures like Jimi Hendrix, Janis Joplin and Mick Jagger reclaimed rock as a vibrant, fiercely anti-Establishment force.

STATESIDE INFLUENCE

Throughout the 1960s a number of scenes co-existed around the world, all of which would feed into each other to create a 'big bang' effect in youth culture. In Southern California, the surf craze owed its soundtrack to Dick Dale, Jan and Dean and, most importantly, The Beach Boys. Led by Brian Wilson, the family-based group took Chuck Berry rhythms, harmony pop and twanging guitars and moulded them into a glorious West Coast sound, which they would then develop into something more complex. Five thousand miles from sunny California, the dingy clubs of London saw young bands influenced by American jazz and blues begin to develop their own exciting style of music.

Venues such as the Flamingo Jazz Club in London were hotspots of American influence on British bands of the decade.

A crop of new groups emerged from under the wing of older players like Cyril Davies and Alexis Korner; The Rolling Stones, The Pretty Things and The Yardbirds were all heavily influenced by the primal beat and sexually explicit lyrics of old blues masters such as Bo Diddley, Muddy Waters and Howlin' Wolf.

FROM THE SOUL

But American black music did not just influence young English middle-class white boys. The decade saw the birth of soul music, a mixture of gospel and rhythm and blues that had begun to emerge in the late 1950s and would flower in the 1960s as a major force in its own right. Soul was different in the way it utilized gospel music, placing more emphasis on vocals and the way it brought together secular and religious themes. Solomon Burke's first recordings for New York's Atlantic Records perfected the soul sound in the wake of pioneers like James Brown, Ray Charles and Sam Cooke. But it was Stax Records in Memphis that became synonymous with the term.

Stax issued hit records by Otis Redding, Wilson Pickett and Joe Tex and by their house band Booker T and The MGs – though they were later rivalled by a run of fabulous singles by the Queen of Soul, Aretha Franklin, for Atlantic. The Memphis scene was further enhanced by the Muscle Shoals studio in the neighbouring town of Florence, Alabama, a hotbed of musical activity. The studio enjoyed a close relationship with Stax and it was from here that many of the label's later hits emerged. Not all black music emerged from a 'stable', as the maverick Sly Stone showed with his multi-gender, multi-racial band The Family Stone.

But arguably the most successful black music concern of the decade was Tamla Motown. Set up by Berry Gordy Jr. in 1959 with a loan of $8,000, Motown was more than just another record label – Gordy's dream was to produce music from the ghetto with a dance beat that would become mainstream, with its own unique sound. Taking its

Berry Gordy's Motown label created an astonishing stable of stars that toured together and recorded the soul soundtrack of the 1960s.

UPTOWN   UPTOWN

THE MIRACLES · MARY WELLS
MARVELETTES
THE CONTOURS MARTHA & THE VANDELLAS
MARVIN GAYE   THE SUPREMES
BILL MURRAY   CHOKER CAMPBELL ORCH

THE MIRACLES · MARY WELLS
MARVELETTES
THE CONTOURS MARTHA & THE VANDELLAS
MARVIN GAYE   THE SUPREMES
BILL MURRAY   CHOKER CAMPBELL ORCH

name from a Debbie Reynolds film, *Tammy*, and Motor Town – Detroit was the home of Ford Motors – Gordy got lucky when he hooked up with a group called The Miracles. It was their lead singer Smokey Robinson (later Gordy's number two) who persuaded him to press and distribute his own records. Gordy never looked back as Motown became a studio and, using one of the most successful songwriting teams ever created worldwide hits for the likes of The Supremes, The Four Tops, Martha and The Vandellas, Marvin Gaye and The Temptations. Another name, Stevie Wonder, would mature from teen sensation to mature genius over the years to come and would remain with Motown – on his own terms – into the next millennium.

THE FAB FOUR

But there was one band and one city in particular that stamped their mark indelibly on the world at large and fired the public imagination – four lads from Liverpool by the name of The Beatles. Their influence on pop and rock was all-encompassing. Over the course of the decade The Fab Four, as they were christened by an eager press, were to prove that there was longevity in the pop phenomenon. Groomed by manager Brian Epstein, the quartet quickly graduated from the clubs of Hamburg's notorious Reeperbahn to the world's living rooms, attracting not just a teenage audience but also a family one as their records gate-crashed the Top 10 on both sides of the Atlantic. They created a pop catalogue that remains unrivalled today, their tunes discussed in detail by serious music critics.

Just as The Beatles crossed international boundaries, their home town of Liverpool and the club that launched them, the Cavern, momentarily became the epicentres of the pop world. Fellow Liverpool acts such as The Searchers, Gerry and The Pacemakers and The Swinging Blue Jeans led the way, and most of the big cities in the UK would be rocked by the ensuing beat boom. Every youngster wanted to play the guitar, it seemed, and a crop of regional heroes soon emerged. Manchester provided the likes of The Hollies, Herman's Hermits and Freddie and The Dreamers, Newcastle's

contribution was the tougher sound of The Animals, whilst Birmingham's wake-up call brought out such bands as The Move and The Moody Blues, acts that would go on to play a prominent part in the 1970s rock scene.

THE MODS AND THE ROCKERS

Black music was popular with an emergent youth cult in Britain known as the Mods, a rebellious group of young men and women who favoured the latest fashions from the Carnaby Street and Swinging London scenes, amphetamines and motor scooters (as opposed to their arch-rivals the Rockers whose predilection was for old-style leather jackets and motorbikes). The seaside towns of the English south coast became the backdrop for skirmishes between the two groups.

Out of mod culture would emerge some of the greatest English rock bands of all time, notably The Who, The Small Faces and The Kinks, who would meld their early rhythm and blues influences with a peculiarly British style that owed a lot to the old music-hall tradition to write sublime songs that perfectly defined the mood and character of the country. In turn, these bands would head off to the US to find varying degrees of fame and fortune. Known as the British Invasion, they became the ambassadors of a new youth culture and were welcomed with open arms by an equally dissatisfied American youth looking for a change of values and lifestyle.

THE BEAT GOES ON

One of the most fertile home-grown scenes in the US in the early part of the decade was the folk movement, whose home was in the bohemian area of New York City. Greenwich Village had long been a centre for arty types, especially from the 1950s onwards when the beat poets like Allen Ginsberg and Jack Kerouac rose to prominence.

Carnaby Street, in London's West End, became the focus of fashionable youth ready to experiment with style, music and drugs.

In the early 1960s, it was home to the beatniks – anybody who wanted to play guitar and sing like the great Woody Guthrie or Leadbelly and who was influenced by the burgeoning civil rights movement.

Many talented singer/songwriters came out of the coffee houses and folk clubs along Bleeker Street – but all were overshadowed by the 1960s' greatest spokesman, Bob Dylan. The former Robert Zimmerman took his direction from Woody Guthrie and Charley Patten and shaped his very own musical vision, one initially caught up in the civil rights movement but which quickly developed into a poetic vision, as much like his namesake Dylan Thomas or Baudelaire as it was Guthrie. Dylan had already issued a number of recordings by the time The Beatles and the Stones were making their presence felt on his side of the Atlantic, and many young American kids were picking up on both Dylan's articulate, very relevant songs and the punchy beat of the Brits none more so than Jim McGuinn, Gene Clarke and David Crosby, three young men in Los Angeles whose vision was to take folk music and merge it with the new sound of electric guitars.

The Byrds' first single, a version of Dylan's 'Mr Tambourine Man', released in early summer of 1965, started off the folk rock phenomenon; there were many imitators like Sonny and Cher and Barry McGuire, but over the next few years McGuinn and company would become one of the most influential groups in the history of rock as they experimented with jazz, Indian music, electronics and country.

FAR OUT

The all-out revolution in American popular music that followed not only drew on different traditional forms, but was also inspired by the prevailing political climate such as the escalating war in Vietnam and by the advent of a new 'wonder drug', LSD. The music's epicentre swung from Liverpool back to America and to another city by the sea,

The light shows pioneered by Jefferson Airplane reflected the drug-enhanced experience of 1960s culture.

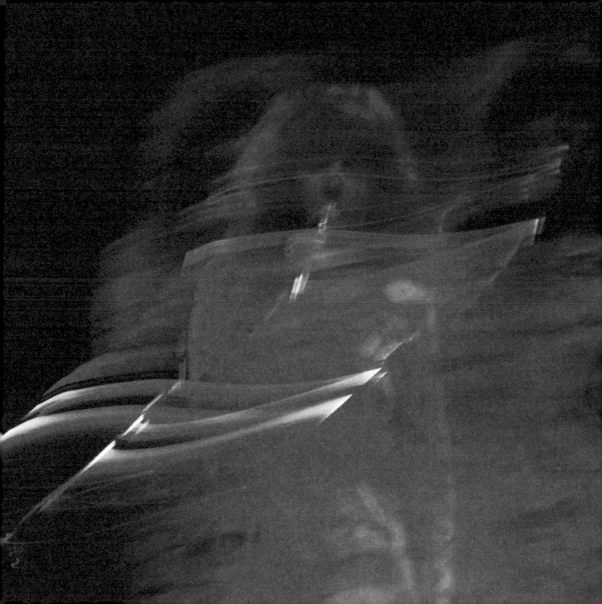

San Francisco. A place with strong bohemian traditions, Frisco was a liberal town and it was there that novelist Ken Kesey – who had undergone tests by the US government for a mind-expanding drug called lysergic acid and found it beneficial – staged the first 'Acid Tests' with his troupe, The Merry Pranksters.

LSD, as it became known, quickly caught on, especially amongst young kids living there who were smitten with the folk rock boom happening down the coast in Los Angeles and eager to plug in. Bands like The Beau Brummels and The Charlatans were the first acts around the city to play a form of electric folk, but it was a second wave that captured the imagination of the media at large.

A notable success was Jefferson Airplane who took folk-rock on to its next stage, bringing folk, blues and elements of pop together with the kind of improvizational ability enjoyed by jazz players such as John Coltrane and Miles Davis. They were soon at the heart of a new scene joined by fellow locals Country Joe and The Fish, Quicksilver Messenger Service, Big Brother and The Holding Company, Moby Grape and The Grateful Dead. If their LA counterparts like Love, Spirit and The Doors excelled at making the most of the studio environment, the San Francisco bands were at their best when they took off on long, spacey explorations, jamming on numbers often over half an hour in length. It was all a far cry from the two-and-a-half-minute pop songs of earlier in the decade.

THE SUMMER OF LOVE

By 1967, the San Francisco sound had become the backdrop to the Summer of Love. Kids across the planet rejected their parents' values and joined together to grow their hair long and espouse brotherly love instead of supporting the expansionist war the Americans were fighting in south-east Asia. The hippie movement had arrived. Indeed, by the

Country Joe and The Fish specialized in rambling jams rather than three-minute pop songs.

middle of the decade rock was developing at a rate never witnessed before or since. Dylan went electric, alienating some of his more traditional fans, while The Beatles quit touring, left their army of screaming devotees behind and concentrated on composition and working in the studio, capturing the *zeitgeist* with *Sgt. Pepper's Lonely Hearts Club Band* (1967). The same year, 1967, saw Lou Reed's Velvet Underground cut their own eponymous art rock masterpiece in New York under the aegis of Pop Art guru Andy Warhol.

At the same time that San Franciscans were experimenting with new sounds, attempting to simulate the sounds of a drug 'trip' with their music, their British counterparts were also undergoing a complete sea change. Guitar technology in particular was improving constantly with bigger, better and louder amplification coming on to the scene. This was the era of the fuzz box, the wah-wah pedal and the Marshall stack, which were embraced by a new breed of British guitarist like Jeff Beck, Eric Clapton and Jimmy Page.

AN ELECTRIC REVOLUTION

The revolution in electric guitar-playing was about to be kick-started by the arrival in London in autumn 1966 of a young black musician, Jimi Hendrix, who took the sound of blues guitar out of the Mississippi delta and launched it into space. Writing tunes that combined LSD-inspired lyrics with other-worldly sounds from his guitar (often achieved by means of feedback), Jimi and his band The Experience were the children of a new tomorrow. During the few short years he was alive, Hendrix became one of the most influential figures in rock.

New types of club sprang up to cater for the new music and the new audience: the grubby little venues that had been such a feature of the beat era were replaced by more elaborate environments such as the Avalon and Fillmore ballrooms in the US and places like the UFO club in London. One feature of these venues never before witnessed

The 1960s ended with a blaze of psychedelic colour, expressed through the intense music and fantastic light shows at ever more elaborate gigs.

was the advent of the light show, where all kinds of images were projected behind the musicians and often on to the audiences in an attempt to recreate the effects of LSD.

One band that pioneered the mixed-media concept and took rock off in yet another direction was Cambridge's Pink Floyd. Led by Syd Barrett, a talented songwriter who took the band into the singles charts, the group's forte was long spacey numbers like 'Interstellar Overdrive', which combined electronics with ethereal keyboard sounds, drones and pounding drums and atonal guitar licks to create a 'far-out' psychedelic effect. Rock began to look to the avant-garde for inspiration and bands like The Soft Machine, Frank Zappa's Mothers Of Invention and Captain Beefheart and His Magic Band became the order of the day.

NEW VIBRATIONS

Rock as a cultural phenomenon was now separating from 'pop'. The grip of Tin Pan Alley had been loosened and bands were now, for the most part, writing their own material. Groups like The Tremeloes in the UK and The Ohio Express in the US still filled the Top 20, as did the 'made-for-TV' Monkees, but many musicians who had started their careers as chart bands were now taking music in a direction never before dreamt of. The 45-rpm single was no longer perceived as the most important medium by which to reach the public – the long-playing (LP) album now held sway. The Beatles and Cream used their pre-eminent position to release double albums, while The Who, whose Pete Townshend had created many classic three-minute singles, was now attempting to break new ground with their epic rock opera *Tommy* (1969).

The sleeves in which records were clothed became almost as important as the music itself. In the States, Rick Griffin's mind-blowing artwork graced the sleeves of LPs by The Grateful Dead; rising underground cartoonist Robert Crumb

The decade's spirit of exploration and experimentation was reflected in both the music and on the cover: Cream's Disraeli Gears (1967).

designed the cover for Big Brother's *Cheap Thrills* (1968), while in the UK Martin Sharp's day-glo designs decorated sleeves for Cream. Tired of screaming girls who did not listen to the music anyway, The Small Faces released one of the most evocative records of the time and arguably the first concept LP, *Ogden's Nut Gone Flake* (1968), in a circular sleeve – then promptly split up in a bid to be taken more seriously!

THE END OF THE LOVE-iN?

The late 1960s saw live music events grow in size as hundreds of thousands of fans got together in tribal gatherings: the Human Be-In in San Francisco and Monterey Pop further down the coast. There were the big Isle of Wight Festivals, free concerts in Hyde Park and, biggest of all, the Woodstock Festival in upstate New York in the summer of 1969. Yet despite all the optimism and figures like John Lennon and Jim Morrison speaking out for the love generation, the 1960s ended on a sour note with The Beatles in disarray, a disillusioned Dylan making a country and western album, and a death at the Altamont Festival when Hell's Angels security guards clashed with an audience member.

After the excesses of psychedelia came a return to roots by musicians on both sides of the Atlantic, all of whom were influenced by the likes of The Byrds' *Sweetheart Of The Rodeo* (1968), The Band's *Music From Big Pink* (1968) and Fairport Convention's *Liege And Lief* (1969). In fact the biggest-selling rock bands in 1969 included California's Creedence Clearwater Revival with their evocative songs extolling simple American values; and Fleetwood Mac, a British quintet who had weathered the blues boom of the previous year to forge a style that encompassed not only blues but folk, classical and the San Franciscan love of extemporization.

The 1960s had been a decade that had achieved so much but, as the 1970s dawned, excess, disillusionment and death replaced the celebration of life and its vibrant spirit. The pendulum was swinging once again….

Woodstock in New York – the most memorable of 1960s festivals – featured Jimi Hendrix, The Who and Crosby, Stills, Nash & Young.

THE SIXTIES: KEY ARTISTS

THE BEACH BOYS (VOCAL/INSTRUMENTAL GROUP, 1961-PRESENT)

Fifties' vocal outfits were the inspiration for Brian Wilson to form his own group – consisting of brothers Brian, Dennis and Carl, cousin Mike Love and Brian's high school friend Al Jardine – and write songs largely built around five-part harmonies. Dennis's love of surfing provided the starting point for the lyrics. The Beach Boys' first release, 'Surfin'' (1961) helped secure a contract with Capitol Records. Their first album, *Surfin' Safari* (1962), and title track ignited the surf-rock craze. Through 1964, they held their own against Beatlemania, courtesy of a string of infectious hits – 'I Get Around' and 'Dance, Dance, Dance' – and beautifully produced tracks like 'Don't Worry Baby', 'The Warmth Of The Sun' and 'All Summer Long'. Brian suffered a nervous breakdown and quit the road. Multi-instrumentalist Bruce Johnston took his place; Brian focused on songwriting.

COMPETING WITH THE BEATLES

Awed and inspired by The Beatles' *Rubber Soul* (1965), Brian took it upon himself to outdo the Fab Four. *Pet Sounds* (1966) contains some of his best material. In summer 1966, in answer to the acid-induced *Revolver*, Brian embarked on a drug-fuelled mission to create an avant-pop masterpiece. The results were fragmented and disjointed, and Brian shelved the project. The group's career has been similarly disjointed since. They have released albums with and without Brian, who remains mentally fragile. Love and Johnstone tour under the Beach Boys' name. Dennis Wilson drowned in 1983, and Carl Wilson died of cancer in 1998. The surviving members reunited for a tour in 2012 and Brian Wilson occasionally tours his 'long lost' masterpiece, *Smile*.

Beach Boys fever began in 1963 when 'Surfin' USA' made the Top 10 in the US.

THE BEATLES (VOCAL/INSTRUMENTAL GROUP, 1960-70)

Consisting of John Lennon on rhythm guitar, Paul McCartney on bass, George Harrison on lead guitar and Ringo Starr on drums, The Beatles evolved from Lennon's skiffle group The Quarry Men to become the most successful and influential act in the history of popular music. Just as the skiffle craze was dying down, Lennon's band received a boost via his recruitment of McCartney, and the subsequent departure of its less talented members. In 1958 Harrison joined the fold and in 1960, during an extended club engagement in Hamburg, West Germany, Pete Best joined as drummer. It was in Hamburg that The Beatles really came of age, fusing as a unit during long, gruelling sessions on stage. On their return to Liverpool, they acquired a new manager, Brian Epstein who approached EMI's small Parlophone label, run by George Martin. Martin signed The Beatles and both parties would never look back. Except it was to be the end of the road for Best, who was replaced by Ringo Starr.

BEATLEMANIA AND BEYOND

The Lennon/McCartney songwriting partnership, now that it had a record company demanding new material, went into another gear, producing songs of incredible range and increasing sophistication, from the infectious 'Please Please Me', 'She Loves You' and 'I Want To Hold Your Hand' that led to Beatlemania in the UK, to hits such as 'A Hard Day's Night' and 'Can't Buy Me Love' that saw them conquer the rest of the world during the halcyon year of 1964. As Beatlemania ran its course, the group withdrew to the studios on Abbey Road. Between 1966 and 1969, they produced recordings of breathtaking scope, imagination and musical and lyrical sophistication. From the albums *Revolver* (1966), *Sgt. Pepper's Lonely Hearts Club Band* (1967) and *The White Album* (1968) to landmark singles like 'Eleanor Rigby' and 'Strawberry Fields Forever', The Beatles created a body of work that, more than 35 years after the band's demise, still has a solid grip on the mass consciousness.

The Beatles' catchy songs and loveable marketability opened the doors for a new era of British pop music.

BOB DYLAN (GUITAR, HARMONICA, SINGER/SONGWRITER, B. 1941)

Born Robert Allen Zimmerman, Bob Dylan learned to play guitar and harmonica as a child while influenced by radio broadcasts of country, blues and, during his mid-teens, rock'n'roll. Quitting college at the end of his freshman year to become a full-time musician, he decided to head for New York City, where gigs brought him to the attention of Columbia Records and led to the release of his eponymous debut album in 1962. *The Freewheelin' Bob Dylan* was released the next year, containing two songs of protest ('Blowin' In The Wind' and 'A Hard Rain's A-Gonna Fall'). Given the political climate of the times, they brought Dylan's name to everyone's attention. *The Times They Are A-Changin'* (1964) continued the cycle of protest songs, its outstanding title track sounding a warning to parents and politicians about the crumbling status quo.

BROADENED APPEAL

Bringing It All Back Home (1965) projected Dylan into the pop mainstream, its first side featuring the main man backed by a heavily amplified five-piece band. He secured a massive worldwide audience with his breakthrough single, 'Like A Rolling Stone', which peaked at No. 2 on the US charts. Lyrically, Dylan was now a streetwise beat poet, and this was an image that he would stick with, reaching its apotheosis on arguably his finest record, the double album *Blonde On Blonde* (1966). Although 1970's *Self Portrait* incited the first uniformly critical drubbing of Dylan's career, the new decade saw him sustain a fairly high degree of success.

Since 1988, Dylan has fronted what has come to be known as his 'Never Ending Tour' of the globe, while returning to form in the studio. *Together Through Life* hit the top slot on both sides of the Atlantic in 2009, making him the oldest living person to go straight into the chart at No. 1.

Bob Dylan's contribution to music is immeasurable. 'Like A Rolling Stone' was named the No. 1 song of all time by Rolling Stone *magazine.*

JIMI HENDRIX (GUITAR, VOCALS, 1942–70)

The left-handed Johnny Allen Hendrix taught himself to play guitar while drawing on blues influences such as Robert Johnson, Howlin' Wolf, Muddy Waters, T-Bone Walker and B.B. King. He began working as a session guitarist with the soul/R&B likes of Sam Cooke, King Curtis, Ike and Tina Turner and Little Richard. Hendrix then opted to switch from sideman to lead guitarist in his own band, Jimmy James and The Blue Flames. Playing gigs around New York City's Greenwich Village throughout late 1965 and much of 1966, Hendrix was spotted by Animals' bassist Chas Chandler who persuaded him to relocate to London, which at that time represented the centre of the creative/cultural universe.

INSTANT FAME

It was in London that The Jimi Hendrix Experience was created, with guitarist Noel Redding on bass and Mitch Mitchell on drums. Within weeks, the trio's performances were creating a major buzz on the London scene, and they also hit the UK Top 10 with the singles 'Hey Joe', 'Purple Haze' and 'The Wind Cries Mary', all from Hendrix's outstanding debut album *Are You Experienced?* (1967). This record, together with his sensational appearance at the Monterey Pop Festival in June 1967, made him a superstar in his home country as well as overseas, just nine months after he had left. Onstage the innately shy Hendrix ignited audiences with his breathtaking musicianship and willingness to put on a show, featuring such antics as setting fire to his guitar.

In June 1969, Hendrix folded The Experience and formed Band Of Gypsies with Billy Cox on bass and Buddy Miles on drums. This was the trio that appeared at Woodstock, where Hendrix's erratic performance was salvaged by his unforgettable and then-controversial rendition of 'The Star Spangled Banner'. The Jimi Hendrix Experience was briefly reformed in early 1970 until Hendrix's death in London from drugs-related causes on 18 September of that year.

Jimi Hendrix the 'semi-demigod', as described by Life magazine.

THE ROLLING STONES (VOCAL/INSTRUMENTAL GROUP, 1962–PRESENT)

Having first met at school, Mick Jagger and Keith Richards were reintroduced to one another at the start of the 1960s by a mutual friend. A high school dropout with a passion for jazz and the blues, Brian Jones was trying to form a band of his own when he met and recruited Jagger and Richards. Bill Wyman was drafted in shortly after, reportedly because he had his own amplifier. Jazz aficionado Charlie Watts completed the line-up. The Stones cultivated a bad-boy image, which did their popularity no harm. 1964 saw the band enjoy UK chart-topping success with covers of 'It's All Over Now' and 'Little Red Rooster'. In 1965, they released the worldwide smash that would become their anthem, '(I Can't Get No) Satisfaction', as well as the chart-topping 'Get Off Of My Cloud'.

EXPERIMENTATION AND TRAGEDY

Experimentation reared its head in *Aftermath* (1966) and *Between The Buttons* (1967), but The Stones returned to crowd-pleasing form with 'Jumpin' Jack Flash' and the *Beggar's Banquet* LP (both 1968). Behind the scenes, however, all was not well. Jones' chronic drug addiction led to him officially quitting the band in 1969 – in actual fact he was fired – and Mick Taylor replaced him. Just over three weeks later Jones was found dead in his swimming pool. Jagger's immersion in the jet-set lifestyle and Richards' retreat into his own drug-induced nightmare increased tensions in the band. Taylor left the group in 1974 and Bill Wyman departed in 1991.

Despite Jagger's assertion that he would 'rather be dead than singing 'Satisfaction' when I'm forty-five,' he continues to break that pledge, as evidenced by mid-period and later albums like *Some Girls* (1978), *Tattoo You* (1981), *Steel Wheels* (1989), *Voodoo Lounge* (1994) and *A Bigger Bang* (2005). In 2016 they went back to their blues roots on their *Blue & Lonesome* album. Their 2018 world tour was the biggest grossing tour of that year.

Inspired by the likes of Muddy Waters, The Rolling Stones started out playing covers of blues songs, which were largely unknown in Britain.

THE WHO [VOCAL/INSTRUMENTAL GROUP, 1964–82, 1989, 1996–PRESENT]

Originally comprising Pete Townshend on guitar, Roger Daltrey on vocals, John Entwistle on bass and Keith Moon on drums, The Who virtually exploded onto the mid-1960s scene in a blaze of power rock that placed them at the forefront of the mod movement. A contract with Decca Records yielded the UK hit singles 'I Can't Explain', 'Anyway, Anyhow, Anywhere' and 'My Generation'. The last of these featured Daltrey alternately stuttering and belting out Townshend's lyrics, and included the anthemic wreckless-youth line, 'I hope I die before I get old'. Onstage this message was reinforced not only by Townshend's guitar-smashing antics, but also by Moon regularly demolishing his kit. This unbridled energy and success continued into 1966 with 'Substitute'.

NEO-CLASSICAL ROCK

In 1967, the band achieved American success when 'Happy Jack' cracked the Top 40 and 'I Can See For Miles' made the Top 10. The Who had finally arrived, yet the mod movement was winding down, prompting Townshend to regroup and compose what many consider to be his masterpiece, the rock opera *Tommy* (1969). Thereafter, The Who would not find it easy to live up to *Tommy*'s reputation, although the band still enjoyed considerable success with further hit singles and acclaimed albums such as *Who's Next* (1971), *Quadrophenia* (1973) and *Who Are You* (1978). The latter turned out to be its last outing with Moon, whose famously debauched sex, drugs and rock'n'roll lifestyle caught up with him at the age of just 31.

And although there would be more recordings and numerous tours with others filling Moon's larger-than-life shoes – even stretching beyond Entwistle's death in 2002 to the present – Townshend, Daltrey and Entwistle would subsequently concede that The Who really died along with its enigmatic, manically virtuosic drummer.

Although they later moved into rock territory, The Who was originally marketed as a mod band.

THE SIXTIES: A-Z OF ARTISTS

THE ANIMALS (VOCAL/INSTRUMENTAL GROUP, 1962-66)

After the million-selling 'House Of The Rising Sun' in 1964, Tyneside's Eric Burdon (vocals), Hilton Valentine (guitar), Alan Price (keyboards), Chas Chandler (bass) and John Steel (drums) racked up further international smashes and by 1965, music press popularity polls had them breathing down the necks of The Beatles and The Rolling Stones. Price then left to pursue a solo career and was replaced by Dave Rowberry from The Mike Cotton Sound. It was business as usual for The Animals until they disbanded after 1966's 'Don't Bring Me Down'. The old line-up reassembled for periodic reunion concerts and for two albums: 1976's *Before We Were So Rudely Interrupted* and, more notably, *Ark* in 1983, which they promoted – along with a re-released 'House Of The Rising Sun' – on a world tour.

THE BAND (VOCAL/INSTRUMENTAL GROUP, 1968-76)

1968's *Music From Big Pink* was, like most subsequent Band albums, a true blend of electric folklore nurtured over rough nights with rock'n'roller Ronnie Hawkins before Robbie Robertson (guitar), Richard Manuel (piano, vocals), Rick Danko (bass), Garth Hudson (organ, saxophone) and Levon Helm (drums) landed a job backing Bob Dylan, who would be in an all-star cast at *The Last Waltz*, a 1976 concert film that marked The Band's farewell to the road..

BLIND FAITH (VOCAL/INSTRUMENTAL GROUP, 1969)

Billed as 'the supergroup of all times', Steve Winwood (keyboards, vocals), Eric Clapton (guitar), Rick Grech (bass) and Ginger Baker (drums) were an amalgam of ex-members of Cream, Traffic and Family. Launched with a free concert in London's Hyde Park, they broke up after a troubled US tour. Winwood then reformed a Traffic that was to recruit Grech in 1970, while Clapton recorded a solo album and Baker formed the percussion-heavy Airforce.

Known for their gritty, bluesy sound, The Animals became a leading exponent of the 1960s psychedelic music scene.

BLOOD, SWEAT AND TEARS (VOCAL/INSTRUMENTAL GROUP, 1967–PRESENT)

They were the most famous rock equivalent of a 'brass band' – founder member Al Kooper's own description. With a sensational horn section always high in the mix, 1968's *Child Is Father To The Man* established them as a musicianly act that was to serve as a role model for Colosseum and The Average White Band and the more sophisticated US jazz rock of Weather Report and Return To Forever. The group survived Kooper's exit later that year by adopting a more mainstream approach, chiefly via the recruitment of David Clayton-Thomas, a singer of aggressively masculine bent, who dominated a million-selling second LP, *Blood, Sweat And Tears*. Four more hits followed, but the outfit proved incapable of major commercial recovery after 1971's 'Go Down Gamblin''. Over 150 members have passed through the group over the years.

BOOKER T AND THE MGS (VOCAL/INSTRUMENTAL GROUP, 1962–71)

Stax Records' house band, Booker T also toured and recorded instrumentals in their own right. More than any other group they defined the sound of 1960s soul with their sparse, funky arrangements. Booker T. Jones, Stax' sax and organ prodigy, formed The MGs (Memphis Group) with Steve Cropper (guitar), Donald 'Duck' Dunn (bass, replacing Lewis Steinberg) and Al Jackson Jr. (drums). Their first release, 1963's 'Green Onions' was a US No. 3, eventually charting at No. 7 in the UK on its re-release. Their 1968 hit 'Soul Limbo' is the BBC's TV cricket theme. Victims of their own success, they split in 1971 because of the demand for their individual services as ace sessioneers.

TIM BUCKLEY (GUITAR, VOCALS, 1947–75)

As one of a bohemian clique of singer/songwriters in mid-1960s New York, Buckley developed a style of *de rigueur* melancholy introspection that was jazzier and more daring than most. However, after 1970's transitional *Blue Afternoon*, offerings like *Lorca* and *Starsailor* were virtually free-form. Buckley died of a heroin overdose, leaving son Jeff to posterity.

Blood, Sweat and Tears had massive success with their 1969 album – it spent two years in the US charts, seven weeks of which were at No. 1.

BUFFALO SPRINGFIELD (VOCAL/INSTRUMENTAL GROUP, 1966–68)

Migrating from New York to Los Angeles, Steve Stills and Richie Furey rehearsed with a third singing guitarist, Canadian Neil Young, who recommended Bruce Palmer (bass) and Dewey Martin (drums). 1967's *Buffalo Springfield* was remarkable for an acoustic bias and clever vocal harmonies. A hit single, 'For What It's Worth', and healthy sales for two further albums did not forestall a rancourous split – though two of the members were to form half of Crosby, Stills, Nash and Young.

THE BYRDS (VOCAL/INSTRUMENTAL GROUP, 1964–73)

Jim (later Roger) McGuinn, David Crosby and Gene Clark were all seasoned folk musicians when, inspired by the sounds of the 'British Invasion', they formed acoustic folk pop group The Jet Set. Chris Hillman (bass) and Michael Clarke (drums) joined the line-up that became The Byrds. A version of Bob Dylan's 'Mr Tambourine Man' (1965) hit the top of the US charts and was quickly followed by another Dylan cover, 'All I Really Want To Do'. The Beatles declared The Byrds to be their favourite American band, while Bob Dylan not only endorsed their covers but actually followed their lead into folk rock. 'Eight Miles High' (1966) heralded the era of psychedelic rock, but turned out to be The Byrds' last Top 20 US single. Crosby and Clarke left the band in 1967. Their 1968 country rock album *Sweetheart Of The Rodeo* signalled the end of the classic Byrds' sound and by 1973, following a one-album reunion, the end of the band itself.

CANNED HEAT (VOCAL/INSTRUMENTAL GROUP, 1967–PRESENT)

Much of this good-time blues outfit's allure lay in the disparate natures of its late front men: jocular Bob 'Bear' Hite (vocals) and intense Al 'Blind Owl' Wilson (vocals, harmonica, guitar). 1968's *Boogie With Canned Heat* and its attendant 'On The Road Again' hit established them as a world-class act. 'Goin' Up The Country' was also a smash, but the group became more renowned for entertainment at outdoor festivals under the leadership of long-time drummer Fito de la Parra.

The Byrds' unique blend of jangling guitars, angelic harmonies and restless eclecticism helped pioneer folk, psychedelic and country rock.

JOE COCKER (VOCALS, 1944–2014)

A UK Top 50 entry with 1968's self-penned 'Marjorine' prefaced a chart-topping overhaul of The Beatles' 'With A Little Help From My Friends'. This domestic success was not repeated in the US. Nevertheless, he became a bigger star there following a show-stealing performance at Woodstock (1969) and hit revivals in 1970 of The Beatles' 'She Came In Through The Bathroom Window' and Julie London's signature tune 'Cry Me A River'. After a tour as *de facto* leader of the Mad Dogs And Englishmen troupe of Hollywood 'supersidemen', progress was erratic until 1983, when 'Up Where We Belong', a duet with Jennifer Warnes, was a US No. 1 and reached the Top 10 in Britain. His popularity assured, he toured and recorded regularly before being diagnosed with lung cancer in 2014.

LEONARD COHEN (GUITAR, VOCALS, 1934–2016)

Despite a humble vocal endowment, this acclaimed Canadian poet and novelist moved to the States in his mid-30s to make his first essay as a recording artist with 1968's sparsely arranged and all-acoustic *Songs Of Leonard Cohen*. Reaching out to self-doubting adolescent diarists, it and its successors – notably *Songs From A Room,* which included the much-covered 'Bird On A Wire', and 1971's *Songs Of Love And Hate* – were big hits, albeit much less so in North America than in Europe, where he was a surprise hit at 1970's Isle of Wight Festival. After weathering punk, in which his wordy gentility had no place, later albums such as *I'm Your Man* (1988) and *Ten New Songs* (2003) brought him to a new young audience, fortuitously, as his long-time manager had fraudulently emptied all his bank accounts. He undertook a series of rapturously received world tours to restore the damage.

CREAM (VOCAL/INSTRUMENTAL GROUP, 1966–68, 2005)

The first and arguably most famous of hard rock's 'supergroups', Cream comprised Eric Clapton on guitar/vocals, Jack Bruce on bass/harmonica/keyboards/vocals and Ginger Baker on drums. The trio's debut album *Fresh Cream* (1966) made the UK Top 10. Clapton's superb blues guitar was perfectly complemented by Bruce's powerful vocals and

The dark sound of Leonard Cohen's debut album Songs Of Leonard Cohen *was widely acclaimed by folk music fans.*

inventive playing. 1967's *Disraeli Gears* yielded 'Sunshine Of Your Love', the group's first Stateside hit single. This album blitzed listeners with a welter of awesome instrumentals, multi-layered textures and dazzling effects. The altogether more patchy *Wheels Of Fire* (1968) contained both the band's worst excesses and some of its finest moments, not least the superb 'White Room' and 'Crossroads'. However, while the record topped the US charts and the group was established as one of the world's top live attractions, the group members shocked everybody by deciding to call it a day. A brief reunion occurred in 2005.

CREEDENCE CLEARWATER REVIVAL (VOCAL/INSTRUMENTAL GROUP, 1967–72)

If John Fogerty (vocals, guitar), Tom Fogerty (guitar), Stuart Cook (bass) and Doug Clifford (drums) were Californian hippy in appearance, their music harked back to the energy and stylistic clichés of 1950s rock'n'roll, and their spiritual home seemed to be the swamplands of the Deep South, as instanced in titles like 'Born On The Bayou'. After 1969's 'Proud Mary' all but topped the US chart, they reached a global audience too with 'Bad Moon Rising' at No. 1 in Australia and Britain, and comparable figures for the likes of 'Green River', 'Travelling Band', 'Up Around The Bend' and attendant albums that met favour with heavy rock and mainstream pop fans alike. The winning streak came to an end in 1972. Following disbandment, chief among composer John Fogerty's solo hits was 1975's 'Rockin' All Over The World', which was adopted as a signature tune by Status Quo.

CROSBY, STILLS AND NASH (VOCAL/INSTRUMENTAL GROUP, 1968–PRESENT)

When on a US tour with The Hollies, Graham Nash (vocals, guitar) had sown the seeds of a 'supergroup' with ex-Byrd Dave Crosby (vocals, guitar) and Steve Stills (vocals, guitar) from Buffalo Springfield. They rehearsed in London for an eponymous album that featured hippy lyricism, flawless vocal harmonies and neo-acoustic backing tracks. Its spin-off single, Nash's 'Marrakesh Express', was a worldwide smash, and, if his trio's warblings were not to everyone's taste, they were well-received at Woodstock where they were joined by Neil Young, a colleague of Stills, who stayed on for

A swamp rock band, Creedence Clearwater Revival had their first big hit with 'Susie Q' from their first album, released in 1968.

1970's *Déjà Vu*, attributed to Crosby, Stills, Nash and Young. The group broke up the following year to pursue solo careers, though they have periodically reunited – when they are not at each other's throats.

THE DAVE CLARK FIVE (VOCAL/INSTRUMENTAL GROUP, 1961-70)

Early on this London combo underwent fundamental personnel reshuffles that resulted in a line-up that remained stable for the rest of its career. Then Dave Clark (drums), Lenny Davidson (guitar), Denis Payton (saxophone), Rick Huxley (bass) and Mike Smith (vocals, keyboards) switched their stylistic emphasis to music with vocals. After a 1964 chart-topper, 'Glad All Over' and its 'Bits And Pieces' follow-up – both written by Smith and Clark – the group racked up heftier achievements in the States as a foremost 'British Invasion' act. Their only major film, *Having A Wild Weekend* (UK title: *Catch Us If You Can*) was a box-office triumph, and – also in 1965 – 'Over And Over' was a US No. 1, but many later releases were characterized by bandwagon-jumping.

THE DOORS (VOCAL/INSTRUMENTAL GROUP, 1966-72)

Jim Morrison (vocals) has been the posthumous subject of a movie that fuelled the myth that he *was* The Doors. If his stage antics brought the Los Angeles outfit much publicity – and notoriety – their hits were either team efforts or written by other personnel, namely Ray Manzarek (keyboards), Robbie Kreiger (guitar) and John Densmore (drums). 1967's 'Light My Fire', a US No. 1, was followed by further high placings in both the single and album lists, peaking in 1968 with the million-sellers 'Hello I Love You' and 'Touch Me'. Then came a concert in Miami, where Morrison was purported to have exposed himself. During a long wait for the trial, he exiled himself in Paris, where he died suddenly in 1971. The Doors disbanded a year later after two albums without him. They occasionally reformed for various projects before a bitter legal dispute between Densmore (and Morrison's estate) and the others. They reconciled before Manzarek's death in 2013.

Jim Morrison, with his darkly poetic lyrics and rich vocals, played a key part in The Doors' success.

FAIRPORT CONVENTION (VOCAL GROUP, 1967–PRESENT)

Not so much a premier folk rock ensemble as one of the most English of veteran rock bands, this band formed in London in 1967 in a vague image of Jefferson Airplane, but traditional folk pervaded their second LP, on which singer Sandy Denny debuted, and those that followed. Representatives of all line-ups have pitched in at Cropredy, the annual festival over which the group preside.

FLEETWOOD MAC (VOCAL/INSTRUMENTAL GROUP, 1967–PRESENT)

Peter Green (vocals, guitar) had been a star of John Mayall's Bluesbreakers, in which John McVie (bass) and Mick Fleetwood (drums) had toiled less visibly. On leaving Mayall in 1967, the three became 'Peter Green's Fleetwood Mac' after enlisting guitarist Jeremy Spencer. Later, a third guitarist, Danny Kirwan, was added. The outfit began moving away from its blues core with 'Albatross', 'Oh Well' and other hits penned by Green. His exit – and that of Spencer – in 1970 brought the group to its knees, despite the enlistment of McVie's wife, Christine Perfect (vocals, keyboards) from Chicken Shack. More upheavals preceded a relocation to California by the mid-1970s and a second, hugely successful career. After long 'wilderness years', Green managed a qualified comeback as a concert attraction in the 1990s.

THE FOUR SEASONS (VOCAL GROUP, 1961–PRESENT)

In 1962, New Jersey session singers Frankie Valli, Tommy DeVito and Nick Massi plus songwriter Bob Gaudio issued a single, 'Sherry', as The Four Seasons. With Valli's shrill falsetto to the fore, it was an international million-seller. Other such triumphs of the same persuasion included 'Big Girls Don't Cry', 'Rag Doll' and 1965's 'Let's Hang On'. By 1968, the momentum had slackened, but the group enjoyed a further brace of chartbusters during the late 1970s disco boom.

FREDDIE + THE DREAMERS (VOCAL GROUP, 1961–2002)

A debut single, 1963's 'If You Gotta Make A Fool Of Somebody', began a two-year British chart run for this Manchester

Peter Green's Fleetwood Mac of the late 1960s and early 1970s was a straight-up blues rock band playing blues classics.

outfit. Moreover, as their fortunes subsided at home, they caught on in North America, scoring a US No. 1 with 'I'm Telling You Now', and amassing advance orders of 142,000 (the biggest in label Mercury's history) for a debut US album. Much of their appeal lay in trademark comic antics centred on bespectacled, geeky Freddie Garrity (vocals). Their latter-day output encompassed a large proportion of humorous material such as an entire LP of Disney film songs. All roads led to the nostalgia trail, and one-shot singles like self-penned 'I'm A Singer In A Sixties Band' by a solo Garrity, who was writing an autobiography when he died after a long illness in 2006.

GERRY AND THE PACEMAKERS (VOCAL/INSTRUMENTAL GROUP, 1959-2017)

In 1963, this Liverpool act's first three singles – 'How Do You Do It', 'I Like It' and 'You'll Never Walk Alone' – all reached the top of the chart in Britain, a hitherto unmatched feat. Self-composed 'I'm The One' almost made it four in a row, but times got harder after 'Don't Let The Sun Catch You Crying' seized up at No. 6, though it did establish the group in North America. Backed by new Pacemakers, Gerry Marsden (vocals, guitar) became a popular draw on Swinging Sixties nostalgia revues before ill health forced him to retire.

THE GRATEFUL DEAD (VOCAL/INSTRUMENTAL GROUP, 1965-95)

Rock's most famous hippie band grew out of a union between singer/songwriter/lead guitarist Jerry Garcia, songwriter/rhythm guitarist Bob Weir and keyboardist/singer Ron McKernan. Their eponymous debut album in 1967, despite providing some indication as to the band's eclecticism, failed to reproduce the range and excitement of its live performances. It was not until the in-concert double album *Live/Dead* (1969) that record buyers could appreciate the improvizational skills of the musicians. McKernan's chronic alcoholism resulted in his death, aged 26. Keith Godchaux replaced him, but substance abuse problems led to his dismissal in 1979; his replacement Brent Mydland was around for just over a decade before he died from a drug overdose. In 1987 The Dead produced their highest-selling album, *In The Dark*. Following Mydland's death, the band continued performing to sell-out crowds until Garcia's death from a heart attack in 1995.

Gerry and The Pacemakers penned the hit single 'You'll Never Walk Alone', which went on to become Liverpool Football Club's anthem.

THE HOLLIES (VOCAL/INSTRUMENTAL GROUP, 1962-PRESENT)

The sound of Manchester's most acclaimed beat group hinged on the jazz sensibility of Bobby Elliott (drums) and the breathtaking chorale of Allan Clarke (vocals), Tony Hicks (guitar, vocals) and Graham Nash (vocals, guitar) who, under the pseudonym 'L. Ransford', also composed many of an unbroken series of smashes. Yet it was a non-original, 1966's 'Look Through Any Window', that broke The Hollies in the US. Though reliant more on outside writers after Nash left to form the Crosby, Stills and Nash 'supergroup', the run of hits continued up to 1974's 'The Air That I Breathe'; in 1983, 'Stop In The Name Of Love' swept into the US Top 20. Clarke retired in 2000 but Hicks and Elliott have carried on. .

THE INCREDIBLE STRING BAND (VOCAL/INSTRUMENTAL GROUP, 1966-74)

On breaking free of the Scottish folk circuit, singing multi-instrumentalists Robin Williamson and Mike Heron charmed a wider world with homespun modal harmonies that reconciled the pibroch with the sitar. They peaked commercially in 1968 with *The Hangman's Beautiful Daughter* in the UK album Top 10. Later output relied more on instrumentation, and their long chromatic melodies and harmonic daredevilry remained intriguing and influential on Led Zeppelin and others.

JEFFERSON AIRPLANE (VOCAL/INSTRUMENTAL GROUP, 1965-73)

When the 'classic' line-up of Marty Balin (vocals), Grace Slick (vocals), Paul Kantner (guitar, vocals), Jorma Kaukonen (guitar, vocals) and Skip Spence (drums) found each other, a merger of an oblique form of folk rock with psychedelia ensured acceptance by their native San Francisco's hippy community. They had success with 1967 singles 'Somebody To Love' and 'White Rabbit', and albums still charting when the group evolved into Jefferson Starship to enjoy another golden age in the 1980s.

JETHRO TULL (VOCAL/INSTRUMENTAL GROUP, 1967-2012)

While this group – originally Ian Anderson (vocals, flute), Mick Abrahams (guitar), Glenn Cornick (bass) and Clive Bunker (drums) – rose on the crest of the British 'blues boom', they absorbed many other musical idioms, principally via

Innovative prog rockers Jethro Tull have an unique sound marked by quirky vocals and the lead flute work of frontman Ian Anderson.

composer Anderson. The image of his matted hair, vagrant attire and antics with his flute during early TV appearances was not easily forgotten, for, as well as being a popular album act, they were also mainstream pop stars by 1969, when 'Living In The Past' all but topped the UK chart. 1971's *Aqualung* heralded a series of conceptual albums that made Jethro Tull hugely successful in the US. At the end of the 1970s, the band turned to folk music for inspiration on albums like *Songs from the Wood* and the Grammy-winning *Crest of a Knave*.

TOM JONES (VOCALS, B. 1940)

This Welshman's piledriving but flexible baritone was first heard on 1965's 'It's Not Unusual', a UK No. 1 that also reached the Top 10 in the States. A lean period ended with UK and US hit 'Green Green Grass Of Home'. Further hits stretched to the early 1970s, partly because the magnificence of his voice was able to ride roughshod over indifferent material. A return to the charts after a 10-year absence with 1987's 'The Boy From Nowhere' brought much of the aura of a fresh sensation to teenage consumers. Suddenly hip, he had another smash in 1990 with a version of Prince's 'Kiss'. He recorded with Robbie Williams, The Stereophonics, Wyclef Jean and other modern chart contenders, intrigued by his unquiet journey to old age and, in 2006, he received a knighthood.

JANIS JOPLIN (VOCALS, 1943-70)

During a troubled adolescence in Texas, Joplin sang in regional clubs before a move to California where she emerged as focal point of San Francisco's Big Brother and The Holding Company, sounding weary, cynical and knowing beyond her years. In 1968, she began a solo career that was triumphant and tragic – for, shortly after a drug-induced death in 1970, she topped both the US album and singles chart with, respectively, *Pearl* and 'Me And Bobby McGee'.

THE KINKS (VOCAL/INSTRUMENTAL GROUP, 1964-96)

The Kinks went through numerous line-up changes, but were always led by singer/songwriter Ray Davies, while his

Janis Joplin, with her charismatic blend of blues, soul and rock, left a profound musical legacy, despite her early death aged only 27.

brother Dave supplied the band's signature rock guitar sound. In 1964, 'You Really Got Me' stormed its way to the top of the UK charts and made the US Top 10. This success was repeated on 'All Day And All Of The Night', which peaked at No. 2 in Britain and No. 7 in the US. As The Kinks grew increasingly out of touch with a contemporary scene that was replete with psychedelia and social upheaval, they released critically acclaimed albums of great artistry: *The Village Green Preservation Society* (1968) and *Arthur (Or The Decline And Fall Of The British Empire)* (1969). The band petered out in the 1990s and Ray Davies embarked on a solo career. Original bassist Pete Quaife died in 2010, but in 2018 Ray Davies stated that he was reforming the band with brother Dave and original drummer Mick Avory.

ALEXIS KORNER (GUITAR, VOCALS, 1928–84)

The late 'Godfather of British blues' emerged from London's traditional jazz scene to found Blues Incorporated in 1962. Among those passing through the ranks of this loose but inspirational amalgam were subsequent members of The Rolling Stones, Cream and Led Zeppelin. In the late 1960s, Korner too made the charts as singer with CCS, whose biggest hit, a cover of Led Zeppelin's 'Whole Lotta Love' became the theme tune to BBC television's *Top Of The Pops*.

THE LOVIN' SPOONFUL (VOCAL/INSTRUMENTAL GROUP, 1964–69, 1991–PRESENT)

Though New Yorkers, this group – John Sebastian (vocals, guitar, autoharp), Zal Yanovsky (guitar), Steve Boone (bass) and Joe Butler (drums) – had musical roots in rural blues and jug bands. Their second million-seller of 1966, 'Summer In The City', was a swipe at seasonal humidity. The group broke up in 1969. Sebastian's solo career embraced a 1976 US No. 1, 'Welcome Back'. Butler and Boone revived the group in 1991.

THE MAMAS AND THE PAPAS (VOCAL GROUP, 1964–68)

Singers Michelle Gilliam, Cass Elliot (real name Naomi Cohen), John Phillips and Denny Doherty had been part of the folk and fringe theatre scene in New York. On trying their luck in Los Angeles – where Phillips had made useful music industry

The songs of The Kinks paired Ray Davies' quick-witted, observant lyrics with his brother Dave's powerful guitar style.

connections – 'California Dreamin'' and 'Monday Monday' were recorded with session musicians underpinning the four's vigorous and contrapuntal chorale. After these both rose high in the US Top 10 in 1966, The Mamas and The Papas reached a global audience too. Further hits included 'Dedicated To The One I Love' and 'Creeque Alley'. Personal traumas and a vexing run of comparative flops led to disbandment, but all ex-personnel remained in the entertainment industry.

MANFRED MANN (VOCAL/INSTRUMENTAL GROUP, 1962–69)

This multifaceted ensemble – Paul Jones (vocals, harmonica), Mike Vickers (guitar, woodwinds), Manfred Mann (keyboards), Dave Richmond (bass) and Mike Hugg (drums) – first reached the national Top 20 with 1963's '54321'. After Richmond was replaced by Tom McGuinness, there was hardly any let-up of hits, despite other personnel changes. Some of the most enduring tracks were written by Bob Dylan, who considered the band the most proficient exponents of his work. Indeed, the group scored a million-seller with his 'Mighty Quinn'. All former members of the group achieved further success as recording artists, most remarkably Jones with two fast UK Top 5 penetrations; McGuinness, doing the same with his McGuinness-Flint unit; and Mann, whose progressive Earth Band enjoyed a run of hits in the 1970s. 'Ob-la-di Ob-la-da', a Beatles cover, at No. 1, and 'Reflections Of My Life', their only major US chartbuster.

JOHN MAYALL (MULTI-INSTRUMENTALIST, VOCALS, B. 1933)

Mayall carved a niche of true individuality in perhaps pop's most stylized form, re-inventing it constantly: duetting with Chicago bluesman Paul Butterfield on a 1967 British EP; recording with a big band on 1968's *Bare Wires* album; and without a drummer for 1969's *The Turning Point*. From the mid-1960s, his albums had been making inroads into the UK list, and his accompanying Bluesbreakers cradled many stars-in-waiting, including guitar heroes Eric Clapton and Peter Green. Initially modest success in the States prompted an uprooting to California, and a preponderance of North American hirelings in the 1970s. He is still a reliable concert attraction and new albums remain worthwhile.

The Mamas and The Papas, whose sweet California-sound harmonies remain popular.

JONI MITCHELL (GUITAR, VOCALS, B. 1947)

Fairport Convention were among several artists who had already covered her songs when this gifted Canadian soprano's debut LP, *Songs To A Seagull*, appeared in 1968. A move to California coupled with relentless touring assisted the passage of the following year's *Clouds* into the US Top 40. However, it was not until she caught the general tenor of the post-Woodstock era that Mitchell truly left the runway with hit single 'Big Yellow Taxi'. *Blue* and 1974's *Court And Spark* – her first with all-amplified accompaniment – were particularly big sellers. A jazzier approach in the later 1970s was received less enthusiastically. Since then, artistic and commercial progress have been patchy and have involved ventures into other cultural areas – most conspicuously exhibitions of her paintings in the mid-1990s – and increasingly longer periods of vanishing from the public eye.

THE MONKEES (VOCAL/INSTRUMENTAL GROUP, 1966-70, 1976-PRESENT)

Four amenable youths – Mike Nesmith (guitar), Peter Tork (vocals), Mickey Dolenz (drums) and Davy Jones (vocals) – were hired by a Hollywood business conglomerate to play an Anglo-American pop combo in a 1966 TV series that was to be networked worldwide. Success was instant, and an international No. 1 with 'I'm A Believer' precipitated further smashes that continued after the final programme in 1968. They lost the rights to the name in 1971, but reformed periodically in various permutations (almost never a complete reunion) on the back of successful re-runs of the series from the mid-1970s. Jones died in 2012.

THE MOODY BLUES (VOCAL/INSTRUMENTAL GROUP, 1964-PRESENT)

Though 'Go Now' was a worldwide smash in 1965, later singles were much less successful for Denny Laine (vocals, guitar), Mike Pinder (keyboards), Ray Thomas (woodwinds, percussion), Clint Warwick (bass) and Graeme Edge (drums), veterans of several beat groups from the British Midlands. With the departures of the late Warwick and Laine (later in Paul McCartney's Wings), the group was sagging on the ropes by 1967. However, with the respective enlistments of John

The Monkees' music stands testament to their value as representatives of 1960s pop culture, even though they were a 'manufactured' band.

Lodge and Justin Hayward, they revived with 'Nights In White Satin', from *Days Of Future Passed*, an ambitious concept LP with orchestra that preceded a series of successful albums in the UK and US. Following a sabbatical for solo projects in the mid-1970s, the group reassembled, minus Pinder, for 1978's *Octave* and further albums that have sold steadily.

THE MOVE (VOCAL/INSTRUMENTAL GROUP, 1966-71)

Carl Wayne (vocals), Roy Wood (guitar), Trevor Burton (guitar), Chris 'Ace' Kefford (bass) and Bev Bevan (drums) burst forth from Birmingham with a run of memorable UK hit singles, including a No. 1 with 1968's 'Blackberry Way'. All were composed by Wood, who had taken over as lead singer by 1970. The group had evolved into The Electric Light Orchestra by 1972.

GENE PITNEY (VOCALS, 1941-2006)

This University of Connecticut graduate was first recognized in the music business as a composer of hits for Ricky Nelson and Bobby Vee. As a performer, Pitney made a US Hot 100 debut with 1961's '(I Wanna) Love My Life Away' before climbing higher with two successive film title songs – 'Town Without Pity' and 'The Man Who Shot Liberty Valence'. Further hits included 'Only Love Can Break A Heart' and 'I'm Gonna Be Strong' – his biggest UK smash apart from a chart-topping duet of 'Something's Gotten Hold Of My Heart' with Marc Almond in 1989 – 'Backstage' and the 1967 solo blueprint of 'Something's Gotten Hold Of My Heart', all sung in his trademark piercing nasal tenor. By the 1970s, Top 40 entries were less frequent, but his regular concert tours remained sellouts. Pitney died suddenly on a UK tour in 2006.

THE PRETTY THINGS (VOCAL/INSTRUMENTAL GROUP, 1963-PRESENT)

Phil May (vocals) and ex-Rolling Stone Dick Taylor (guitar) formed this London R&B outfit in 1963. A long-haired reprobate image held instant appeal and they made the UK Top 20 with 'Don't Bring Me Down'. Unfortunately, sales did not match critical acclaim for albums such as *S.F. Sorrow* (1968) – unarguably the first 'rock opera' – and 1969's *Parachute*, *Rolling Stone* magazine's Album Of The Year.

Gene Pitney is one of the few great artists and songwriters that survived the 1960s intact and went on to continue a successful career.

PROCOL HARUM (VOCAL/INSTRUMENTAL GROUP, 1966–PRESENT)

Propelled by the 'holy' organ of Matthew Fisher, 'A Whiter Shade Of Pale' spent six weeks at No. 1 in Britain and rose high in the US Hot 100 during 1967's flower-power summer. The 'Homburg' follow-up – also written by Gary Brooker (vocals, piano) and lyricist Keith Reid – was almost as big a hit worldwide, but further chart strikes were less impressive until a reissue of the evergreen 'A Whiter Shade Of Pale' restored them to the domestic Top 20 in 1972.

THE RIGHTEOUS BROTHERS (VOCAL DUO, 1962–70)

Bill Medley and the late Bobby Hatfield struck gold in 1965 with 'You've Lost That Lovin' Feeling", a simple song inflated by producer Phil Spector's trademark 'wall of sound'. Another year of hits in the same vein closed with Medley going solo. A reunion with Hatfield spawned a US-only smash, 1974's 'Rock And Roll Heaven'. In 1990, a re-release of 1965's 'Unchained Melody' – featured in the movie *Ghost* – topped the UK chart.

SANTANA (VOCAL/INSTRUMENTAL GROUP, 1966–PRESENT)

A Latin-American take on what became known as jazz rock, the group led by Mexican Carlos Santana (guitar) was a palpable hit at Woodstock in 1969. This coincided with an eponymous debut album penetrating the US Top 10. An optimum commercial period – embracing US chart-toppers *Abraxas* and *Santana III* – was followed by dwindling success until 'Smooth', from 1999's guest star-studded *Supernatural*, spent weeks at No. 1 in the US and elsewhere.

THE SEARCHERS (VOCAL/INSTRUMENTAL GROUP, 1961–PRESENT)

Tidy harmonies and restrained fretboard interaction became stylistic trademarks after Tony Jackson (bass), John McNally (guitar), and Mike Pender (guitar) with Chris Curtis (drums), had a UK No. 1 with 'Sweets For My Sweet' in 1963. Belated success in the States was followed by personnel changes and commercial decline, though years on the cabaret trail were punctuated by two well-received albums of new material in the late 1970s.

The Santana Blues Band first found success in the late 1960s with their immensely popular blend of salsa, rock, blues and jazz styles.

THE SHANGRI-LAS (VOCAL GROUP, 1964-68)

New York schoolgirls Margie and Mary Ann Ganser and Betty and Mary Weiss were thrust into the US and UK Top 20s with 1964's 'Remember (Walking In The Sand)'. After 'Leader Of The Pack', a teenage morality play, topped the US chart, its mordant theme was investigated from new angles with such songs as 'Dressed In Black' and the world-weary 'Past Present And Future'. Repromotions of 'Leader Of The Pack' twice climbed the British Top 20 in the 1970s.

DEL SHANNON (GUITAR, VOCALS, 1939-91)

Stating his intent with 1961's million-selling – and self-penned – 'Runaway', this square-jawed hunk from Michigan continued an exploration of small town soul-torture with the likes of 'Hats Off To Larry', 'Little Town Flirt' and 'Stranger In Town'. Other chartbusters included 'The Swiss Maid', 'From Me To You' – the first Beatles composition to penetrate the US Hot 100 – and 1964's 'Keep Searchin''. He also reached the national Top 10 by proxy when Peter and Gordon recorded his composition 'I Go To Pieces'. When the hits petered out, he remained a respected figure in the industry. He even managed a one-off return to the charts with 'Sea Of Love' nine years before his suicide in 1991.

SIMON AND GARFUNKEL (VOCAL DUO, 1956-71)

As 'Tom and Jerry', Paul Simon (vocals, guitar) and Art Garfunkel (vocals) had a minor US Hot 100 success as teenagers in 1957 with 'Hey Schoolgirl'. Both attempted to forge solo careers, with Simon becoming a reliable draw in the British folk clubs. Back in the US by 1964, he recorded an album, the acoustic *Wednesday Morning 3am*, with Garfunkel. Its highlight was 'The Sound Of Silence', which was issued as an amplified rock single and topped the US charts. With Simon taking most of the creative initiative, later hits included 'Homeward Bound', 'Mrs Robinson' (from 1968's *The Graduate* film soundtrack) and 'The Boxer'. The new decade began with a No. 1 in both Britain and the States with 'Bridge Over Troubled Water', in which Garfunkel's breathy tenor floated effortlessly over orchestrated accompaniment. Both he and Simon have given good individual accounts of themselves in the charts since.

Simon and Garfunkel are best known and loved for their hits 'The Sound Of Silence', 'Mrs Robinson' and 'Bridge Over Troubled Water'.

THE SMALL FACES (VOCAL/INSTRUMENTAL GROUP, 1965-69)

After entering the UK Top 20 with 1965's 'Whatcha Gonna Do About It', this pre-eminent mod group – Steve Marriott (vocals, guitar), Jimmy Winston (keyboards), Ronnie Lane (bass, vocals) and Kenney Jones (drums) – suffered a miss with the self-composed 'I Got Mine'. They replaced Winston with Ian McLagan, and got back on course with the chart-topping 'All Or Nothing' and lesser hits before a post-1967 creative peak with 'Itchycoo Park', 'Tin Soldier', and 'Lazy Sunday'. 'Itchycoo Park' was the vehicle of a US advance that was thwarted by Marriott's departure to form Humble Pie. The others rallied by teaming up with Ron Wood (guitar) and Rod Stewart (vocals) from The Jeff Beck Group as 'The Faces'. A brief Small Faces reunion in the late 1970s was notable for market indifference towards two comeback albums, against UK Top 40 placings for re-promoted 1960s singles.

SONNY AND CHER (VOCAL DUO, 1964-76)

Hollywood songwriter and arranger Sonny Bono linked up, both professionally and romantically, with Cher La Pier, a session singer, for a handful of misses before striking gold with 1965's chart-topping 'I Got You Babe'. Its vague if fashionable 'protest' tenor, the overnight sensation's proto-hippy appearance and an element of boy-girl ickiness that some find endearing, helped keep the momentum going with further smashes, both together and as soloists. Cher also scored three US No. 1s in the early 1970s when hits attributed to 'Sonny and Cher' had become intermittent, and the now-married couple were making the most of past glories in a cabaret netherworld. Following their divorce in 1976, Cher enjoyed an eventual career revival as both a film actor and solo chart contender. Sonny achieved political office as mayor of Palm Springs before his death in 1998.

STEPPENWOLF (VOCAL GROUP, 1967-PRESENT)

After they migrated from Toronto to Los Angeles, the group scored a million-seller with the 1968 biker anthem, 'Born To Be Wild', the theme song to the *Easy Rider* movie. Other hits included the self-penned 'Magic Carpet Ride', 'The

The Small Faces' blend of R&B, mod and psychedelic pop had a great influence on the Britpop movement of the 1990s.

Pusher', 'Rock Me' and 1970's 'Hey Lawdy Mama'. Ebbing record sales led to brief disbandment in the mid-1970s, but, with German-born vocalist John Kay (Joachim Krauledat) the only original member, the group remain a potent draw on the 1960s nostalgia circuit.

THE STEVE MILLER BAND (VOCAL/INSTRUMENTAL GROUP, 1966–PRESENT)

A cauldron of blues and psychedelia, 1968's *Children Of The Future* was a US Top 30 entry for a California-based outfit in which the only constant would be Miller (guitar, vocals), though first singer Boz Scaggs enjoyed solo success. Becoming more radio-friendly, Miller made greater impact from the early 1970s with US chart-toppers 'The Joker', 'Rock 'N' Me' and 1982's 'Abracadabra'. As a postscript, a 1990 re-issue of 'The Joker' went to No. 1 in Britain, thanks to its use in a TV commercial. Miller continues to tour and record, and in 2016, he was inducted into the Rock and Roll Hall of Fame.

AL STEWART (GUITAR, VOCALS, B. 1945)

Once lead guitarist with Bournemouth's Tony Blackburn and The Rovers, Stewart's commercial discography as a solo artist commenced with a 1966 cover of a Yardbirds LP track, 'Turn Into Earth'. Very bound up in himself lyrically, he made minor media waves over his insertion of a rude word in the autobiographical 'Love Chronicles', title track of a 1969 album that laid out the parameters of his folky singer/songwriter career.

THE STOOGES (VOCAL/INSTRUMENTAL GROUP, 1967–74)

This Detroit quartet's focal point was Iggy Pop (James Osterberg, vocals), fronting Ron Asheton (guitar), Scott Asheton (drums) and Dave Alexander (bass). Tiring of psychedelia, they had dug down to a raw three-chord bedrock for an eponymous maiden album in 1969. Two more albums, *Fun House* and 1973's *Raw Power*, were appreciated mostly in retrospect after internal ructions and drug abuse prompted disbandment.

Steppenwolf greatest hit 'Born To Be Wild' contains the lyric 'heavy metal thunder', which gave a name to an emerging new genre.

THEM (VOCAL/INSTRUMENTAL GROUP, 1963-66)

This Irish R&B group entered the UK Top 10 in 1965 with 'Baby Please Don't Go' and 'Here Comes The Night'. The latter also made the US Top 40, as did 'Mystic Eyes'. However, a self-written B-side, 'Gloria', was to be their most renowned number after it became a US garage band standard. It was, however, a mismanaged tour of North America that proved the last straw for Van Morrison (vocals, harmonica), who subsequently commenced a climb to international solo stardom.

THE 13TH FLOOR ELEVATORS (VOCAL/INSTRUMENTAL GROUP, 1965-68)

They surfaced at the tail-end of the 'British Invasion' from a mid-Texas scene as self-contained in its way as Merseybeat had been. 'You're Gonna Miss Me' was a regional hit, but later releases obeyed a law of diminishing returns, both artistically and commercially. Today, The Elevators are remembered for being the group in which Roky Erickson (vocals, guitar) cut his teeth before achieving solo renown.

TRAFFIC (VOCAL/INSTRUMENTAL GROUP, 1966-75)

From various also-ran beat groups, Dave Mason (vocals, guitar), Chris Wood (woodwinds) and Jim Capaldi (drums) joined forces with Steve Winwood (vocals, keyboards, guitar) of The Spencer Davis Group. Though 'Paper Sun' and 'Hole In My Shoe' and the *Dear Mr Fantasy* (1967) LP all charted in Britain, tensions between Winwood and Mason caused the latter's brief exit early in 1968 and a permanent one after a second album, *Traffic* (1968). Capaldi and Wood's help during subsequent sessions for a proposed solo offering by Winwood came to be issued in 1970 as a Traffic album, *John Barleycorn Must Die*. The group reached a commercial summit with 1971's *Low Spark Of High-Heeled Boys* before an over-reliance on long-winded improvizations failed to mask a creative bankruptcy, though there was a return to form with 1974's *When The Eagle Flies* finale. In 1994, Winwood and Capaldi reformed Traffic for an album, *Far From Home*, and correlated concerts before Capaldi died in 2005.

Largely considered an interim band for Steve Winwood, Traffic forged a highly successful path through the rock scene of the 1960s and 1970s.

THE TROGGS (VOCAL GROUP, 1964-PRESENT)

After 'Wild Thing' charged into the UK chart in 1966, its follow-up, 'With A Girl Like You', penned by mainstay Reg Presley (vocals), actually seized the top spot. These were smashes in North America too. Intermittent successes later and the recurrence of Troggs numbers in the repertoires of countless US garage bands were a solid foundation for a lucrative post-Top 40 career that has embraced a link-up with R.E.M. for 1991's *Athens To Andover* album, and a 1994 chart-topping hit revival of 1967's 'Love Is All Around' by Wet Wet Wet. Presley died of lung cancer in 2013, but the band continues, led by original guitarist Chris Britton.

THE VELVET UNDERGROUND (VOCAL/INSTRUMENTAL GROUP, 1965-73, 1992-94)

Lou Reed met John Cale in New York. Both were interested in trying to merge rock with the avant-garde. Together they formed The Velvet Underground and in 1965 Pop Art guru Andy Warhol happened to catch a performance and decided to manage them. Warhol added former model Nico to the line-up, to contribute dusky lead vocals. *The Velvet Underground And Nico* (1967) wasn't a commercial success, but it would have an indelible influence on subsequent generations of offbeat musos. Next, The Velvets recorded *White Light, White Heat* (1968) without Nico or Warhol. It was even more extreme than their previous outing, epitomized by the record's closer, 'Sister Ray', a 17-minute exercise in musical pandemonium. In 1968, Cale was ousted and replaced by Doug Yule. The band continued to fragment, and by 1973 and the poorly-received *Squeeze*, Yule was left to front a band that was The Velvet Underground in name only. Nico died in 1988, but Reed and Cale reformed the rest of the band for a European tour in 1993. US dates were cancelled after the pair fell out.

THE WALKER BROTHERS (VOCAL/INSTRUMENTAL GROUP, 1964-67, 1975-78)

The unrelated Walkers, Scott Engel (vocals, bass), John Maus (vocals, guitar) and Gary Leeds (drums), sought their fortunes in Britain, where 'Love Her' made the Top 20 in 1965. Then came bigger smashes and, with Engel on lead

Hailed as an inspiration for garage rock and punk rock, The Troggs chalked up a number of hits in the UK and US.

vocals, the trio emerged as the darlings of young ladies in the UK and, to a smaller degree, in the States. However, provoked by both bickering between Engel and Maus and falling sales, The Brothers went their separate ways. Engel's *Scott* and 1968's chart-topping *Scott 2* albums established him as both the Belgian *chansonnier* Jacques Brel's principal interpreter, and as an intriguing composer in his own right. The Walker Brothers did, however, score a UK hit in 1976 with 'No Regrets'. There followed three contrasting albums before Engel resumed a snail's-paced solo career.

JOHNNY WINTER (GUITAR, VOCALS, 1944–2014)

A lengthy 1968 eulogy in *Rolling Stone* broadened this boss-eyed and albino Texan's work spectrum and placed an eponymous debut album in the national Top 30. Among famous admirers were The Rolling Stones and John Lennon, who each proffered songs for his consideration after he began touring beyond North America, backed by ex-members of The McCoys and Winter's brother Edgar (keyboards, saxophone), who went solo in 1970. *Johnny Winter And* was the first of several concert albums to enter international charts, but in ratio to Johnny's increasing drug dependency was a deterioration in quality of successive releases. A merger with Edgar for 1976's *Together* collection made commercial sense but, by then, Johnny's time in the sun was past.

STEVIE WONDER (PIANO, VOCALS, B. 1950)

Born Steveland Judkins and blind virtually from birth, Stevie Wonder had mastered the piano, harmonica and drums by the age of seven. This musical prodigiousness saw the child star grow into the soul man; his trademark vocal tone – pure, full and warm – was the embodiment of R&B. He went on to become a master of Motown and was one of the very first pop artists to embrace the emerging world of electronic keyboards, becoming an icon not just of soul music, but of the whole African-American community.

The Walker Brothers had only minor success in the US but reached No. 1 in the UK with the hit single 'Make It Easy On Yourself' (1965).

THE YARDBIRDS (VOCAL/INSTRUMENTAL GROUP, 1963-68, 1995-PRESENT)

The nurtured prowess of successive lead guitarists Eric Clapton, Jeff Beck and Jimmy Page helped make The Yardbirds one of the most innovative rock groups of the 1960s. More discreetly influential, however, were the members: Keith Relf (vocals, harmonica), Chris Dreja (rhythm guitar), Paul Samwell-Smith (bass) and Jim McCarty (drums), especially after 1965's 'For Your Love' came close to topping both the UK and US charts. In 1966, Samwell-Smith left, and Page agreed to play bass until Dreja was able to take over. Beck and Page then functioned as joint lead guitarists until the former's departure in the middle of a harrowing US tour. The group hired pop producer Mickie Most for the releases that preceded a final performance until McCarty and Dreja reformed the group in 1995. Dreja retired in 2013.

FRANK ZAPPA (GUITAR, VOCALS, 1940-93)

In 1964, Zappa formed The Mothers Of Invention, whose albums resembled pop-Dada aural junk-sculptures, laced with outright craziness; influences included 1950s pop, jazz, schmaltz and the pioneering tonalities of Varèse and Webern. However, Zappa's concern over social issues was never so stifled by burlesque that it could not be felt. 1968's *We're Only In It For The Money* charted but, too clever for Joe Average, the now greatly augmented Mothers were disbanded in 1970 by Zappa, who then issued *Hot Rats*, a demonstration of his guitar playing. In the decade before his death, he went some way towards establishing himself as a 'serious' composer in the same league as Varèse.

THE ZOMBIES (VOCAL/INSTRUMENTAL GROUP, 1962-69)

1964's 'She's Not There' nestled uneasily among more extrovert offerings of the day in the UK Top 20. It also topped the US Hot 100 and smaller hits followed for Colin Blunstone (vocals), Paul Atkinson (guitar), Rod Argent (keyboards), Paul Arnold (bass) and Hugh Grundy (drums). Furthermore, The Zombies had actually disbanded when 1969's 'Time Of The Season' put them suddenly back near No. 1 in the US again, with commensurate sales for a final album, *Odessey And Oracle* [sic] (1968).

Frank Zappa was one of the most creative musicians and composers of his time. He released over 60 albums in his lifetime.

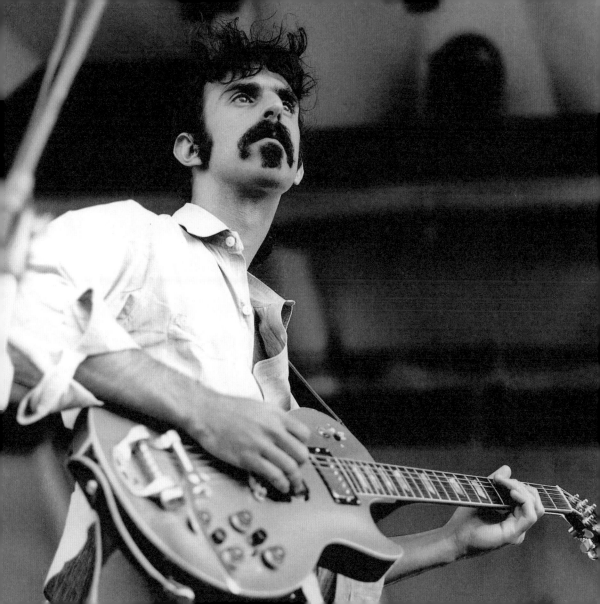

After the seismic shifts of the previous decade, the 1970s reflected faster-moving, less permanent crazes, beginning with glam rock and ending with the new wave.

Glam rock saw the likes of Alice Cooper and Kiss taking make-up to extremes, while the comparatively anonymous Eagles and Bruce Springsteen respectively updated the blueprints established the previous decade by country rocker Gram Parsons and singer/songwriter Bob Dylan.

As Motown moved from Detroit to the West Coast, it would be the likes of Stevie Wonder who kept black music progressing alongside former Impression Curtis Mayfield. Disco was more faceless if further-reaching, but a true icon of black music appeared from left field in the shape of reggae pioneer Bob Marley.

The introduction of the synthesizer to work alongside the now-established electric guitar fuelled progressive rock as well as influential European groups like Can and Kraftwerk. Progressive music from Yes, Pink Floyd and Mike Oldfield also used keyboards to best-selling effect.

The arrival of punk and its nihilistic philosophy in the mid-1970s gave music a much-needed kick up the backside. Elements like its newspaper and cut-up graphics and ripped clothes would have a lasting cultural impact and, while the music was blunt and direct, its plea for social change and racial harmony was as timely as the hippie movement had been a decade previously.

THE SEVENTIES

THE SEVENTIES: SOUNDS + SOURCES

This was the decade that saw popular music turn into one of the biggest money-making industries of recent times – oil crises and vinyl shortages did not stop promoters, record companies and acts realizing their wildest dreams of fame and fortune as sales of records, concert tickets and associated merchandising went through the roof.

Utopian values turned to greed as musicians abandoned their integrity to go for the big bucks. Of course, as was the norm, the 1970s only began in earnest a few years in: 1970–71 continued the trends set in the late 1960s. But eace and love were being replaced by profit and the bottom line.

GOING ONE STEP FURTHER

The predilection for big outdoor events grew even bigger with huge festivals at Bath, the Isle of Wight, Lincoln and Weeley in the UK, while Watkins Glen in New York State in July 1973 saw upwards of 500,000 music fans come together to see The Band, The Grateful Dead and The Allman Brothers star in what was claimed to be the biggest rock show of all time. Many musicians who rose to prominence in the 1960s became the rock Establishment of the new decade. Most of the ex-Beatles continued to sell albums, and Dylan returned to form, releasing his 1975 masterpiece *Blood On The Tracks*. He was joined by the likes of Van Morrison, Crosby, Stills, Nash & Young, The Grateful Dead and Frank Zappa as top-grossing US-based acts of the era. The return-to-roots movement that started with The Band in the late 1960s gathered momentum, especially in the UK where folk rock became hugely popular. Following the example of Fairport Convention, the likes of Steeleye Span and Lindisfarne sold out tours and even scored hits in the Top 20.

The Isle of Wight Festival was part of a surge of similar events in the 1970s, as they became money-spinning opportunities for big business.

Even US groups like The Grateful Dead left behind their psychedelic days for the more tranquil waters of backwoods America on albums like *Workingman's Dead* (1970).

COUNTRY ROCKERS AND SONG-SINGERS

Indeed, the move towards country and western started by the likes of The Byrds and The Flying Burrito Brothers created a new style of music: country rock. This borrowed heavily from the Nashville sound but was smoothed at the edges to create a more easy-going, radio-friendly ambience. Bands like The Eagles hit gold perfecting this style and in their wake came a shoal of soft rock bands. Nashville would become one of the most important cities of the 1970s as country went mainstream via such figures as George Jones, Tammy Wynette and Dolly Parton.

The early 1970s saw the rise of the singer/songwriter, especially in the US, with Joni Mitchell, Carole King, Jackson Browne, James Taylor and Carly Simon among those matching critical acclaim with high earnings for baring their innermost souls. The UK would match them with Cat Stevens, Rod Stewart and Elton John – artists who had cut their teeth in the 1960s but were now spokespeople for the new 'me generation' – writing introspective songs from their viewpoint and experience.

ROCK ON

Rock in the early 1970s was hard and heavy as perfected by a new breed of British bands like Black Sabbath, Free and Deep Purple, all of whom soared to popularity with mega-selling albums in 1970–71. But undoubtedly the biggest phenomenon was Led Zeppelin who, formed from the ashes of The Yardbirds, became the biggest band on the planet in 1970s. The new band had originally thought they would go down like the proverbial 'lead balloon' – yet by 1971 they were outselling practically every other act as their LP *Led Zeppelin IV* demolished the charts on both sides of the Atlantic with its

Free's Paul Kossoff was a characteristic heavy rocker whose hard-drinking, hard-riffing lifestyle ended in tragedy.

mixture of bone-crushing riffs, airy acoustic interludes, unbridled sexuality and stunning musicianship. Their 'Stairway To Heaven', which combined all these attributes in one song, became an anthem. And because Zeppelin refused to release singles, in the UK at least, you had to buy the album to get hold of it.

The tastes of the rock audience had swung back to alcohol and downers rather than pot and LSD, and The Rolling Stones remained superstars, producing two of their finest records in *Sticky Fingers* (1971) and *Exile On Main St.* (1972). These were delivered in a style that had not deviated much from their roots of a decade before – rollicking 12-bar blues, top-heavy with slide guitars. Their American counterparts were the likes of The Allman Brothers, Lynryd Skynryd and The Doobie Brothers, who all purveyed no-frills basic rock – 'heads-down no-nonsense mindless boogie', as British satirists Alberto Y Lost Trios Paranoias put it.

MEGA ROCK

At the other extreme was 'progressive rock', which took popular music into the realms of opera, classical and electronics. Marrying complex pieces of music with poetic lyrics, the prog rock masters were fond of using full orchestras and the very latest cutting-edge musical instruments such as mellotrons (which replicated the sound of strings), Moog and other synthesizers. Rock became high art as supergroups like Emerson, Lake and Palmer, all gifted musicians, covered classical pieces by the likes of Mussorgsky as well as writing long, complicated suites, and taking rock into large arenas and stadiums with often overblown stage shows.

Another act to take this route was Pink Floyd, who lost their arty/underground image of the 1960s to become megastars of the 1970s. Top-selling albums *Dark Side Of The Moon* (1973) and *Wish You Were Here* (1975) established them as rock colossi, while their elaborate live act featured, at various times, giant inflatable pigs, Spitfire aircraft and the demolition of

Bands like Kraftwerk were able to sculpt their sound without guitars or drums by taking advantage of the advent of the electronic keyboard.

a huge brick wall. Other kings of prog rock included Yes, King Crimson, Genesis, Jethro Tull, Queen and Mike Oldfield, whose instrumental concept LP *Tubular Bells* came out of left field in 1973 to become a top-selling record.

Although pop music had usually emanated from the shores of either Britain or America, another country became a major player in the 1970s: Germany. The country was still split in two following the Second World War and, because of the post-war deprivations, German musicians of the 1970s were of a harder, more radical hue. They played a variety of styles – Amon Duul II from the southern city of Munich purveyed an intense hybrid of spacey, psychedelic West Coast-influenced rock whilst the bands from the *Ruehrgebiet* were more industrial and electronic and became highly influential. From the robotic sounds of Neu and Kraftwerk to the white-noise overkill of Can, their influence would become stronger and stronger through the late 1970s and onwards.

GLAM-TASTIC

The 1970s saw the advent of glam, which had its frivolous and serious sides. As early as 1971 the charts were alive with the sounds of Slade, T. Rex and The Sweet, all of whom played a revved-up rock dressed in sequins, sparkle and satin. But glam, despite its teen appeal, had a more serious, theatrical side – its cue taken from a band that only enjoyed cult status in the 1960s but whose influence would reach through the next 30 years and beyond. The Velvet Underground had stepped out of the shadow of their mentor Andy Warhol and explored the darker side of life. By 1971, most of their key members had left – including leader Lou Reed, whose arrival in London along with another American, ex-Stooges leader Iggy Pop, had a profound effect on British rockers like Mott the Hoople, Roxy Music and David Bowie.

Cross-dressing and a flirtation with the burgeoning gay scenes in both London and New York created an exciting new direction in rock. Bowie suddenly caught on with his ambitious concept album *The Rise and Fall of Ziggy Stardust and the*

Gay and lesbian rights became big news in the 1970s and this was reflected in the new-found freedom of expression in all musical forms.

Spiders from Mars (1972). Mascara, lipstick and sexual ambiguity became the order of the day as bands like the New York Dolls followed in his wake. But the chameleon-like Bowie managed to stay one step ahead, toying with different styles and personas as he went from rock through soul to electronica to become one of the biggest figures of the decade.

A NEW BLACK SOUND

Black music continued to be a huge force, both as an influence and as a mainstream phenomenon. The end of the 1960s had seen the emergence of acts like the Chambers Brothers and Sly and The Family Stone who mixed fiery danceable soul and rhythm and blues with psychedelic effects and radical politics. The 1970s would see the emergence of a more sophisticated but no less radical form of soul as figures like Isaac Hayes, Gil Scott Heron and Curtis Mayfield married the latest sounds of white rock with black politics for big crossover appeal. They were joined by such 1960s survivors as The Isley Bros and Stevie Wonder, the latter producing classic progressive soul albums like *Talking Book* (1972) and *Innervisions* (1973).

The Philadelphia sound was now challenging the Motown tradition, though the latter's Jackson Five carried on where The Four Tops left off. But one of the most interesting outfits to come along was Parliament, whose mixture of theatrics, politics, psychedelia and funk broke new barriers. Funk was to become one of the buzzwords of the decade. Taking its cue from 1960s soulster James Brown, funk combined syncopated rhythms, dominant bass lines, sharp rhythm guitars and brass, with acts as diverse as Earth Wind and Fire, The Meters, The Commodores, Miles Davis and Herbie Hancock.

But in terms of influence there was one style of black music and one figure in particular that changed the face of 1970s music – the sound of reggae and the advent of its most famous ambassador, Bob Marley. There had been a long tradition of music coming out of Jamaica since the 1950s – calypso and mento were, followed in the 1960s by bluebeat and ska. But it was reggae, with its reliance on skanking rhythms and a tough, slow backbeat, that became the most

Parliament created such dance-floor favourites as 'Tear The Roof Off The Sucker (Give Up The Funk)', 'Aqua Boogie' and 'Flashlight.'

popular. The original Wailers, back in the ghetto of Trenchtown, had been Marley, Peter Tosh and Bunny Livingston, but by the time the group recorded a breakthrough live album in London in 1975 only Marley remained. Marley soon had a big following, not only of whites but also a young black audience consisting of kids whose parents had arrived in the UK from the Caribbean in the 1950s. The charismatic singer had the knack of communicating a message of universal brotherhood and was soon to unite audiences around the globe, especially after conquering the United States. The music he played informed the direction of many 1960s survivors such as The Stones, Dylan and Eric Clapton. Punks like The Clash also embraced reggae, while new wave trio The Police successfully appropriated its rhythms.

POP WON'T STOP

Pop continued to sell, thanks to acts like Elton John, Rod Stewart and Queen, who all crossed over from rock into the mainstream. The 1970s was also the era of teenybopper pop – indeed, the roots of the perennially popular boy-band phenomenon can be traced back to the early 1970s when clean-cut singers like The Osmonds took care of the mainly female teen audience. As the decade progressed they were followed by rougher-hewn acts like The Bay City Rollers and David Essex. The intelligent, original and wholly irresistible pop of Swedish singing quartet ABBA left an indelible mark on the pop scene with a string of catchy, finely crafted tunes such as 1974's Eurovision-winning 'Waterloo'. The decade was seen out with acts embracing disco – artists like Donna Summer and 1960s' rejects The Bee Gees, who completely revitalized their career writing a number of disco-based anthems.

THE DAWN OF PUNK

Few had seen the storm clouds gathering mid-decade that heralded one of the most important and drastic sea changes in the history of popular music. Rumours began to circulate in 1975 of a new type of rock that was a return to basics but

Punks lived by a do-it-yourself attitude, creating their own clothes and even record labels in order to sell their music.

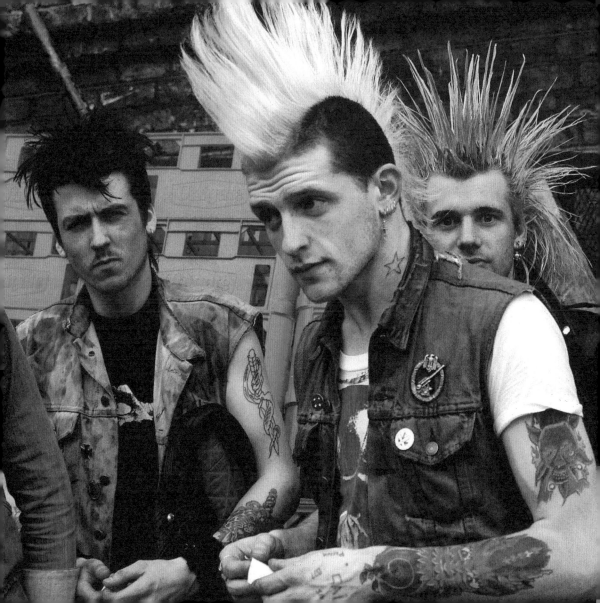

delivered with such speed, conviction and force that it was like a blow to the head. Punk rock, with its simple, basic three-chord guitar attack, was delivered without finesse but with the kind of attitude that had not been seen since the 1950s. Punk did not come out of nowhere – there had always been bands that had delivered their music concisely with a sneer, bite and excitement. 1960s garage rockers like The Standells and The Strangeloves had their tracks collected together as *Nuggets* by Lenny Kaye for Elektra Records as far back as 1972. Kaye was also the guitarist and musical director for poet/singer Patti Smith, whose visionary *Horses* album had been an arms call for a return to simpler guitar rock whilst still possessing a fiery, passionate and poetic heart, and had been declared best album of 1975 by many critics.

Smith and her band were part of a select, incestuous scene in New York that had congregated at little clubs like CBGBs in the Bowery. It was The Ramones, another member of this clique from the Lower East Side, whose sound was to become the blueprint for a thousand imitators. The cartoon-character-like brothers' snappy, amphetamined anthems caught the imagination of the new 'blank generation', whilst in London manager Malcolm McLaren and designer Vivienne Westwood, influenced by this hotbed of activity in the Big Apple, set about fashioning their own 'punks'.

They created The Sex Pistols, whose look was based on the torn T-shirts of Richard Hell, a bassist, writer and mover/shaker of the NYC scene. But singer Johnny Rotten had his own ideas – a working-class lad hell bent on rejecting not just British middle-class values but all that the 1970s rock Establishment held so dear. His bug-eyed stare and dishevelled demeanour sent a frisson through the Establishment – though he was as much music-hall jester as he was foul-mouthed rebel.

Things happened swiftly in 1976, the year The Ramones played London's Roundhouse. Many of the capital's pub-rockers, a back-to-basics movement that spawned Dr. Feelgood and Ian Dury's Kilburn and The High Roads, were soon to re-appear as part of the punk boom. Independent labels like Stiff Records were soon in action, issuing records by the likes of the aforementioned Hell and British combo The Damned. However, many of the bigger bands signed to major labels – The

The celebrated New York 'Country Bluegrass Blues And Other Music For Uplifting Gormandizers' club, better known as the CBGBs club.

Clash were with CBS while the Pistols went through EMI and A&M before settling with Virgin. But it did not stop Rotten and company delivering their controversial nihilistic message, a four-letter word row on prime-time TV that ensured their notoriety went before them. Bands, labels and venues mushroomed in Britain as teenagers awoke to the filth and the fury of such anthems as 'Anarchy In The UK' and 'No Future' – such was the paranoia engendered by the new revolution that questions were asked in the House of Commons. Inevitably the big labels got in on the act and, slowly but inevitably, punk was watered down to become new wave, sucking in a disparate array of bands in the process.

A NEW ORDER

The Establishment had momentarily been toppled. Labels like Virgin dropped their hippie bands and only signed outfits with short haircuts and snappy suits. As punk rose to a crescendo in the summer of 1977, the death of one rock icon seemed to usher in a new era as Elvis Presley died in sad and bloated circumstances. The Pistols split in 1978, their bass player Sid Vicious dying of a heroin overdose a year later, but the avalanche they had started could not be stopped. The rock world of the end of the 1970s was completely re-shaped, with the DIY example of punk being adopted by new kids starting out. The scene was characterized by a new order – bands with literate, charismatic frontmen like The Boomtown Rats; Elvis Costello and The Attractions; and Ian Dury and The Blockheads, the last two escapees from the pub rock era.

Biggest of all the new wavers was Blondie, whose figurehead, Debbie Harry, became the most photographed face of 1979 and whose radio-friendly pop songs climbed the charts one after another. Rock's conscience, meanwhile, was safe in the hands of the British 2-Tone bands like The Specials, whose music drew on bluebeat and ska but whose vision was informed by inner-city decay, racism and the anti-working-class policies of the incoming Thatcher government. As the Tory party and the US Republicans came to power, the scene was set for the 1980s, an era during which, as one wag put it, it was as if punk never happened.

Debbie Harry leapt from the platform of CBGBs and forged the new wave pop sound.

THE SEVENTIES: KEY ARTISTS

DAVID BOWIE (VOCALS, 1947–2016)

One of the great chameleon figures in rock, David Bowie has also been among the most influential. In 1969, he caught the British public's imagination with the quirky 'Space Oddity', which became a Top 5 hit soon after the first manned moon landing. When he created the messianic rock star character Ziggy Stardust and glam-rock concept album *The Rise And Fall Of Ziggy Stardust And The Spiders From Mars* (1972), a legend was born. After an interlude with *Pin-Ups* (1973), a covers album, Bowie returned with *Diamond Dogs* (1974). The album's bleak, Orwellian theme and the extravagant stage show he devised gave Bowie his American breakthrough, encouraging him to relocate there. Another stylistic switch, based around the soul sound of Philadelphia, produced *Young Americans* (1975), which brought him a US No. 1 single with 'Fame'. By *Station To Station* (1976), Bowie's stage persona had morphed into the 'Thin White Duke'.

A LASTING IMPRESSION

Frazzled from the perks and pressures of fame, Bowie retreated into seclusion, but began working with pioneering electronic sound musician Brian Eno. The resulting *Low* (1977) was another radically different musical direction. But in 1983, he returned to the mainstream with *Let's Dance*, which yielded three international hits – 'China Girl', 'Modern Love' and 'Let's Dance'. In 1989, Bowie formed a band called Tin Machine with the rhythm section from Iggy Pop's band, and made two self-titled, rock-oriented albums. But their appeal was limited and Bowie returned to his solo career. He continued to experiment with modern musical styles, drawing on industrial rock for *1. Outside*

David Bowie was the master chameleon, constantly re-inventing both his persona and music to the changing moods of the time.

(1995) and incorporating jungle beats on *Earthling* (1997). *Hours* (1999), *Heathen* (2002), and *Reality* (2003) found Bowie in relaxed form, taking facets of his earlier career and updating them. He continued to be musically active until his unexpected death from liver cancer in January 2016, two days after the release of his final album, *Blackstar*.

THE EAGLES (VOCAL/INSTRUMENTAL GROUP, 1970-80, 1994-PRESENT)

The Eagles defined the sound of California in the 1970s. Guitarist Glenn Frey, drummer Don Henley, guitarist Bernie Leadon and bassist Randy Meisner were recruited as Linda Ronstadt's group for her *Silk Purse* album in 1970, after which they decided to form their own band.

Their debut album, *The Eagles* (1972), went gold in America, spawning three hit singles: 'Witchy Woman', 'Take It Easy' and 'Peaceful Easy Feeling'. *Desperado* (1973) was less successful, although it featured 'Tequila Sunrise', one of their most popular songs. The slicker, sharper sound of *On The Border* (1974) brought them their first US No. 1 with 'Best Of My Love'. *One Of These Nights* (1975) topped the US charts for five weeks and included three big hits – 'One Of These Nights', 'Lyin' Eyes' and 'Take It To The Limit'.

REACHING NEW HEIGHTS

Hotel California (1976) was The Eagles' pinnacle. Painstakingly recorded, it caught the full decadence of their vision of the American dream in a blaze of guitars, acerbic lyrics and tight harmonies. It was No. 1 in America for eight weeks, producing two No. 1 singles – 'New Kid In Town' and the title track – and won five Grammy Awards. Their long-awaited follow-up, *The Long Run* (1979), continued to break the band's own records, spending nine weeks at No. 1 and featuring three more major hits: 'Heartache Tonight', 'The Long Run' and 'I Can't Tell You Why'. But by

The laid-back style of The Eagles' early PR shots was in stark contrast to their intense, carefully sculpted songs.

the time *Live* (1980) came out, the band had broken up, although it was not made official until 1982. Whenever Henley was asked when The Eagles would reform he replied, 'When Hell freezes over'. *Hell Freezes Over* (1994) was the result of two years' inching towards a reunion. Since then they have toured periodically and recorded *Long Road Out Of Eden* (2007). The band have continued to tour despite Frey's death in 2016.

LED ZEPPELIN (VOCAL/INSTRUMENTAL GROUP, 1968–80, 2007)

A versatile guitarist, Jimmy Page was an in-demand session player in the mid-1960s. In the summer of 1968, he recruited bassist John Paul Jones. Next to join was Robert Plant, who recommended drummer John Bonham. Led Zeppelin was born. Their eponymous debut album of 1969 contained heavy, stylized versions of Willie Dixon's 'You Shook Me' and 'I Can't Quit You Baby', self-written tracks like the frenetic 'Communication Breakdown' and the slow-building, explosive 'Dazed And Confused'.

Led Zeppelin II (1969) and *Led Zeppelin III* (1970) saw the band's status and ambition spiral hugely. *Led Zeppelin IV* (1971) is widely regarded as their finest album – containing the epic 'Stairway To Heaven' – and heralded the golden age of Led Zeppelin. By now they were touring in a private jet with their logo emblazoned on the side.

TRAGEDY AND SUCCESS

On tour in 1977, Plant was told that his five-year-old son had died suddenly and all group operations were suspended. They reconvened in late 1978 to work on *In Through The Out Door* (1979). It topped the US charts for seven weeks. That month, they made their live return at the UK's Knebworth Festival, mounting the biggest rock production yet seen in Britain. In the summer of 1980, they toured Europe and were rehearsing for an American tour when John Bonham

During long guitar solos Robert Plant, used his trademark howl to accompany the soaring, epic guitar work of Jimmy Page.

was found dead on 25 September, having choked on his own vomit after drinking more than a bottle of vodka. In December, the remaining band members announced that they 'could not continue as we were'. However, in 1985, the surviving members performed as Led Zeppelin at Live Aid, with drummers Phil Collins and Tony Thompson.

In 1994 Page and Plant teamed up for an MTV show, *Unledded*. The resulting album, *No Quarter* (1994), was a Top 5 US success. In 1998 they recorded an album of new songs, *Walking Into Clarksdale*, that went Top 10. In 2007 they reunited for a one-off show at London's O2 Arena with Jason Bonham replacing his father.

PINK FLOYD (VOCAL/INSTRUMENTAL GROUP, 1965–94)

Pink Floyd were formed in London in 1965 by singer/guitarist Syd Barrett, bassist Roger Waters, keyboard player Richard Wright and drummer Nick Mason. The band's debut album, *Piper At The Gates Of Dawn* (1967) made No. 6 in the UK charts. By the end of 1967, however, Barrett's increasingly unstable behaviour was becoming a liability. He left in March the following year, with David Gilmour taking his place. Their second album, *A Saucerful Of Secrets* (1968), couldn't match the success of the first, and *Ummagumma* (1969), though it reached No. 5, had a palpable lack of direction. They returned to form with *Atom Heart Mother* (1970), which gave them their first UK No. 1, and *Meddle* (1971), which peaked at No. 3 and stayed in the charts for over a year and a half.

EPIC MASTERPIECES

In 1973 they released *The Dark Side Of The Moon*, a groundbreaking concept album themed around the pressures of modern life, paranoia and schizophrenia. The album caught the zeitgeist but its appeal remains timeless. Worldwide sales of *Dark Side...* are now over 30 million and rising. Floyd's most ambitious concept,

Originally called Tea Set, the name Pink Floyd was adopted when the band found themselves on the same bill as a band with the same name.

The Wall (1979), dealt with the barriers created by society and individuals. It featured 'Another Brick In The Wall Part 2', an anti-education rant that was a spectacularly successful single. *The Wall* spent 15 weeks at the top of the US album charts.

In 1986 Waters announced that he had left Pink Floyd, who were 'a spent force, creatively'. But Gilmour and Mason disagreed and confirmed their intention to continue. Still recording and performing, in 1994 they released *The Division Bell*. The subsequent tour was lavish, even by Pink Floyd standards, and included a complete performance of *The Dark Side Of The Moon*. However, after the tour, Pink Floyd was wound down. Waters rejoined the band for an emotional one-off reunion at Live 8 in 2005. Barrett died in 2006, and Wright died in 2008.

QUEEN (VOCAL/INSTRUMENTAL GROUP, 1971–PRESENT)

The gorgeously flamboyant Queen was formed in 1970 in London by singer Freddie Mercury, guitarist Brian May and drummer Roger Taylor, with bassist John Deacon completing the line-up in 1971. Their eponymous debut in 1973 quickly won them a loyal following. But it was the tight harmonies and dynamic playing of 'Killer Queen', from their third album *Sheer Heart Attack* (1974), that really caught the band's character and marked them out from the fading glam rock wave. Queen delivered the *coup de grâce* in 1975 with 'Bohemian Rhapsody', a six-minute epic that blended operatic vocals with metal guitars. The single, boosted by a groundbreaking video, stormed the British charts, staying at No. 1 for nine weeks.

JAZZ, POP, ROCK AND DISCO

1980 saw a shift from the bombastic rock of the previous decade. *The Game* was a deliberate pop album. It was a

Freddie Mercury was a glamorous, flamboyant frontman who filled the stage with his histrionic vocal pyrotechnics.

UK No. 1 and their biggest US success, topping the charts for five weeks with two No. 1 singles – the jaunty 'Crazy Little Thing Called Love' and the feisty 'Another One Bites The Dust'.

The next album, *Hot Space* (1982), flirted with disco and funk and featured a collaboration with David Bowie, 'Under Pressure'. *The Works* (1984) was a broader musical sweep embracing synth pop ('Radio Ga Ga'), hard rock ('Hammer To Fall') and pop ('I Want To Break Free'). The following year they were one of the highlights of Live Aid. *A Kind Of Magic* (1986) included 'One Vision'. It was three years before *The Miracle* (1989), which featured 'I Want It All' and 'Breakthru'. The last album recorded with Mercury, *Innuendo* (1991), included 'Headlong' and the grandiose 'The Show Must Go On'. In November 1991 Mercury announced that he had AIDS. Two days later, on 24 November, he died. Periodically, the remaining group members revive the band with another singer, but everyone knows that Mercury can never be replaced.

A TRIBUTE IN FILM

Freddie and the band were finally memorialized in movie form in 2018, with the long awaited biopic, *Bohemian Rhapsody*. Though it received mixed reviews and was criticized for playing fast and loose with historical accuracy, it succeeded for many fans in celebrating the music and the man – the gifted musician and performer that was Freddie Mercury – and was deemed by many to be at least 'triumphant entertainment' in which 'Rami Malek does a commanding job of channelling Freddie Mercury's flamboyant rock-god bravura'.

The magic of Freddie Mercury and Brian May's musical partnership endures despite Mercury's death in 1991.

THE SEVENTIES: A-Z OF ARTISTS

ABBA (VOCAL/INSTRUMENTAL GROUP, 1972-83)

ABBA was formed in 1972 in Sweden, by Benny Andersson, Bjorn Ulvaeus and their girlfriends Frida Lyngstad and Agnetha Faltskog. Their glam rock singalong 'Waterloo' won the 1974 Eurovision Song Contest convincingly and became a No. 1 single. For the rest of the decade they dominated the British and European charts with a string of brilliantly conceived hits.

AC/DC (VOCAL/INSTRUMENTAL GROUP, 1973-PRESENT)

A hard-rocking quintet whose no-frills approach garnered them a huge following, AC/DC were formed in Sydney in 1973 by expatriate Scottish brothers Angus and Malcolm Young (both guitar). Bon Scott became lead singer in 1974. After two Antipodes-only albums, the band moved to America, where their fifth album for Atlantic Records, *Highway To Hell* (1979), sold over six million copies. Scott died from alcohol poisoning in 1980 and was replaced by singer Brian Johnson. The transition was seamless; AC/DC's *Back In Black* (1980) provided their only UK No. 1. AC/DC have stuck to a winning formula, eschewing the vagaries of fashion despite the departures of Malcolm Young in 2014 due to ill health (he died in 2016) and Brian Johnson in 2016 because of hearing problems.

AEROSMITH (VOCAL GROUP, 1973-PRESENT)

This best-selling American heavy rock band centred on the relationship between principal members Steven Tyler (vocals) and Joe Perry (guitar). The pair came together in Boston, with Joey Kramer (drums), Brad Whitford (guitar) and Tom Hamilton (bass). Their first album, *Aerosmith* (1973), was an immediate success. Antagonism between Tyler and Perry led to the latter's departure in 1980, to be replaced by Jimmy Crespo. Differences were set aside four years later

AC/DC's appeal lay in their direct and unfussy hard rock.

Colac

when Perry returned to the fold. The band's profile was raised by the ground-breaking collaboration with rappers Run DMC on the single 'Walk This Way', which led to a triumphant resurgence in Aerosmith's fortunes with *Pump* (1989) and *Get A Grip* (1993). Aerosmith were a key influence on 1990s American hard rock. Their farewell tour, begun in 2017, appears to be open-ended.

ALAN PARSONS PROJECT (VOCAL/INSTRUMENTAL GROUP, 1977–90)

Studio engineer Parsons (b. 1948) had been involved with the engineering of The Beatles' *Abbey Road* (1969) before he became a producer and, briefly, artist in conjunction with songwriter Eric Woolfson. A string of immaculately played and produced concept albums featuring guest singers and musicians charted big in the States, but remained a studio-bound operation. Woolfson died in 2009 and Parsons continues to release albums.

ALICE COOPER (VOCALS, B. 1948)

Although over time the name Alice Cooper came to attach itself to singer Vincent Furnier, it originally applied to the rock band that he fronted, the classic line-up of which comprised Furnier, Glen Buxton (guitar), Michael Bruce (guitar), Dennis Dunaway (bass) and Neal Smith (drums). The 1972 single and album *School's Out* made Cooper a major star in America and Britain. After several hits, Cooper succumbed to alcoholism in the late 1970s and his star waned until the success of the 1989 album *Trash* and single 'Poison' resurrected his career.

THE ALLMAN BROTHERS (VOCAL/INSTRUMENTAL GROUP, 1969–76, 1978–82, 1989–2014)

A southern American blues-rock band comprising Duane Allman (guitar), Gregg Allman (vocals, organ), Dickey Betts (guitar, vocals), Berry Oakley (bass), Butch Trucks and Jai Johanny 'Jaimoe' Johanson (both drums). The Allmans' incendiary guitar sound was captured on *Live At The Fillmore East* (1971). Despite the deaths of Duane Allman (1971) and Oakley (1972) in eerily similar motorcycle accidents, the band played on until 2014. Gregg Allman died in 2017.

Steve Tyler and Joe Perry propelled Aerosmith to the very tip of American rock, where their influence is still felt today.

JEFF BECK (GUITAR, VOCALS, B. 1944)

Regarded as one of Britain's finest rock guitarists, Beck left The Yardbirds in 1968 to form the Jeff Beck Group. The band's second incarnation made two ground-breaking albums that mixed rock and pop with jazz and R&B. In 1972, the guitarist became part of the short-lived power trio Beck, Bogert and Appice, before making an all-instrumental jazz-fusion album *Blow By Blow* (1975). After a live album with Hammer's group in 1977, Beck did not record again until 1980's *There And Back*. His career in the 1980s and 1990s was sporadic and littered with guest appearances, notably on Tina Turner's *Private Dancer* (1984). Latterly, he has developed a style that mixes electronics with blues-rock.

BLACK SABBATH (VOCAL/INSTRUMENTAL GROUP, 1970-2017)

Pioneers of heavy metal, Sabbath hailed from Birmingham, England, and comprised John 'Ozzy' Osbourne (vocals), Tony Iommi (guitar), Terence 'Geezer' Butler (bass) and Bill Ward (drums). Their second album's title track 'Paranoid' was a rare hit, as Black Sabbath's reputation was built on a series of 1970s albums featuring doom-laden lyrics. Osbourne was fired in 1979, but finally rejoined the band in 1997. They disbanded after a farewell tour in 2017.

BLONDIE (VOCAL/INSTRUMENTAL GROUP, 1976-83, 1997-PRESENT)

An internationally popular New York outfit, Blondie's founders were Debbie Harry (vocals) and Chris Stein (guitar) with an eventual supporting cast of Clem Burke (drums), Nigel Harrison (bass), Jimmy Destri (keyboards) and Frank Infante (guitar). More pop-orientated than their contemporaries, Blondie topped the charts on both sides of the Atlantic with *Parallel Lines* (1978), which contained the smash 'Heart of Glass', the first of six UK No. 1 singles. Blondie dabbled in reggae ('The Tide Is High') and calypso ('Island Of Lost Souls') and can claim to have made the first white rap song, 'Rapture'. After the lacklustre *The Hunter* (1982), Blondie disbanded. The group reformed 15 years later and hit the UK No. 1 spot again with 'Maria'.

Blondie was formed around the core of Chris Stein and Debbie Harry. Their pop-driven new wave remains hugely popular.

BOSTON (VOCAL/INSTRUMENTAL GROUP, 1976–PRESENT)

A mainstream American rock band whose meticulously layered music was largely the brainchild of songwriter, guitarist and producer Tom Scholz, Boston's line-up was completed by Brad Delp (vocals), Barry Goudreau (guitar), Sib Hashian (drums) and Fran Sheehan (bass). The all-conquering first album *Boston* (1976) became the biggest-selling debut of all time and yielded the hit single 'More Than A Feeling'. Eight years after the successful *Don't Look Back*, Boston's next album, *Third Stage* (1986), emerged boasting the US No. 1 single 'Amanda'. For 1994's *Walk On*, Delp was replaced as vocalist by Fran Cosmo, although he returned for *Corporate America* (2002). Delp died in 2007. Despite this, they continued to tour and record, and in 2013 they brought out their sixth studio album, *Life, Love & Hope*, featuring lead vocals recorded by Delp before his death.

CHICAGO (VOCAL/INSTRUMENTAL GROUP, 1967–PRESENT)

This horn-backed septet fronted by bassist-vocalist Peter Cetera and keyboardist-vocalist Robert Lamm morphed into soft-rock balladeers in the mid-1970s, thanks to the chart-topping 'If You Leave Me Now' (1976). Many buyers would not have connected them with brash, brassy early hits like '25 Or 6 To 4' (1970), but the change of musical direction ensured the band played on. In 2016 they were inducted into the Rock and Roll Hall of Fame.

THE CLASH (VOCAL/INSTRUMENTAL GROUP, 1976–86)

If The Sex Pistols were the face of UK punk, The Clash was the soul. Their eponymous debut album (1977) was one of the definitive punk albums featuring the rallying anthem 'White Riot' and caustic rockers 'London's Burning' and 'Janie Jones'. *London Calling* (1979) cracked the US Top 30 and *Sandinista!* (1980) had similar success. *Combat Rock* (1982) had a big rock sound, recapturing their best songwriting on 'Rock The Casbah' (their only US Top 10 hit). But even as the album was released the band was starting to fall apart. The next album *Cut The Crap* (1985) served only to prove that they had lost their way, and they disbanded in early 1986.

Committed and powerful, The Clash's live gigs were joyful displays of perspiration and fervour.

ELVIS COSTELLO (GUITAR, VOCALS, B. 1955)

One of the new wave's most celebrated songwriters, Costello (Declan Patrick MacManus) initially portrayed himself as a revenge-obsessed young man before steadily maturing into a genre-straddling elder statesman. His cheeky appropriation of the name 'Elvis' was in tune with the iconoclastic mood of 1977, when his debut album *My Aim Is True* was released. Backed by The Attractions – Bruce Thomas (bass), Steve Nieve (real name Nason, keyboards) and Pete Thomas (drums) – their early work together established Costello as a major artist. Costello went on to work with a variety of collaborators including the songwriter Burt Bacharach, opera singer Anne-Sofie von Otter and New Orleans musician Allen Toussaint.

THE DAMNED (VOCAL/INSTRUMENTAL GROUP, 1976–PRESENT)

A trailblazing outfit responsible for the first British punk single, 'New Rose' in 1976. The original line-up of Dave Vanian (real name Letts, vocals), Brian James (guitar), Captain Sensible (Ray Burns, bass) and Rat Scabies (Chris Miller, drums) disintegrated after the second album *Music For Pleasure* (1978). They later reformed, minus James, and have had changing personnel since. The Damned progressed beyond punk to embrace psychedelia in the mid-1980s, their most successful period commercially.

DEEP PURPLE (VOCAL/INSTRUMENTAL GROUP, 1968–PRESENT)

Deep Purple have sold over 100 million records in a 38-year career – continuous apart from a hiatus between 1976 and 1984 – so are one of the more commercially successful rock bands. They cut one of the all-time classic concert albums in 1972's *Made In Japan*, which included air-guitar anthem 'Smoke On The Water'. Their classic line-up, captured on 1970's *In Rock*, was Ritchie Blackmore (guitar), Jon Lord (keyboards), Ian Gillan (vocals), Ian Paice (drums) and Roger Glover (bass). The latter three were still in harness in 2006 with Don Airey (keyboards) (Lord had retired in 2002 and died in 2012) and sole American Steve Morse (guitar), and now play extensively to South American and former Iron Curtain countries, where their popularity endures. The band started their Long Goodbye Tour in 2017 with no end in sight.

Elvis Costello has battled from new wave conventions to more experimental songwriting and retains a loyal fan base.

EMERSON, LAKE AND PALMER (VOCAL/INSTRUMENTAL GROUP, 1970-78, 1992-2010)

A British supergroup who pioneered progressive rock in the early 1970s, comprised former Nice keyboardist Keith Emerson, Greg Lake, latterly of King Crimson (guitar, bass, vocals), and ex-Atomic Rooster drummer Carl Palmer. ELP's music was a fusion of classical music and rock. Most of the band's lyrics were written by former King Crimson wordsmith Peter Sinfield. ELP made their first major appearance at the Isle of Wight Festival in 1970. Their best-known work, 1973's *Brain Salad Surgery*, was dominated by the epic 'Karn Evil 9'. Notorious for their extravagant live shows, ELP fell from fashion during the punk era, disbanding in 1978 but reforming in the 1990s. Emerson and Lake both died in 2016.

THE FALL (VOCAL/INSTRUMENTAL GROUP, 1976-2017)

Emerging from Manchester in 1976, The Fall are led by vocalist Mark E. Smith, who has employed over 50 different musicians. The Fall's music has remained largely unaltered: a basic garage band throb over which Smith sings and rants his obscure lyrics. They had some chart success with their cover version of The Kinks' 'Victoria' but they have remained a cult attraction. Championed by legendary DJ John Peel, The Fall's output has been prolific, recording some 25 studio albums, 24 live albums, five part-live, part-studio albums and 45 singles and EPs. Thirty-three Fall compilations have been released, of which only *50,000 Fall Fans Can't Be Wrong* (2004) covers the band's entire career. Smith died in 2018.

THE FLYING BURRITO BROTHERS (VOCAL GROUP, 1969-99)

Having invented country rock in The Byrds, Chris Hillman and Gram Parsons (both guitar, vocals), recruited pianist/bassist Chris Ethridge and guitarist 'Sneaky' Pete Kleinow and formed The Burritos to further explore the genre's possibilities. *The Gilded Palace Of Sin* (1969) featured some of Parsons' finest work but he was sacked after 1970's *Burrito Deluxe*. Bernie Leadon and former Byrds drummer Michael Clarke joined and, in 1972, Hillman departed a constantly shifting line-up.

The appeal of Emerson, Lake and Palmer lay in the extravagant complexity of their progressive music.

FREE (VOCAL/INSTRUMENTAL GROUP, 1968–73)

Comprising Paul Rodgers (vocals), Simon Kirke (drums), Paul Kossoff (guitar) and Andy Fraser (bass), Free made headlines in 1970. Their primal blues-rock power made them the stars of that year's Isle of Wight Festival. Hit single 'All Right Now' reached No. 2, and they looked set for lasting stardom. But *Highway* (1970), a hurried follow-up to No. 2 hit album *Fire And Water* (1970), failed to break the UK Top 40. Kossoff's drug problems spiralled (he died in 1976), songwriters Rodgers and Fraser clashed and a potentially world-beating band limped to a sorry conclusion in 1973. Rodgers and Kirke, the only originals, continued in Bad Company, who stripped out the commercial aspects of Free's raw blues songs and turned them into radio- and stadium-friendly chest-beaters. Rodgers has also sung with Queen and The Firm (featuring Jimmy Page) while pursuing a solo career. Fraser died in 2015.

GENESIS (VOCAL/INSTRUMENTAL GROUP, 1967–2007)

The core of Genesis – Peter Gabriel (vocals), Tony Banks (keyboards) and Mike Rutherford (bass) – met at school in the mid-1960s. The recruitment of Steve Hackett (guitar) and Phil Collins (drums) in 1970 completed the classic line-up. Tensions between Gabriel and his colleagues following the ambitious concept album *The Lamb Lies Down On Broadway* (1974) saw the singer quit, to be replaced by the slightly reluctant Collins. *Trick Of The Tail* (1976) became the band's biggest US success so far. Genesis continued to prosper as a trio when Hackett departed after 1977's *Wind And Wuthering*. In the 1980s, a more radio-friendly approach yielded the band's most commercially successful period. Collins left in 1997 and Genesis made one more album with singer Ray Wilson. Collins returned for a reunion tour in 2007.

GEORGE HARRISON (GUITAR, VOCALS, 1943–2001)

Harrison was initially the most successful solo Beatle with *All Things Must Pass* (1971). Removing himself from music to focus on fundraising, he resumed his career with 1972's *Living In The Material World*. But later albums couldn't match

Genesis's success was derived from the complex styling of the vocals and music.

earlier success. He bounced back with 1987's smash 'Got My Mind Set On You'. Harrison's last solo studio album would be *Brainwashed* (2002), released posthumously.

HAWKWIND (VOCAL/INSTRUMENTAL GROUP, 1969–PRESENT)

London space rockers Hawkwind have had many line-ups, but at the time of the UK No. 3 'Silver Machine' in 1972, the core members were ever-present founder Dave Brock (guitar, vocals), Nik Turner (saxophone, vocals), Del Dettmar (synthesizer), Dik Mik (audio generator), Lemmy (bass, vocals), Simon King (drums) and poet/writer Robert Calvert. 1973's double live set *Space Ritual* caught Hawkwind at their peak. Over the years, the band slipped into the margins but their sci-fi psychedelia influenced heavy rock and the rave generation.

IGGY POP (VOCALS, B. 1947)

Iggy Pop (real name James Osterberg) was hailed as the godfather of punk, but when The Stooges called it a day in 1971, he was viewed as a spent force. It was only the persistence of David Bowie that led to them reconvening. The band fell apart again in 1974 and Iggy attempted to kick heroin. Bowie maintained contact, which led to the pair creating Iggy's two 1977 albums in Berlin. The burgeoning punk movement also helped re-ignite Iggy's career. 1979's *New Values* reunited him with some former Stooges colleagues and after *Zombie Birdhouse* (1982) he took a break, returning in 1986 with *Blah Blah Blah*, which again featured Bowie. He continues to record and perform.

THE JAM (VOCAL/INSTRUMENTAL GROUP, 1977–82)

A three-piece from Woking, Surrey, The Jam comprised Paul Weller (guitar, vocals), Bruce Foxton (bass, vocals) and Rick Buckler (drums). Emerging with punk, the band embraced the movement's energy but scorned its negative aspects. After a promising debut, *In The City* (1977), follow-up *This Is The Modern World* (1977) was rushed and unconvincing. *All Mod Cons* (1978) marked the start of a remarkable resurgence. 1979 saw their first Top 10 single, 'The Eton Rifles',

Hawkwind, like many of their psychedelic contemporaries, went through a great many changes of personnel.

and the quasi-concept album *Setting Sons*. The Jam became the UK's most popular group with four No. 1 singles, 'Going Underground', 'Start', 'Town Called Malice' and 'Beat Surrender'. Increasingly uncomfortable with the trio's musical limitations and demands of The Jam's huge audience, Weller disbanded the group in 1982 to form The Style Council.

ELTON JOHN (PIANO, VOCALS, B. 1947)

Elton John became one of the most extrovert performers of the 1970s. He has sold over 250 million records worldwide and is now a national institution. Between 1971 and 1976 he released over a dozen albums, seven of which went to No. 1 in the US. Elton's 'Candle In The Wind', sung at the funeral of Princess Diana in 1997, became the world's biggest-selling single with sales of over 33 million.

JOY DIVISION (VOCAL/INSTRUMENTAL GROUP, 1977–80)

One of the UK's most important post-punk bands, Joy Division's often bleak and claustrophobic music continues to inspire. Enthused by The Sex Pistols' legendary Manchester gig in 1976, school friends Bernard Sumner (guitar) and Peter Hook (bass) formed Stiff Kittens, quickly renamed Warsaw. Recruiting Ian Curtis (vocals) and Steven Morris (drums), they became Joy Division in 1977. Working for independent label Factory Records, they arrived at a unique sound that varied from their live shows. *Unknown Pleasures* (1979) was immediately hailed as a classic by the British music press, while *Closer* (1980) was richer in texture but no less austere in outlook. Standalone single 'Love Will Tear Us Apart' went Top 20 but only after Curtis, who suffered from epilepsy, hanged himself in May 1980, ending the band's career. The others went on to form New Order.

KISS (VOCAL/INSTRUMENTAL GROUP, 1973–2019)

Kiss, founded by New Yorkers Gene Simmons (bass, vocals) and Paul Stanley (guitar, vocals), combined the showmanship of glam rock and the drive of heavy metal. Recruiting Peter Criss (drums, vocals) and Paul 'Ace' Frehley

Elton John burst on to the 1970s pop scene with his talent for hit songs and sheer entertainment

(guitar, vocals) and adopting costumes and elaborate stage make-up, Kiss's early albums made little impact but their reputation grew via an increasingly extravagant stage show. The classic live album, 1975's *Alive*, went quadruple platinum in the States. The ambitious *Destroyer* (1976) and *Love Gun* (1977) consolidated Kiss's position as America's top rock act. All four members released solo albums simultaneously in 1978. Criss and Frehley had departed by the time Kiss unmasked in 1983 although they, and the make-up, would return. Their farewell tour took place in 2019.

KRAFTWERK (VOCAL/INSTRUMENTAL GROUP, 1970-PRESENT)

This German electronic group's pioneering use of synthesizers made them a very influential band. Co-founders Florian Schneider and Ralf Hütter set up Kling Klang Studio, where the pair made three albums. They were augmented by electronic percussionists Wolfgang Flür and Karl Bartos on a tour to promote the band's fourth album, *Autobahn* (1974), completing Kraftwerk's classic line-up. The three albums that followed, *Radio-Activity* (1975), *Trans-Europe Express* (1977) and *The Man Machine* (1978), were to alter the course of popular music, highlighting the possibilities of the synthesizer as a lead instrument. Live performances played up the mechanical angle, using life-size robot replicas of the band members. Kraftwerk continue to record and tour, albeit intermittently. Schneider left in 2008.

JOHN LENNON (GUITAR, VOCALS, 1940-80)

Lennon's post-Beatles solo career began with *John Lennon/Plastic Ono Band* (1970), a harrowingly honest record inspired by the Primal Scream therapy that Lennon was undergoing. *Imagine* (1971) featured his best-loved song and was a more sugar-coated affair. The workmanlike *Mind Games* (1973) was recorded in the shadow of Lennon's separation from Yoko Ono. His infamous 'lost weekend' in LA produced 1974's *Walls And Bridges*, a partial return to form. He was reunited with Yoko Ono in 1974 and, after the birth of son Sean in 1975, Lennon temporarily retired from music. Shortly before his murder in 1980, he re-emerged with *Double Fantasy*, an album shared equally between Lennon and Ono.

Kiss combined New York glam with heavy metal licks and became one of the biggest-selling US bands of the 1970s.

LYNYRD SKYNYRD (VOCAL/INSTRUMENTAL GROUP, 1973–2018)

This southern rock band came together in Jacksonville, Florida, around the core of Ronnie Van Zant (vocals), Allen Collins (guitar) and Gary Rossington (guitar), plus Billy Powell (keyboards), Larry Junstrom (bass), and Bob Burns (drums). An air crash shortly before the release of their sixth album *Street Survivors* in 1977 claimed the lives of Van Zant and additional guitarist Steve Gaines, although the band continued. Skynyrd remain best known for the anthemic 'Freebird'. They announced their farewell tour in 2018.

BOB MARLEY (GUITAR, VOCALS, 1945–81)

The man responsible for popularizing reggae, Bob Marley's career began with the Wailers. Marley later met the Barrett brothers – Aston (bass) and Carlton (drums) – and the new Wailers were formed in 1974. Signed in 1973 to Island Records, Marley had to wait until 1975 for his breakthrough – 'No Woman No Cry'. *Exodus* (1977) and *Kaya* (1978) were massive sellers internationally. *Uprising* (1980) was to be his last studio album before his death from cancer in 1981.

PAUL McCARTNEY AND WINGS (VOCAL/INSTRUMENTAL GROUP, 1971–80)

McCartney put together Wings in the summer of 1971, featuring his wife Linda on keyboards in a line-up that saw many changes in the band's nine-year career. *Band On The Run* (1973) was a commercial success and a world tour followed in 1975–76, but the band splintered in 1977. The ex-Beatle's arrest for possession of cannabis in 1980 caused a cancelled tour and the end of Wings. McCartney has continued his solo career ever since.

VAN MORRISON (VOCALS, B. 1945)

After leaving Irish beat group Them, Van Morrison relocated to the States in 1967 to launch a solo career. His debut single 'Brown Eyed Girl' was a hit in America but not Britain. His second album *Astral Weeks* (1968) was a massively influential work that added Celtic and jazz influences to his R&B and soul roots. Particularly prolific in the mid-1970s,

For many, Bob Marley was a Rasta poet with a rare vision and a charismatic performer who appealed across the barriers of race and colour.

Morrison has made over 40 albums in his career; his 40th studio album, *The Prophet Speaks*, was released in late 2018. He was knighted for services to music in 2016.

MOTT THE HOOPLE (VOCAL/INSTRUMENTAL GROUP, 1969–74)

A riotous rock band from Shrewsbury comprising Ian Hunter (vocals, keyboards), Mick Ralphs (guitar), Pete 'Overend' Watts (bass), Verden Allen (organ) and Dale 'Buffin' Griffin (drums), Mott were about to split when offered 'All The Young Dudes' by David Bowie in 1972. This began a string of five hits and two successful albums: *Mott* (1973) and *The Hoople* (1974). The band split in 1974, but their enduring influence on British rock was proven by an unlikely 2009 reunion.

THE NEW YORK DOLLS (VOCAL GROUP, 1971–77, 2004–11)

A trailblazing quintet with an energetic and shambolic style. The New York Dolls were formed in 1971 by David Johansen (vocals) and Johnny Thunders (guitar, died 1991), adding Sylvain Sylvain (guitar), Arthur Kane (bass) and Billy Murcia (drums), who died in 1972 and was replaced by Jerry Nolan. The 1973 debut *New York Dolls* was promoted by a legendary appearance on British television. The album was not a big seller and record company Mercury dropped The Dolls after a similar failure of the 1974 follow-up, *Too Much Too Soon*. Future Sex Pistols manager Malcolm McLaren took charge of the band's final days as they flirted with communist iconography. Folding in 1977, surviving Dolls Sylvain and Johansen released new albums in 2006 and 2009, playing festivals to acclaim. They have been inactive since 2011.

GARY NUMAN (VARIOUS INSTRUMENTS, VOCALS, B. 1958)

Numan's electronic music was influenced by Berlin-era Bowie and set in a dystopian future of his own imagining. The hypnotic synthesizers and emotionless vocals earned him a second 1979 chart topper, 'Cars', which was also a smash in America. Mainstream success proved difficult to sustain but Numan still commands a devoted cult following with a new, more industrial sound.

The New York Dolls brutally challenged the attitudes of pop's smart set by cross-dressing in messy drag.

MIKE OLDFIELD (MULTI-INSTRUMENTALIST, B. 1953)

Prodigiously talented, Oldfield played all the instruments on 1973's *Tubular Bells*. It was a transatlantic best-seller, helped by the use of its main theme in *The Exorcist* (1973). *Hergest Ridge* (1974) was a British No. 1 whilst *Ommadawn* (1975) and *Incantations* (1978) displayed African and folk influences. Oldfield has since reworked *Tubular Bells* several times.

RAINBOW (VOCAL/INSTRUMENTAL GROUP, 1975–84, 1994–97, 2015–PRESENT)

Formed by ex-Deep Purple guitarist Ritchie Blackmore, Rainbow' debut album *Ritchie Blackmore's Rainbow* (1975) featured hit 'Man On The Silver Mountain'. 1979's *Down To Earth* saw the band's first major singles chart successes, 'All Night Long' and 'Since You Been Gone'. In 1980, the band headlined the inaugural Monsters of Rock Festival at Castle Donington. The group split in 1984, but a new Rainbow was revived by Blackmore in the 1990s, and again in 2015.

THE RAMONES (VOCAL/INSTRUMENTAL GROUP, 1974–96)

The Ramones – Joey (vocals), Johnny (guitar), Dee Dee (bass) and Tommy (drums) – were the definitive American punk rock group. They played their first gig in 1974 and quickly gained a reputation with their 20-minute sets of two-minute songs. They toured the US and UK frequently and finally cracked the UK Top 30 with 'Sheena Is A Punk Rocker' from their third album, *Rocket To Russia* (1977). *End Of The Century* (1980) was their most commercially successful album, going Top 20 in the UK and Top 50 in the US. The title track of *Brain Drain* (1989) was used for the Stephen King movie *Pet Sematary*, and they released *Loco Live* (1991), *Mondo Bizarro* (1992) and an album of covers, *Acid Eaters* (1994), before the appropriately titled *Adios Amigos* (1995). Joey, Johnny and Dee Dee all died between 2001 and 2004.

ROXY MUSIC (VOCAL/INSTRUMENTAL GROUP, 1972–83, 1998–2011)

Fronted by singer Bryan Ferry, the line-up included synthesizer player/tape operator Brian Eno, Phil Manzanera (guitar), Andy McKay (saxophone), Paul Thompson (drums) and various bassists. When Eno left after *For Your Pleasure*

The Ramones' no-nonsense two-minute songs drove the sound of punk from the mid-1970s.

(1973), Roxy's music lost some of its experimental edge. After 1976's *Siren*, Roxy Music took a break. Their return with *Manifesto* (1978), followed by *Flesh + Blood* (1980) and *Avalon* (1983), was more commercial. They disbanded in 1983, but reformed in 1998. They have been inactive since a 2011 tour, although Ferry continues a solo career.

RUSH (VOCAL GROUP, 1968–PRESENT)

This Canadian power trio went through a number of line-up changes before settling with Geddy Lee (bass, keyboards, vocals), Alex Lifeson (guitar) and Neil Peart (drummer, lyricist). Their blend of progressive rock and heavy metal was at its peak on the concept album *2112* (1976). *Permanent Waves* (1980) and *Moving Pictures* (1981) were punchier and new wave influenced. After the extensive use of synthesizers in the mid-1980s, Rush returned to their roots in the 1990s.

THE SEX PISTOLS (VOCAL/INSTRUMENTAL GROUP, 1975–78)

Malcolm McLaren was responsible for bringing together bassist Glen Matlock, guitarist Steve Jones, drummer Paul Cook and singer John Lydon (Johnny Rotten). In October 1976, The Sex Pistols signed to EMI and released a single, 'Anarchy In The UK'. Matlock was replaced by Sid Vicious, and in 1977, The Sex Pistols released 'God Save The Queen'. Banned by the BBC, it reached No. 2 amid a widespread belief that it had been kept from the top. At the beginning of 1978, Rotten quit, and in October, Vicious was charged with his girlfriend's murder. Released on bail, he died of a heroin overdose. *The Great Rock'n'Roll Swindle* (1979) was the soundtrack to McLaren's film about The Sex Pistols. It yielded two more Top 10 singles – 'Silly Thing' and 'C'Mon Everybody' – but by then, there was no band.

CARLY SIMON (SINGER/SONGWRITER, B. 1945)

Growing up in a musical New York family, Carly Simon won a Grammy for Best New Artist in 1971. Her first big hit, 'You're So Vain' (1972), sparked an enduring interest in the song's subject that she has coyly never clarified. That same year she married fellow singer-songwriter James Taylor. They had several hits together and separately before divorcing

Rush were proud exponents of pomp rock, with their flashy two-neck guitars and power rock sound.

in 1981. Simon broadened her musical horizons and continued her hit career. Several of her songs were featured in popular films, including 'Nobody Does It Better' from 1977's James Bond outing, *The Spy Who Loved Me*.

PAUL SIMON (GUITAR, VOCALS, B. 1941)

Paul Simon (1972) was an eclectic affair followed a year later by *There Goes Rhymin' Simon*. His third solo album, *Still Crazy After All These Years* (1975), featured a reunion with Art Garfunkel on the duet 'My Little Town'. The singer's most popular and influential work was *Graceland* (1986), which utilized African musicians, helping popularize what would be dubbed 'World Music'. He retired after a farewell tour in 2018.

SIOUXSIE AND THE BANSHEES (VOCAL/INSTRUMENTAL GROUP, 1976–96)

A legendary punk band, The Banshees consisted of vocalist Siouxsie, Steve Severin (bass), John McKay (guitar) and Kenny Morris (drums). McKay and Morris left abruptly in 1979 to be replaced by Budgie (ex-Slits) and John McGeoch, formerly of Magazine, whose more sophisticated, nimble-fingered guitar steered the band away from the punk assault of old and into their most popular phase.

PATTI SMITH (SINGER/SONGWRITER, B. 1946)

Patti Smith started her career writing poetry, as well as a play, lyrics and sleeve notes. In 1974 she released independent single, 'Hey Joe'/'Piss Factory' – punk poetry set to rock music. Turning to music, she released defiantly avant-garde *Horses* in 1975, which made a brief appearance in the US Top 50; 'Because The Night', co-written with Bruce Springsteen, was a 1978 hit. In 1980 Patti married Fred Smith and retired from music to bring up a family. When Fred died in 1994, her response was to start performing again, confronting her life as mother, widow and artist on *Gone Again* (1996) and *Peace And Noise* (1997). In 2007, she was inducted into the Rock And Roll Hall Of Fame, and in 2011 she was awarded the Polar Music Prize. Smith continues to record and perform.

Patti Smith's uncompromising delivery of her poetry and lyrics won her the approval of fans and contemporaries alike.

BRUCE SPRINGSTEEN (GUITAR, VOCALS, B. 1949)

Hailed as the new Dylan after two albums, Springsteen fully realized his potential with the widescreen *Born To Run* (1975). Managerial problems delayed *Darkness On The Edge Of Town* (1978), a more sombre but no less compelling work. 1984's *Born In The USA* catapulted Springsteen into the mainstream, selling 14 million copies worldwide. Backed by the E Street Band, Springsteen was without equal as a live performer, with gigs often lasting over four hours, as documented on the 1986 five-record epic *Live 1977–85*. He opted for a more intimate approach for *Tunnel Of Love* (1987), which detailed the breakdown of his first marriage and was Springsteen's last work with the E Street Band until a 1999 reunion tour. He continues to record and tour and has also appeared in the one-man show, Springsteen On Broadway.

STATUS QUO (VOCAL/INSTRUMENTAL GROUP, 1967–PRESENT)

The great survivors of British rock, Quo are synonymous with the three-chord boogie, but first came to public attention in 1967 with psychedelically-flavoured single 'Pictures Of Matchstick Men'. A change of direction to their more familiar style was explored on the 1970 album *Ma Kelly's Greasy Spoon*. The line-up coalesced around the ever-present duo of Francis Rossi (guitar, vocals) and Rick Parfitt (guitar) with Alan Lancaster (bass) and Richard Coughlan (drums). Bedecked in denim and plimsolls, Quo were a potent live force, consolidating their popularity with a string of consistent albums, such as *Hello!* (1973), *On The Level* (1975) and *Blue For You* (1976). Their many hits include 'Caroline', their only UK singles chart-topper 'Down Down', 'In The Army Now' and the song that would open Live Aid, John Fogerty's 'Rocking All Over The World'. Parfitt retired in 2016 after health problems and died later that year, but the band boogies on.

STEELY DAN (VOCAL/INSTRUMENTAL GROUP, 1972–81, 1993–PRESENT)

This critically acclaimed New York outfit was formed around the nucleus of songwriters Walter Becker (bass, vocals) and Donald Fagen (keyboards, vocals). Drummer Jim Hodder and guitarists Denny Dias and Jeff 'Skunk' Baxter completed the line-up, along with vocalist David Palmer. Their debut *Can't Buy A Thrill* (1972) contained the radio staples 'Reeling In The

Bruce Springsteen has a distinctive line in gritty storytelling. His 1970s shows, though, were lively, dynamic and bombastic.

Years' and 'Do It Again'. Palmer left before the less impressive follow-up *Countdown To Ecstasy* (1973), but the Dan were back on peak form on 1974's *Pretzel Logic*, at which point Fagen and Becker started to rely on session musicians, whose ranks included keyboardist/singer Michael McDonald. After a hiatus following 1980's *Gaucho*, Steely Dan reformed in 1993 and, surprisingly, have returned to the live arena. Becker died in 2017 but Fagen has kept the band going.

THE STRANGLERS (VOCAL GROUP, 1974–PRESENT)

Formed in 1974 in Guildford, Surrey, The Stranglers were relatively experienced musicians when they broke through at the same time as punk in 1977. Comprising Hugh Cornwell (guitar, vocals), Jean-Jacques Burnel (bass, vocals), Dave Greenfield (keyboards) and Jet Black (drums), the band's early sound was notable for The Doors-like keyboards and grumbling bass. The Stranglers' two 1977 albums, *Rattus Norvegicus* and *No More Heroes*, made them the new wave's best-selling band. *Black And White* (1978) and *The Raven* (1979) kept their profile high. A more experimental direction was forged with 1981's *Gospel According To The Meninblack* whilst *La Folie* (1982) yielded the band's biggest hit, 'Golden Brown'. After 10 albums, Cornwell quit for a solo career in 1990. The Stranglers remain a popular live act.

STYX (VOCAL/INSTRUMENTAL GROUP, 1972–80, 1996–PRESENT)

This Chicago quintet were leaders of the pomp-rock genre, peaking in the 1977–80 period with albums like *The Grand Illusion* (1977), *Cornerstone* (1979) and conceptual *Paradise Theater* (1981). Fronted by Dennis DeYoung but essentially faceless, they were prime US radio fodder, alongside bands such as Boston and REO Speedwagon, before punk arrived on those shores. The band had a couple of breaks in the 1980s and 1990s and DeYoung left in 1999, but the others have continued.

SUPERTRAMP (VOCAL/INSTRUMENTAL GROUP, 1970–PRESENT)

Keyboard player Rick Davies assembled Supertramp under the patronage of a Dutch millionaire. His most important

Some regarded The Stranglers as punk poseurs for jumping on the bandwagon, but their polished, incisive performances won them a huge following.

recruit was singer Roger Hodgson. After several line-up changes, Dougie Thomson (bass), Bob Siebenberg (drums) and John Helliwell (saxophone, keyboards) joined for the third album, *Crime Of The Century* (1974), which was their commercial breakthrough. Supertramp relocated to the States and their material became more pop orientated. 1979's *Breakfast In America* scaled the heights worldwide, spawning hits with the title track, 'The Logical Song' and 'Take The Long Way Home'. Citing musical differences with Davies, Hodgson left after *Goodbye Stranger* (1982). Davies has kept Supertramp alive with a combination of old and new members, while Hodgson continues to tour his version of the band but without the name.

T. REX (VOCAL/INSTRUMENTAL GROUP, 1970–77)

The first glam rock band evolved from acoustic duo Tyrannosaurus Rex, formed by Marc Bolan (guitar, vocals) and multi-instrumentalist Steve Peregrine-Took. Mickey Finn (bongos) replaced Took in 1969 as Bolan began to deploy electric instruments. Shortening the name to T. Rex heralded a chart breakthrough in October 1970 with the single 'Ride A White Swan'. Steve Currie (bass) and Bill Legend (drums) were added and T. Rex achieved further Top 10 success, including four No. 1s. However, by 1973, T. Rex were losing ground not only to glam rivals Slade, but also to pin-up boy David Cassidy. Bolan's popularity slipped away until a new generation hailed him as one of punk's forefathers. Bolan died in a car accident in September 1977.

TANGERINE DREAM (VOCAL/INSTRUMENTAL GROUP, 1970–PRESENT)

A German electronic outfit founded by Edgar Froese (guitar), whose main lieutenants were Christophe Franke (drums) and Peter Baumann (organ). Operating as a keyboard trio, their experimental 1970s work fitted the progressive zeitgeist. They achieved unexpected UK chart success with 1973's Phaedra, the first commercial album to feature the sequencer. The band continued their pioneering work in electronic music, bringing out soundtracks, including to the game *Grand Auto Theft V*, and over 100 albums, the most recent being *Quantam Gate* (2017).

Supertramp, in full flares and white suits, left the UK to become superstars in the US, with the best-selling album Breakfast In America.

JAMES TAYLOR (GUITAR, VOCALS, B. 1948)

Discovered by The Beatles' Apple label for whom he recorded his first album in 1968, Taylor moved back to America to seek a cure for heroin addiction. He signed to Warner Bros. and unleashed the three-million-selling *Sweet Baby James* in 1970. Although his early work typified the sensitive early 1970s singer/songwriter, 1977's *JT* displayed a more upbeat approach. His 1976 *Greatest Hits* collection was certified diamond for 10 million sales.

TELEVISION (VOCAL/INSTRUMENTAL GROUP, 1973-78, 1992-PRESENT)

An art punk group formed in New York in 1973, Television originally included Richard Hell (bass), along with guitarists Tom Verlaine and Robert Lloyd and Billy Ficca (drums). Hell soon left due to friction with Verlaine. Fred Smith, briefly a member of Blondie, took over on bass. The interlocking guitars of Verlaine and Lloyd provided the band's trademark and set them apart from their peers. Television's first release was a pioneering independent single, 'Little Johnny Jewel'. The debut album *Marquee Moon* (1977) was immediately hailed by critics as a classic but the band split after the disappointing follow-up, *Adventure* (1978). Television reformed in 1992 for a third, eponymous album and have performed together occasionally since, although Lloyd left in 2007.

10CC (VOCAL/INSTRUMENTAL GROUP, 1972-95)

Eric Stewart, Lol Creme (both guitar, keyboards), Graham Gouldman (bass) and Kevin Godley (drums) wrote, sang and produced four albums of inventive pop/rock from 1973 to 1976. Their 1975 No. 1 'I'm Not In Love' was also a Stateside smash. 10cc split in two in 1976 with Gouldman and Stewart retaining the name while Godley and Creme recorded as a duo, later becoming sought-after video directors.

THIN LIZZY (VOCAL/INSTRUMENTAL GROUP, 1970-83)

This Irish hard rock band were led by the charismatic Phil Lynott (bass, vocals), with Brian Downey (drums) and, for

Television originated from the same New York new wave scene as Blondie, gigging regularly at the influential CBGBs.

the classic line-up, the twin lead guitars of Scott Gorham and Brian Robertson. The 1976 smash 'The Boys Are Back In Town' marked the start of the band's golden period, culminating in the classic *Live And Dangerous* (1978). Thin Lizzy split in the 1980s. Lynott died in 1985 of drug-related problems, but various ex-members periodically revive the Thin Lizzy name for tribute shows.

ULTRAVOX (VOCAL/INSTRUMENTAL GROUP, 1977–85, 2009)

Originally consisting of John Foxx (Dennis Leigh, vocals), Chris Cross (Chris Allen, bass), Billy Currie (keyboards, synthesizer), Steve Shears (guitar) and Warren Cann (drums), Ultravox were one of the first new wave bands to utilize the synthesizer. Foxx departed after three albums to be replaced in 1979 by Midge Ure, under whose influence a more accessible sound abounded.

WHITESNAKE (VOCAL/INSTRUMENTAL GROUP, 1977–91, 1994, 1997–98, 2002–PRESENT)

Founded by ex-Deep Purple vocalist Dave Coverdale, Whitesnake released debut EP *Snakebite* (1978), which spawned their first hit and a staple of their live set, 'Ain't No Love In The Heart Of The City'. *Ready An' Willing* (1980) was a breakthrough hit for the band, reaching the UK Top 10 and becoming their first entry into the US Top 100. The signing of a record deal with Geffen in 1984 coincided with a shift from blues rock to a harder sound. Constant line-up changes have resulted in some 40 musicians passing through the band.

XTC (VOCAL/INSTRUMENTAL GROUP, 1977–92, 1999–2006)

Influential Swindon new-wavers, fronted by Andy Partridge (guitar, vocals) with Colin Moulding (bass, vocals), Barry Andrews (keyboards) and Terry Chambers (drums, until 1985). After two 1978 albums, *White Music* and *Go 2*, Andrews departed and the band's sound was overhauled when guitarist Dave Gregory was recruited. After a seven-year lay-off, Partridge and Moulding revived XTC in 1999 as a studio-based outfit.

Phil Lynott was a brilliant frontman for Thin Lizzy and brought them great success.

YES (VOCAL/INSTRUMENTAL GROUP, 1968-PRESENT)

The quintessential progressive rock outfit, Yes were formed by bassist Chris Squire, singer Jon Anderson and drummer Bill Bruford. *The Yes Album* (1970) featured new guitarist Steve Howe and established them as a major force. The classic line-up was completed when keyboard maestro Rick Wakeman joined. 1971's *Fragile* and 1972's *Close To The Edge* saw Yes at the peak of their powers. Alan White replaced Bruford on *Tales From Topographic Oceans* (1973), a double set containing four side-long compositions. Since then, the band has enjoyed a successful but convoluted career that rarely featured the same line-up on consecutive albums.

NEIL YOUNG (GUITAR, VOCALS, B. 1945)

This highly respected Canadian musician's solo career began in 1969 with *Neil Young*. For his next album, *Everybody Knows This Is Nowhere* (1969), he recruited Danny Whitten (guitar), Billy Talbot (bass) and Ralph Molina (drums), collectively known as Crazy Horse. Shortly afterwards, Young joined Crosby, Stills and Nash for an album and tour. 1972's country-tinged 'solo' album *Harvest* was a huge seller, but darkness engulfed Young's work following the sacking and subsequent death by overdose of Whitten. His album *Zuma* (1975) featured one of Young's most celebrated songs, 'Cortez The Killer'. 1978's *Rust Never Sleeps* represented a positive reaction to punk, befitting an artist who has never allowed himself to become complacent and has consistently produced some of rock'n'roll's most vital music.

ZZ TOP (VOCAL/INSTRUMENTAL GROUP, 1970-PRESENT)

A visually distinctive Texan trio comprising Billy Gibbons (vocals, guitar), Dusty Hill (bass, vocals) and Frank Beard (drums), ZZ Top honed their sound through constant gigging. Supporting The Rolling Stones brought them to a wider audience and the third album *Tres Hombres* (1973) was the band's commercial breakthrough. They went on to experience million-selling success with 1983's *Eliminator* and have cleverly reworked that formula ever since.

Neil Young's whining delivery and anarchic guitar style won over a generation of fans.

This was a decade when the impact of dance culture on rock and vice versa sometimes led to exciting results: the 1980s opened with 'Thriller' and closed with the Madchester scene of The Happy Mondays.

Punk had subsided to become the less threatening new wave movement, which, along with the new romantics, dominated the early days of the decade. And as with the 1960s, producers emerged with their own distinctive sound.

The synthesizer was the decade's dominant sound, with many groups replacing guitars with synths. One exception was Dublin's U2, who started the decade supporting Talking Heads and ended it a supergroup. With live rock thin on the ground, a new wave of heavy metal swept Britain before the rise of 'hair-band' rock from the States later in the decade redressed the transatlantic balance. Meanwhile, hip hop was beginning to be heard via the likes of Afrika Bambaataa and Grandmaster Flash.

The fall of the Berlin Wall in 1989 threatened to open new markets to rock, both live and via the new compact disc medium, while even China had allowed western bands to penetrate the Bamboo Curtain. Popular music was now truly an international language.

THE EIGHTIES

THE EIGHTIES: SOUNDS + SOURCES

Just as the 1970s will be recalled for punk's anti-fashion statements, so the decade that followed will be remembered as much for artists' return to the dressing-up box as much as the music they made. Duran Duran, Adam and The Ants, Spandau Ballet, Soft Cell, Simple Minds, The Human League and Depeche Mode were just some of the bands to spring from so-called new romantic roots.

FUN AND FASHION

David Bowie was the single main influence on the movement, his 1980 hit 'Fashion' becoming something of an anthem. London clubs such as Billy's (which became the Blitz) gave the likes of doorman Steve Strange (Visage) and cloakroom attendant Boy George (Culture Club) their first leg-up to fame.

Instead of guitars, these new bands for the most part preferred synthesizers and rhythm machines. The synth was now considerably less expensive and, inspired by Gary Numan's late-1970s hits, British youth was favouring the instrument over the previously ubiquitous six-string.

America's Talking Heads would attempt to forge a link between new wave and black music, more than doubling their quartet with an influx of funk musicians. New Order, who sprang from the ruins of Joy Division after Ian Curtis's 1980 suicide, had a greater impact with their dance-oriented 'Blue Monday', which proved to be one of the most influential dance tracks of the era.

The 1980s audience was more manicured and self-conscious with their fashion than in the late 1970s.

A NEW ATTITUDE

The previous decade had gone out with a bang in the spitting, snarling shape of punk. But while The Sex Pistols played their final gig in San Francisco, the impact of punk and its nihilistic attitude had not really been felt in the land of the greenback. So US musicians and producers took the energy and lost the attitude, resulting in 'new wave', a highly marketable proposition.

The biggest single promoter of 1980s music was MTV (Music Television), which first broadcast its mix of videos in the States in 1981. It would take until the end of the decade for satellite television to reach Britain, but by that time it and sister channel VH1 (Video Hits 1, launched in 1985) had proved themselves starmakers of the highest order. Their VMAs (Video Music Awards) would become as important as the Grammys in reflecting public taste, which the channel itself had helped shape.

POPTASTIC

Former Jackson Five singer Michael Jackson created the soundtrack for the 1980s dancefloor in the shape of the 1982 50-million-seller *Thriller*. 'Jacko' was also the first black artist to break big on MTV, thanks in no small part to his ground-breaking videos and also the shrewd device of inviting guitar god Eddie Van Halen to contribute to 'Beat It'. The echoes of *Thriller* were still being felt two decades later via artists such as Justin Timberlake.

Jackson's female counterpart was Madonna Veronica Louise Ciccone, whose certainty was such that she could afford to jettison all but the first of her names in her successful quest for fame. She made an indelible mark on both sides of the Atlantic, and no female performer, with the exception of the resurgent Tina Turner, would

Madonna constantly reinvented herself throughout the decade, shaping the sounds and moves of the 1980s dance floors.

remain untouched by her influence. Her fashions, attitude, willingness to mock religion and sell her sexuality put her on top of the charts and on the cover of *Time* magazine. And she would reinvent herself to remain relevant in the current millennium.

Britain's biggest pop-dance star in the making was George Michael of Wham!. He emerged from his group to find solo fame with a more adult brand of music, as did Sting when the three egos that comprised The Police could co-exist no more. The brand of intelligent adult rock Sting offered found a similar audience to that which allowed Phil Collins to forge a multi-platinum solo career.

Prince emerged from left field to become first a 'more credible Jacko' and then something intangibly more. His edgy songs and liberal obscenities/profanities kept him deliberately on the fringes of popular acceptability, but by donating songs to the likes of Sheena Easton, Chaka Khan, The Bangles and Sinead O'Connor he could lay claim to being the decade's Stevie Wonder figure.

POLITICAL AWARENESS

America's Bruce Springsteen finally took the last step to global superstardom in 1984 with 'Born In The USA' and its attendant album. The song, musing on post-Vietnam America, became unintentionally ironic when taken up (without prior permission) by Ronald Reagan, a heavy-handed president who was rapidly becoming the most unpopular with the younger generation since Nixon. Paul Simon, long amicably divorced from Art Garfunkel, had yet to approach the success that duo had obtained, but his *Graceland* album (1986), recorded in defiance of the cultural boycott of South Africa with black musicians of that country, would see him reinvent himself to register one of the first best-sellers of the infant compact-disc era, as well as putting world music well and truly on the map.

The Band Aid Christmas single, 'Do They Know It's Christmas', brought together the might and majesty of modern pop royalty.

The 1980s was arguably the decade when rock rediscovered its conscience. Boomtown Rat Bob Geldof followed up 1984's charity single 'Do They Know It's Christmas?', inspired by watching BBC news reports of the famine in Africa, with simultaneous all-star concerts at Wembley Stadium and JFK Stadium, Philadelphia, in 1985, featuring supergroups like Queen, U2 and the reformed Led Zeppelin. Of the bands that featured, Ireland's U2 would prove to display the most lasting political awareness, appearing calculatedly controversial with songs like 'Sunday Bloody Sunday', yet they were always at the forefront when it came to promoting good causes. Two decades after Live Aid, Bono, along with Geldof, was instrumental in the G8 countries affording Africa a debt relief. As the decade rolled on, 'conscience rock' did its bit for Farm Aid, Red Wedge, Amnesty International and Ferry Aid. The Nelson Mandela 70th Birthday Tribute Concert in 1988 was an awareness-raiding exercise that both hastened the release of the future South African president and made an overnight star of Tracy Chapman.

iN WiTH THE NEW

The compact disc arrived in Europe in 1983 and, by the end of the decade, the traditional vinyl record was on the way out. While players were prohibitively expensive when the first CD album, Billy Joel's *52nd Street*, was launched (in Japan only) in 1982, the sales of Dire Straits' album *Brothers In Arms* three years later showed the compact disc was indeed here to stay.

Black music regrouped to make a new mark in the post-disco world when Kurtis Blow became the first rap act to be signed by a major label. The likes of Grandmaster Flash and Afrika Bambaataa (who jointly headlined the first rap festival in Britain in 1986) would follow, but it would take three middle-class white Jewish boys from New York – The Beastie Boys – to make the biggest commercial impact this decade with their tongue-in-cheek take on the genre.

Ozzy Osbourne was one of many aging rockers who revived their reputation at Live Aid, one of the 1980s' most memorable and impactive events.

Heavy rock enjoyed boosts at the beginning and the end of the decade. The first flowering came in the shape of the so-called New Wave of British Heavy Metal (NWOBHM), which spawned the long-running likes of Saxon, Iron Maiden and Def Leppard. Metallica were big fans of this grass-roots movement based around live performance.

BIG HAIR AND BIG SELLERS

By the end of the decade the US answer to NWOBHM had materialized in the shape of 'hair' bands, so-called because of the preposterous bouffants sported by some of the participants. These bands cleverly allied rock power with MTV-friendly image and videos, resulting in mammoth sales for the likes of Bon Jovi, whose 1986 *Slippery When Wet* album was the *Thriller* of its genre. It sold 10 million copies in the US alone and spawned two No. 1 singles. From Britain, Def Leppard managed to catch the coat-tails of the movement to enjoy Stateside success that continues today.

Maybe the slowest-burning success story of the 1980s was R.E.M., who entered the recording world with the indie single 'Radio Free Europe' in 1981 and closed the decade signed for major label Warner Brothers. The four-piece from Athens, Georgia, were the visible part of an 'iceberg' known as US college radio. Britain's equivalent was The Smiths, fronted by Morrissey, a similarly androgynous figure to Michael Stipe. However, they failed to see out the decade in a welter of recrimination between 'Moz' and guitarist/songwriting partner Johnny Marr.

With legwarmers, 'Frankie Says' T-shirts and Spandau Ballet's kilts, the 1980s could claim to be the decade popular music dressed to impress. It was also the decade when video killed the radio star: from now on, you would have to look the part as well as sound it.

Def Leppard flew the stadium rock flag for Britian, capturing the spirit of the age almost as well as the hairstyles..

THE EIGHTIES: KEY ARTISTS

BON JOVI (VOCAL/INSTRUMENTAL GROUP, 1983-PRESENT)

Bon Jovi was formed in 1983 in New Jersey by singer Jon Bon Jovi, guitarist Richie Sambora, keyboard player David Bryan, bassist Alec John Such and drummer Tico Torres. Their eponymous debut (1984) stalled just outside the US Top 40. *7800 Fahrenheit* (1985) peaked just inside the Top 40. Their make-or-break album, *Slippery When Wet* (1986), stormed to the top of the US charts, propelled by two No. 1 singles – 'You Give Love A Bad Name' and 'Livin' On A Prayer'. In the UK it reached No. 6 and stayed in the charts for two years. *New Jersey* (1988) was a No. 1 album in the UK and the US where it topped the charts for four weeks, providing five Top 10 singles, including two No. 1s: 'Bad Medicine' and 'I'll Be There For You'.

INTERNATIONAL POPULARITY

After a gruelling international touring schedule, the band took a break in 1990. In 1992 they reassembled to record *Keep The Faith*. *Crossroads* (1994) was a greatest hits collection that featured two new songs that became hits as well: 'Always' and 'Someday I'll Be Saturday Night'. For *These Days* (1995) Bon Jovi produced a leaner sound that kept them in touch with the new generation of rock fans. Another world tour, another extended break. But *Crush* (2000) showed that it had not damaged Bon Jovi's status. It was a worldwide No. 1, helped by the smash hit 'It's My Life'. Such was their international popularity that the *Crush* world tour was extended from six months to a year. *Bounce* (2002) restored their popularity in America, reaching No. 2 in the US and UK. They then reinterpreted their hits on *This Left Feels Right* (2003). *Have A Nice Day* (2005) was followed up with another world tour. Sambora left in 2013 and they are no longer innovators, but they retain their enormous popularity.

Though now more a happy-clappy stadium soft rock band, Bon Jovi's pop-metal had some edge in the mid-1980s.

MICHAEL JACKSON (VOCALS, 1958-2009)

The self-proclaimed 'King of Pop', Michael Jackson was undeniably the biggest star of the 1980s. Jackson had enjoyed early success as the youngest member of The Jackson Five and as a solo artist with two US Top 5 singles – 'Got To Be There' and 'Rockin' Robin' – but it wasn't until 1977, when he teamed up with producer Quincy Jones, that things got really interesting. With *Off The Wall* (1979) Jackson became the first solo artist to have four US Top 10 singles from one album. Then *Thriller* eclipsed even the high standards of *Off The Wall* with seven US Top 10 singles including two No. 1s – 'Billie Jean' and 'Beat It'. The album was also visually choreographed by videos, including a mini-epic for 'Thriller'. *Thriller* was an impossible album to follow and while *Bad* (1987) could not compete in chart terms, it still sold 22 million copies and produced a record five US No. 1 singles. It was the last album Jackson made with Jones.

A TROUBLED STAR

Success continued with *Dangerous* (1991), but the promotional tour ended prematurely in 1993 when Jackson was engulfed in scandal. Fans had been tolerant of his eccentricities, but allegations of child abuse did irreparable damage to his reputation.

HIStory (1995) was a double CD of greatest hits and new songs, and became another US and UK No. 1. *Blood On The Dancefloor* (1997) featured remixes from *HIStory* and new songs. *Invincible* (2001) was Jackson's first album of all-new material since *Dangerous* and debuted at No. 1 in the US, selling over 11 million worldwide. But controversy was never far away. He inexplicably dangled his child over a hotel balcony in Berlin; an image-restoring TV documentary had the opposite effect; and in 2005 he faced more child-abuse allegations. Finally, his mysterious death in June 2009, on the eve of a much-trumpeted live comeback, saw him deified by millions of devastated followers.

Michael Jackson's solo career gave him a worldwide popularity that would eclipse all other 1980s pop acts.

THE POLICE (VOCAL/INSTRUMENTAL GROUP, 1977-84, 1986, 2007-08)

The Police were founded in London at the height of the punk boom in 1977 by drummer Stewart Copeland with singer/bassist Sting (real name Gordon Sumner) and guitarist Henry Padovani, later joined by guitarist Andy Summers. Padovani soon departed and the remaining three developed a unique sound in the blend of Summers' crisp guitar, Sting's distinctive vocals and Copeland's clattering drums. Heavily influenced by reggae, their first two singles, 'Roxanne' and 'Can't Stand Losing You', did not chart when first released in 1978 as the BBC took a dim view of the subject matter – prostitution and suicide, respectively. Reason prevailed the following year when the success of the reactivated singles launched the debut album *Outlandos D'Amour* (1978) into the UK chart for a two-year residency. *Reggatta De Blanc* (1979) quickly followed and went to No. 1 in Britain, along with the first two singles, 'Message In A Bottle' and 'Walking On The Moon', confirming The Police as the country's most popular new group.

GOING SOLO

Mainstream success in America arrived when *Zenyatta Mondatta* (1980) went Top 5 and spawned two US Top 10 singles, 'Don't Stand So Close To Me' and 'De Do Do Do, De Da Da Da'. In 1982 Summers, Copeland and Sting took a year out for solo projects, reconvening to record *Synchronicity* (1983). Despite tensions, particularly between Sting and Copeland, The Police managed to produce their most crafted and diverse album, which included the classic, subtly sinister 'Every Breath You Take'. The Police played their final shows in Melbourne, Australia in March 1984. There was no official announcement that the band had split up, although Sting was quick to launch his solo career. The Police have reconvened occasionally since, playing at Sting's wedding in 1992 and performing three numbers to celebrate their induction into the Rock And Roll Hall Of Fame in 2003. They reformed in 2007 to celebrate their thirtieth anniversary with a bout of world touring.

Despite The Police being at the height of their worldwide fame in 1983, Sting soon after embarked upon an almost equally successful solo career.

PRINCE (GUITAR, VOCALS, 1958-2016)

Born Prince Rogers Nelson, the enigma that is Prince is the most innovative, mercurial and controversial black rock star since Jimi Hendrix. His debut, *For You* (1978), was a blend of R&B, rock and pop, with titles like 'Soft And Wet' creating an early notoriety. His breakthrough came with *1999* (1982), which yielded a total of four US Top 10 singles. But it was *Purple Rain* (1984) that vaulted Prince to superstardom, topping the US charts for 24 weeks. The soundtrack to an autobiographical movie, it featured two US No. 1 hits – 'When Doves Cry' and 'Let's Go Crazy'. The album also made the UK Top 10.

A prolific artist, in 1985 alone, he won two Grammys and an Oscar, wrote Sheena Easton's US Top 10 hit 'Sugar Walls', donated '4 The Tears In Your Eyes' to *USA For Africa*, and released *Around The World In A Day*, which topped the US charts for three weeks and made the UK Top 5.

HIGHLY INDEPENDENT

Parade (1986), his eighth album in as many years, went Top 5 in the US and UK and included the US No. 1 (and UK No. 4) 'Kiss'. A series of critically acclaimed and successful albums followed. *Symbol* (1992) gave him his fourth UK No. 1 (US No. 6). Prince then changed his name to the unpronounceable symbol and became embroiled in a contractual dispute with Warner Bros. The independently released 'The Most Beautiful Girl In The World' was a No. 1 hit around much of the world in 1994.

Prince celebrated independence from Warner with *Emancipation* (1996), which went Top 20 in the US and UK. But subsequent albums were increasingly self-indulgent until the focused *Musicology* (2004) made No. 3 in the UK and US. His 2007 album *Planet Earth* he chose to give away free with a newspaper. He continued to tour and record until April 2016 when he was found dead at his Paisley Park residence from an accidental overdose of the opioid fentanyl.

Prince was the first artist since The Beatles to simultaneously have a film, album and single at No. 1 after the release of Purple Rain.

U2 (VOCAL/INSTRUMENTAL GROUP, 1976-PRESENT)

U2 are unique in having kept a stable line-up throughout a lengthy career. Singer Bono (Paul Hewson), guitarist The Edge (David Evans), bassist Adam Clayton and drummer Larry Mullen Jr. formed a band at school in Dublin in 1976 and came to England in 1980. Their debut album *Boy* (1980) was well received and constant gigging helped establish their reputation as live performers. The breakthrough came with the passionate 'New Year's Day', from 1983's *War*. The live mini-album *Under A Blood Red Sky* (1984) was a largely successful attempt to capture U2's live act and earned them their first US Top 30 placing. Momentum continued to gather with *The Unforgettable Fire* (1984), featuring 'Pride (In The Name Of Love)'. It cracked the Top 20 in America, fittingly for an album that revealed U2's growing fascination with the United States.

TOPPING THE CHARTS

U2's next album, the eagerly anticipated *The Joshua Tree* (1987) delivered three hit singles – 'Where The Streets Have No Name', 'I Still Haven't Found What I'm Looking For' and 'With Or Without You'. *The Joshua Tree* went on to sell 25 million copies worldwide. It was quickly followed by *Rattle And Hum* (1988), a part-live/part-studio double set that gave the band their first UK No. 1 single, 'Desire'. *Achtung Baby* (1991) was a deliberate attempt to forge a new direction, incorporating elements of dance and electronica. Even more ambitious was *Zooropa* (1993), an ambient-leaning album featuring sampling and treated sounds, totally unlike their previous work. *Pop* (1997) completed U2's transformation into a post-modern rock band. It was one of their lesser-selling albums, although 'Discotheque' was a British No. 1. This was followed by the back-to-basics approach of *All That You Can't Leave Behind* (2000), which yielded a UK chart topper in 'Beautiful Day'. *How To Dismantle An Atomic Bomb* (2004) spawned yet more UK No. 1s in 'Vertigo' and 'Sometimes You Can't Make It On Your Own'. In 2017 they celebrated the 30th anniversary of *The Joshua Tree* with a world tour, playing the album in its entirety. In 2018 another world tour promoted their latest album, *Songs Of Experience*.

U2 on stage in 1983, around the time of their Steve Lillywhite-produced breakthrough album, 1983's War.

THE EIGHTIES: A-Z OF ARTISTS

ADAM AND THE ANTS (VOCAL/INSTRUMENTAL GROUP, 1977–82)

The charismatic Adam Ant (b. Stuart Goddard) was a prominent figure in the boutiques and clubs of the punk scene, and the band released *Dirk Wears White Sox* in 1979. After his backing band became Bow Wow Wow, he started from scratch, gaining huge fame with 1980's *Kings Of The Wild Frontier*. Powered by African-style drumming and Link Wray-influenced guitar, the hits streamed out. 'Dog Eat Dog', 'Ant Music', 'Stand And Deliver', 'Prince Charming' and 'Ant Rap' were all boosted by videos that emphasized flamboyance and helped define the new romantic movement. Adam's solo output included the chart-topper 'Goody Two Shoes', which became his first US smash in 1982. He disbanded the Ants that year, continuing as a solo artist.

ANTHRAX (VOCAL/INSTRUMENTAL GROUP, 1981–PRESENT)

Formed in New York with Dan Spitz (guitar), Scott Ian (guitar), Dan Lilker (bass) and Charlie Benante (drums). After adding Joey Belladonna (vocals) they hit paydirt, recording *Spreading The Disease* for Island in 1986. They gained an awesome live reputation, while issuing blistering records (*State Of Euphoria*, 1988, and *Sound Of White Noise*, 1993), including a team-up with rapper Chuck D, 'Bring The Noise'. They remain one of the most interesting and charismatic modern metal bands.

THE B52s (VOCAL/INSTRUMENTAL GROUP, 1976–PRESENT)

The B52s' kitsch dress sense and spiky, surreal updating of 1960s dance music won a huge college following during the punk/new wave years, but guitarist Ricky Wilson died from AIDS in 1985, leaving original members Kate Pierson (organ, vocals), Cindy Wilson (guitar, vocals), Fred Schneider (keyboards, vocals) and Keith Strickland (drums). In 1986, an updated version of 1978's 'Rock Lobster' became a UK Top 20 smash. 'Love Shack', 'Roam' and 'Meet The Flintstones' followed it up the charts.

One of the key progenitors of thrash metal, Anthrax fused heavy metal proficiency and punk energy to create their influential sound.

THE BEASTIE BOYS (VOCAL/RAP/INSTRUMENTAL GROUP, 1981–2012)

The Beastie Boys – Michael 'Mike D' Diamond, Adam 'MCA' Yauch and Adam 'King Ad-Rock' Horovitz – began life as a New York hardcore punk band, but became the first important white rap act. Debut *Licensed To Ill* (1986) was a good-time rap-metal crossover, spawning the hit singles 'Fight For Your Right To Party', 'No Sleep Till Brooklyn' and 'She's On It'. These bratty anthems and the band's over-the-top stage show caused as much controversy as first-wave punk. After a hiatus, the unexpectedly diverse and thoughtful *Paul's Boutique* arrived in 1989, followed by equally interesting collections. Yauch died in 2012 from cancer and the others disbanded the group.

PAT BENATAR (VOCALS, B. 1953)

Brooklyn-born Benatar established herself as queen of arena rock with a trio of fine albums. Her poppier debut *In The Heat Of The Night* (1979) was followed by the heavier, Grammy-winning *Crimes Of Passion* (1980) and her only No. 1, *Precious Time* (1981). Her expressive tones powered several hit singles including 'Hit Me With Your Best Shot', 'Love Is A Battlefield' and 'We Belong'. Husband Neil Giraldo provided guitar support while Benatar blazed a trail for women rockers.

NICK CAVE (VOCALS, B. 1957))

Nick Cave (vocals) began his fascinating career in Boys Next Door, who became The Birthday Party (Mick Harvey, guitar; Tracy Pew, bass; Phil Calvert, drums). A gothic, blues punk band of fearsome intensity, showcasing Cave's brutal, Captain Beefheart-style lyrics, they released three albums, 1981's *Prayers On Fire* being the pick. Cave later regrouped, retaining Mick Harvey and adding guitarist Blixa Bargeld to form Bad Seeds. Their highly influential mixture of corrupted lounge music, gothic gospel and misanthropic post-punk balladry is displayed on many fine albums, including *From Her To Eternity* (1984), *Henry's Dream* (1992), *Murder Ballads* (1996), and the very witty *Abattoir Blues/Lyre Of Orpheus* (2004). Cave is a Leonard Cohen for Generation X.

Nick Cave formed The Birthday Party before becoming one of the most respected solo artists of the past two decades.

ROBERT CRAY (GUITAR, VOCALS, B. 1953)

By the 1970s the blues was a debased currency amongst Afro-Americans. Robert Cray was the first young black artist to rehabilitate the genre, releasing *Who's Been Talkin'* in 1980. *Bad Influence* emerged in late 1983 (1984 in the UK) with Eric Clapton sitting in. *Showdown* (1985), shared with two of Cray's heroes, Albert Collins and Johnny Copeland, displayed the tradition Robert was coming from. Where he was going to was pointed out on his soul-tinged breakthrough, *Strong Persuader* in 1986, which married Cray's full-toned, economic guitar style and his beautiful, gospely voice. His career now spans more than 20 albums.

THE CULT (VOCAL/INSTRUMENTAL GROUP, 1984–95, 2001–02, 2006–PRESENT)

Centred on singer Ian Astbury and Billy Duffy (guitar), The Cult (initially Southern Death Cult), released goth/psychedelic *Dreamtime* in 1984. Third album *Electric* was influential on many nu-metal bands and Guns N' Roses (who stole drummer Matt Sorum). *Sonic Temple* (1989) was more mainstream rock, making the US Top 10. They still record and tour.

THE CURE (VOCAL/INSTRUMENTAL GROUP, 1976–PRESENT)

This influential post-punk outfit, led by Robert Smith (vocals, guitar) with Lol Tolhurst (drums) and Michael Dempsey (bass; later replaced by Simon Gallup), debuted in 1978 with the Albert Camus-inspired 'Killing An Arab'. The tone got even darker with *Seventeen Seconds* (1980), *Faith* (1981) and *Pornography* (1982). 'Let's Go To Bed' (1982) showed Smith's quirky pop sensibility, which would resurface on hits such as the jazzy 'Lovecats'. American breakthroughs followed, with 1987's *Kiss Me, Kiss Me, Kiss Me* and 1989's 'Lovesong'. Smith's writing still hinted at deep depression, but his music displayed great eclecticism and the group are often hailed as fathers of goth. They remain surprisingly active.

THE DEAD KENNEDYS (VOCAL/INSTRUMENTAL GROUP, 1978–86)

This controversial bunch of San Franciscans were one of the truly great punk bands. Debut 1979 single 'California Uber

The Cure were definable not only by singer Robert Smith's distinctive look, but also by their catchy, edgy, pop songwriting.

Alles' set the template, with Jello Biafra (Eric Boucher) trashing the American dream, voice quavering with menace, and East Bay Ray Glasser's guitar, Klaus Flouride (Geoffrey Lyall)'s bass and Bruce Slesinger's drums in thunderous support. Debut album *Fresh Fruit For Rotting Vegetables* (1980) became a cult classic. Biafra now pursues a spoken word career.

DEF LEPPARD (VOCAL/INSTRUMENTAL GROUP, 1977–PRESENT)

Formed in Sheffield, Def Leppard's fresh brand of poppy heavy metal, led by Joe Elliott (vocals) and Pete Willis (lead guitar), soon won them fans. Debut album *On Through The Night* (1980) just missed the US Top 50; but with 1983's *Pyromania* they became giants of the genre, hitting No. 2 Stateside. 1987's *Hysteria* made US No. 1, and UK No. 2. Guitarist Steve Clark died from drink and drugs in 1991, but the band returned, topping the charts with *Adrenalize* (1992). Since those heady days – with smashes such as 'Love Bites' and 'Let's Get Rocked' – they have modernized successfully on *Slang* (1996), *Euphoria* (1999) and *X* (2002). Their pioneering, catchy pop rock still draws crowds.

DEPECHE MODE (VOCAL/INSTRUMENTAL GROUP, 1976–PRESENT)

Essex schoolboys Vince Clarke (keyboards), Martin Gore (vocals, guitar, keyboards), Andy Fletcher (keyboards) and singer Dave Gahan formed to create melancholic but hooky synth-pop and succeeded with the Top 10 album *Speak And Spell* (1981) and classic dance track 'Just Can't Get Enough'. After Clarke departed to create Erasure, they racked up hits that combined Gahan's world-weary delivery with a riffy, industrial-lite appeal – 'Everything Counts', 'People Are People' (their first US hit) and 'Master And Servant'. Deeply depressive collections such as *Some Great Reward* (1984), *Black Celebration* (1986) and *Music For The Masses* (1987) cemented their US reputation, while 1990's *Violator* and its premier single 'Personal Jesus' marked a move to a more guitar-oriented sound. Varied outings since prove the band have plenty of life left.

DIRE STRAITS (VOCAL/INSTRUMENTAL GROUP, 1977–95)

Led by guitarist Mark Knopfler with brother David (guitar), John Illsley (bass) and Pick Withers (drums), Dire Straits went

New wavers Depeche Mode combined post-punk urgency with dancefloor synth pop to create an exciting new sound.

from playing the London pub circuit to a US hit album, thanks to Knopfler's inventive guitar playing, street-poet lyrics and fine pop rock tunesmithery. Debut single 'Sultans Of Swing' was a punchy helping of Dylanesque roots rock. *Communiqué* (1979) and *Love Over Gold* (1982) paved the way for the multiple-platinum *Brothers In Arms* (1985), with 'Money For Nothing' satirizing the very business they were in. After 1991's slightly disappointing *On Every Street*, Knopfler embarked on a solo career. Dire Straits will be remembered as an intelligent but accessible band who could run the gamut from the borderline experimental (the intro to 'Private Investigations', 1982) to the chug-a-long pop rock of 'Walk Of Life' (1985).

DURAN DURAN (VOCAL/INSTRUMENTAL GROUP, 1978–PRESENT)

The most glamorous of the new romantic bands, Duran Duran had a string of Top 10 hits, including 'Girls On Film' (1981), 'Hungry Like The Wolf', 'Save A Prayer' and 'Rio' (all 1982), 'The Reflex' and 'Wild Boys' (1984). In 1985, Simon Le Bon (vocals), Nick Rhodes (keyboards) and Roger Taylor (drums) worked on side project Arcadia, while the Taylors – Andy (guitar) and John (bass) – joined The Power Station. 1993's *The Wedding Album* yielded the hit 'Ordinary World'.

EURYTHMICS (VOCAL/INSTRUMENTAL GROUP, 1980–90, 1999–2000)

Dave Stewart (keyboards, guitars) and Annie Lennox (vocals) were Eurythmics. In 1983, the title track of *Sweet Dreams (Are Made Of This)* went to No. 1 in the US. The synth-powered pop noir of 'Who's That Girl' was followed by tropical-tinged 'Right By Your Side', proving their adaptability and intelligence. (Lennox's versatile, soulful voice is almost unparalleled in modern pop.) Another 1983 album, *Touch*, yielded the yearning 'Here Comes The Rain Again'. On *Be Yourself Tonight* (1985) their bluesier side emerged, with hits such as 'Sisters Are Doin' It For Themselves' with Franklin. The album's beautiful 'There Must Be An Angel' became their only UK No. 1. Their truly great albums behind them, they still released hit singles in 'Missionary Man' (1986) and 'I Need A Man' (1988) before solo careers beckoned.

FOREIGNER (VOCAL/INSTRUMENTAL GROUP, 1976–PRESENT)

These AOR giants established themselves in 1977 with their eponymous debut album and single 'Feels Like The First

Duran Duran ruled the charts through part of the 1980s with singles like 'Girls On Film' and 'Rio'.

Time', both reaching US No. 4. The band was founded by Englishman Mick Jones (guitar) with Lou Gramm's dramatic tenor vocals. The original line-up was completed by Ian McDonald (guitar, keyboards), Al Greenwood (keyboards, replaced by Rick Wills, 1979), Ed Gagliardi (bass) and Dennis Elliott (drums). Further hits such as 'Cold As Ice' and 'Double Vision' piled up in America; 1981's 4 attained the UK Top 5. Their monster smash, power ballad 'I Want To Know What Love Is', arrived in 1984. Tensions between Jones and Gramm led to Gramm quitting – twice. While things have been smoothed over and the band still tours – recently celebrating all manner of 40th anniversaries – you can never be sure which original members will actually show up.

PETER GABRIEL (SINGER/SONGWRITER, B. 1950)

Gabriel left Genesis in 1975. His first solo album produced the intriguing hit 'Solsbury Hill', which told of that exit. In 1980, the avant-pop of 'Games Without Frontiers' began a run of accessible art rock albums and singles, including the political 'Biko', 1982's Peter Gabriel (Security in the US), and 1986's triumphant world-music influenced So and its mega-hit 'Sledgehammer'. The gap between his albums and tours has got longer, but the quality of both remains high.

GUNS N' ROSES (VOCAL/INSTRUMENTAL GROUP, 1985–PRESENT)

Axl Rose (b. William Bailey, vocals) and Izzy Stradlin (b. Jeffrey Isbell, guitar) were joined by Slash (b. Saul Hudson, guitar), Duff McKagan (bass) and Steve Adler (drums) to form a band that gave the heavy rock scene a mighty shaking. Their debut album, Appetite For Destruction (1987), combined the attack of AC/DC with a punk aesthetic and powerful lyrics. It went to the US No. 1 spot, as did 'Sweet Child O' Mine'. The next few years saw much debauchery, and the releases of the massive-selling Use Your Illusion I and II (1991) and The Spaghetti Incident (1993). It was 15 years before the next album, Chinese Democracy, by which time all the original band and most of their replacements had quit or been fired by Rose. Slash and McKagan were back in 2016 for the Not In This Lifetime... Tour. There is no sign of another album just yet.

The baddest boys of the 1980s: Guns N' Roses brought down-and-dirty rock'n'roll behaviour back into the pop-tastic decade.

THE HAPPY MONDAYS (VOCAL/INSTRUMENTAL GROUP, 1985–92, 1999, 2006–PRESENT)

Led by vocalist Shaun Ryder, the band were at the forefront of the 'Madchester' scene. They appropriated licks from psychedelia, soul and hip-hop to come up with a danceable brand of rock that reached its apotheosis on 1990's *Pills 'n' Thrills And Bellyaches*, which included UK Top 5s 'Step On' and 'Kinky Afro'. Ryder went on to form Black Grape but periodically reforms The Happy Mondays.

DEBBIE HARRY (VOCALS, B. 1945)

Even before Blondie disbanded in 1982, Debbie Harry had launched her solo career. *Kookoo*, released in 1981, was produced by Chic's Nile Rodgers and Bernard Edwards, but failed to yield any hits. Through the 1980s and 1990s she was more popular in Europe than her native America, with hits like 'I Want That Man' and 'French Kissin'. She has collaborated with Iggy Pop, REM, the Jazz Messengers and Elvis Costello on various projects.

THE HOUSEMARTINS (VOCAL/INSTRUMENTAL GROUP, 1983–88)

Formed in Hull by Paul Heaton (vocals), Stan Cullimore (guitar, vocals), Ted Key (bass) and Hugh Whitaker (drums), the band were the epitome of unassuming British indie pop. Their up-tempo melodic songs belied some abrasive, politically charged lyrics on the likes of 'Sheep' and their first big hit, 'Happy Hour'. They scored a UK No. 1 with the gospelly 'Caravan Of Love'. Heaton went on to form The Beautiful South, while latter-day bassist Norman Cook became Fatboy Slim.

HÜSKER DÜ (VOCAL/INSTRUMENTAL GROUP, 1979–87)

Bob Mould (vocals, guitar), Grant Hart (drums, vocals) and Greg Norton (bass) were forefathers of emo, and an immensely important bridge between hardcore and alternative rock. The Minneapolis trio are cited by the likes of The Pixies and Nirvana as a massive influence. Their third album *Zen Arcade* (1984) is an exemplary collection of punk pop.

The Happy Mondays were the epitome of late-1980s/early-1990s rave culture, renowned for their (frequently) drink- and drug-fuelled behaviour.

INXS (VOCAL/INSTRUMENTAL GROUP, 1977–2012)

Michael Hutchence (vocals), Tim Farriss (guitar), Andrew Farriss (keyboards, guitar), Garry Gary Beers (bass), Kirk Pengilly (guitar, saxophone, vocals) and John Farriss (drums) paid their dues on the Australian pub circuit. Taking elements of The Stones, Doors and funk rock, the band broke into the American market with *Shabooh Shoobah* (1982). 1985's *Listen Like Thieves* consolidated their position, while *Kick* (1987) and 'I Need You Tonight' confirmed them as global superstars. 1990's 'Suicide Blonde', from their hit album, *X*, had a prophetic ring. Hutchence, a genuine rock god, was dating petite blonde Kylie Minogue; he later partnered peroxide blonde Paula Yates, and his death in 1997 came by his own hand. Hutchence was replaced with *Pop Idol*-style talent-contest winner J.D. Fortune for one tour, after which the band fell silent.

IRON MAIDEN (VOCAL/INSTRUMENTAL GROUP, 1976–PRESENT)

Original lead vocalist Paul Di'Anno led this east London heavy metal outfit to No. 4 on the UK chart in 1980 with their self-titled debut. New singer Bruce Dickinson went three places better with 1982's *The Number Of The Beast*. Iron Maiden soon became Britain's top metal group, with their hard-rocking, if slightly tongue-in-cheek approach. They progressed steadily upwards until Dickinson quit in 1993. They faltered with replacement singer Blaze Bayley from Wolfsbane until Dickinson was induced to return in 1999. Since then, they have conquered the globe with a succession of multi-million selling albums and DVDs, skilfully managed and touring the world in their customized Boeing 747 piloted by Dickinson.

JAPAN (VOCAL/INSTRUMENTAL GROUP, 1974–82, 1991)

This south-east London band led by singer David Sylvian (real name Batt), with Mick Karn (bass, saxophone), Rob Dean (guitar), Richard Barbieri (synthesizers) and Steve Jansen (b. Stephen Batt, drums), started out playing guitar-based glam and tried to fit in with punk, but found their forte in the new romantic era. They finally made inroads with their third album, *Quiet Life* (1980), due to its intricate, intelligent synth-based pop. *Tin Drum* (1981) produced one of the most captivating Top 5 singles of the time, 'Ghosts'. The band reconvened as Rain Tree Crow for one final album in 1991.

Merging rock and dance influences, Australian group INXS became one of the late 1980s' biggest success stories.

JEAN-MICHEL JARRE (COMPOSER, B. 1948)

Frenchman Jarre is best known for his 1977 hit 'Oxygene', taken from the album of the same name, which reached No. 2 in the UK. He was one of the first rock musicians to employ synthesizers. A series of instrumental albums in the 1970s and 1980s repeated the pattern, including *Equinoxe* (1978), *Magnetic Fields* (1981) and the 1982 *Concerts In China* live album. His gigs, such as his 1989 show in London's Docklands, are huge *son et lumière* spectacles. He continues to make varied albums and performances.

THE JESUS AND MARY CHAIN (VOCAL/INSTRUMENTAL GROUP, 1983–98)

This much-lauded Scottish crew featured Reid brothers, William and Jim (both vocals, guitar), and, for a while, Bobby Gillespie of Primal Scream (drums). They took The Velvet Underground's art rock and overlaid surprisingly poppy melodies. Their Top 20 UK singles included the classic 'Some Candy Talking'. Ultimately, the siblings launched interesting solo ventures.

KILLING JOKE (VOCAL/INSTRUMENTAL GROUP, 1979–PRESENT)

Jeremy 'Jaz' Coleman (vocals), Geordie Walker (guitar, synthesizers), Youth (b. Martin Glover, bass, vocals) and Paul Ferguson (drums) formed one of the most alluring post-punk bands. They are now considered forefathers of American nu-punk. Their compulsive, tribal blasts on debut *Killing Joke* (1980) and *Revelations* (1982) created a legion of rabid fans and a handful of hit singles, including 1985's 'Love Like Blood'. The band still crops up with strong albums.

GRACE JONES (SINGER/SONGWRITER, B. 1948)

Jamaican-born Grace Jones moved to New York aged 13, where she became an archly stylish artist on the gay disco scene in the 1970s and a successful model thanks to her 1.8m (6ft) frame and provocative style. Her recording career took off in the early 1980s when she switched to a post-disco fusion of reggae and rock, and she eventually broke through from the dance charts to the mainstream when 'Slave To The Rhythm' cracked the UK Top 20 in 1985.

Grace Jones' statuesque and flamboyant look ensured that she would always stand out from the crowd.

CYNDI LAUPER (SINGER/SONGWRITER, B. 1953)

Taking advantage of the emergence of MTV, Brooklyn-raised Cyndi Lauper had a big hit with what was arguably the first Girl Power anthem, 'Girls Just Wanna Have Fun', in 1984. She had four more hits from her debut album, *She's So Unusual*, and was briefly ahead of her rival Madonna. She was back on top of the charts a couple of years later with the title track from her *True Colors* album. Her eclectic style and music has ensured a varied career.

THE LEMONHEADS (VOCAL/INSTRUMENTAL GROUP, 1983-96, 2005-PRESENT)

Evan Dando (vocals, guitar, drums) and Ben Deily (guitar, drums) were the main movers behind the indie rock of Boston's Lemonheads, with *Hate Your Friends* and *Creator* (both 1988) and *Lick* (1989). An acrimonious split with Deily eventually brought Dando's girlfriend, Juliana Hatfield, into the fold for the melodic grunge and Americana of *It's A Shame About Ray* (1992). A version of Simon and Garfunkel's 'Mrs Robinson' saw British chart action, though the US remained fairly indifferent – 1993's *Come On Feel The Lemonheads* was a UK Top 5 entry, but did not even make the American Top 50. The band reformed in 2005 and subsequent albums have been interesting without catching their earlier spark.

HUEY LEWIS AND THE NEWS (VOCAL/INSTRUMENTAL GROUP, 1979-PRESENT)

Huey Lewis (b. Hugh Cregg III, vocals, guitar) and Sean Hopper (vocals, guitar) were refugees from country rock band Clover who found global success with the pop-inflected blue-collar rock of their next incarnation. Their third album, *Sports* (1983), became an American No. 1, and bore three Top 10 US tracks including 'Heart And Soul'. 'The Power Of Love' established the band in the UK.

MADONNA (SINGER/SONGWRITER, B. 1958)

The first female pop star to have complete control of her music and image, Madonna has brilliantly manipulated the media to ensure an iconic status that has outstripped her musical achievements. After her disco beginnings in New

Cyndi Lauper's distinctive look, eclectic fusion of pop, rock, reggae and funk and strong vocals made her a darling of the MTV generation.

York where she moved to from her native Michigan, Madonna broke through with 'Borderline' in 1984 and began an extraordinary run of 17 consecutive Top Ten US singles, including seven No. 1s and four No. 2s. By 1990, she was a worldwide megastar and, despite a chequered film career, she has remained a global icon ever since, with a cunning mix of music and controversy.

MARILLION (VOCAL/INSTRUMENTAL GROUP, 1978–PRESENT)

Fish (b. Derek Dick) was the band's charismatic vocalist until 1988, penning complicated but engaging neo-prog rock of *Script For A Jester's Tear* (1983) and *Fugazi* (1984). The band also landed UK hits with 'Kayleigh', 'Lavender' and 'Incommunicado'. Since Steve Hogarth took over they have kept the unfashionable banner of prog flying with aplomb while updating their sound. Recent albums have been fan-funded.

MEAT LOAF (VOCALS, B. 1947)

Born Marvin Lee Aday, Meat Loaf's musical theatre background was apparent in the camp but appealing excess *Bat Out Of Hell* in 1977. His melodramatic delivery and massive stature made him an unlikely rock icon; the album eventually sold over 40 million copies. Its successor, *Dead Ringer* (1981), topped the UK charts, as did 'Dead Ringer For Love', featuring Cher as co-vocalist. Meat Loaf released several pot-boiling collections before *Bat Out Of Hell II: Back Into Hell* (1993), which was a transatlantic No. 1, as was its main single 'I'd Do Anything For Love (But I Won't Do That)'.

MEGADETH (VOCAL/INSTRUMENTAL GROUP, 1983–PRESENT)

Ex-Metallica guitarist Dave Mustaine hardened and sped up his erstwhile band's already ferocious thrash metal. His pessimistic, politicized lyrics drive the likes of *Peace Sells … But Who's Buying?* (1986), with *Rust In Peace* (1990) being the most critically acclaimed album. After an attempt to go more mainstream, the band returned to form with *The System Has Failed* (2004), peaking with *United Abominations* (2007) and *Endgame* (2009).

Named after J.R.R. Tolkien's Silmarillion, Marillion were perhaps the biggest of the new wave of prog rock artists in the 1980s.

MIDNIGHT OIL (VOCAL/INSTRUMENTAL GROUP, 1971-2002, 2009, 2016-PRESENT)

Fronted by the striking, bald, six-and-a-half-footer Peter Garrett, this 1960s-influenced, politically committed Australian band still have plenty to say. They played hundreds of gigs before making their US and UK album debut with *10,9,8,7,6,5,4,3,2,1* in 1983 and it was not until 'Beds Are Burning', from the superb *Diesel And Dust* (1988), that they became internationally renowned. They reformed for a 77-date world tour in 2016.

MÖTLEY CRÜE (VOCAL/INSTRUMENTAL GROUP, 1980-2002, 2006-15)

Vince Neil (vocals), Mick Mars (guitar), Nikki Sixx (bass) and Tommy Lee (drums) became the world's most notorious heavy metal band, as much for their off-record excesses as for their music. Over the years, the production got slicker, but their subject matter (sex'n'drugs'n'rock'n'roll) remained the same. *Shout At The Devil* (1983) became their US Top 20 debut. *Theatre of Pain* (1985) and *Girls Girls Girls* (1987) kept the ball rolling. *Dr Feelgood* (1989) was their first No. 1 (UK No. 4). Egos and drugs brought them down in 2002, but they were back four years later before closing down for good in 2015.

MOTÖRHEAD (VOCAL/INSTRUMENTAL GROUP, 1975-2015)

The seemingly indestructible Lemmy Kilmister (vocals, bass) was a former member of Hawkwind, and Motörhead are named after a Hawkwind song he penned. The line-up settled in the late 1970s with 'Fast' Eddie Clarke (guitar) and Phil 'Filthy Animal' Taylor (drums). The title track of 1980's *Ace Of Spades* was a UK hit and set the band's sound: ear-shatteringly loud guitar, chordal bass and Kilmister's gruff vocals shouted over the top. Clarke quit in 1982 and Taylor was fired in 1992, but Lemmy ground remorselessly on, addicted to the rock'n'roll lifestyle. He finally proved mortal at the end of 2015, aged 70. Taylor had died a month earlier and Clarke died in 2018.

MY BLOODY VALENTINE (VOCAL/INSTRUMENTAL GROUP, 1983-97, 2007-PRESENT)

MBV began as a thrashy 1960s garage band and ended up redefining the sound of rock guitar on the swirling,

The most iconic of the hair metal bands, Mötley Crüe's wild rock'n'roll lifestyle ultimately overshadowed any musical merit.

distorting but lambently beautiful *Loveless* (1991). *Isn't Anything*, from 1988, features slightly more recognizable tunes and forms. Vocalist/guitarist Bilinda Butcher contributed lyrics and guitarist/vocalist Kevin Shields the revolutionary sounds, with Deb Googe on bass and Colm O'Ciosoig on drums. It took until 2013 – which included a 10-year hiatus – for the third album, *m b v*, to arrive. Now there's talk of another.

NEW ORDER (VOCAL/INSTRUMENTAL GROUP, 1980-93, 1998-2006, 2011-PRESENT)

Formed by the remaining members of Joy Division after Ian Curtis's suicide, New Order added extra groove and technology to the angular post-punk beats of their former band, thus heavily influencing the 'Madchester' and dance music scenes of the late 1980s and 1990s. The darkly throbbing anthem 'Blue Monday' came from 1983's essential *Power, Corruption And Lies* album. The electro-dominated *Technique* went to No. 1 in 1989. The group took two breaks, the first to indulge in side projects. During the second, Peter Hook quit and the split turned bitter and legal. The others released *Music Complete* (2015) without him and continued touring.

OZZY OSBOURNE (VOCALS, B. 1948)

After his departure from Black Sabbath and now under the management of future wife Sharon, Ozzy Osbourne formed a band around Lee Kerslake (drums), Bob Daisley (bass), Don Airey (keyboards) and Randy Rhoads (guitar). Debut effort *Blizzard Of Ozz* (1980) was a commercial success and one of the few albums of the decade to achieve multi-platinum status without the benefit of a Top 40 single. To date, Ozzy has released 19 albums (though none since 2010) and tours regularly, including his own Ozzfest, whenever he isn't reuniting with Black Sabbath. The latest No More Tours II Tour (No More Tours I Tour was in 1992) indicates that things may be coming to a close… or not..

TOM PETTY (SINGER/SONGWRITER, 1952-2017)

Petty, born in Gainsville, Florida, was the frontman of his long-time backing band The Heartbreakers. An eponymous

New Order successfully moved from being moody rockers into an ahead-of-the-curve electro-synthpop band.

album in 1977 was a hard-hitting brand of country rock, with plenty of modern attack and rootsy authenticity. The UK was impressed, but it was not until 1979's *Damn The Torpedoes* that the US took its native son to its breast. Alongside Springsteen, Petty helped revitalize the reputation of intelligent blue-collar rock, while tapping into its folkier heritage. He was a member of The Travelling Wilburys with Bob Dylan, Roy Orbison, Jeff Lynne and George Harrison during the 1980s before resuming his own career. He released some 16 albums before his death in 2017.

THE PIXIES (VOCAL/INSTRUMENTAL GROUP, 1986–92, 2004–PRESENT)

One of the most important alt rock bands ever came together in Boston with Charles Thompson IV, who styled himself Black Francis (vocals, guitar), Joey Santiago (guitar), Kim Deal (bass, vocals) and Dave Lovering (drums). Lyrically, Thompson explored religion, weird sex and sci-fi, singing with a preternaturally forceful yelp, fitted to an eclectic array of styles. Punk, surf, pop, hardcore and Spanish elements all collided on a succession of superb albums: the raging *Surfer Rosa* (1988), 1989's *Doolittle*, *Bossanova* (1990) and *Trompe Le Monde* (1991). They were a strong influence on many indie rockers, not least Nirvana. Ultimately, Deal wanted more of her songs used. Frank Black, as he soon became in his solo career, refused so she left and formed The Breeders. The Pixies reunited to play ecstatically received gigs in 2004 and have pursued a break-up/reunion pattern ever since.

THE POGUES (VOCAL/INSTRUMENTAL GROUP, 1982–2014)

Formed in north London around gifted songwriter Shane MacGowan (vocals), the Pogues' other long-term members include Spider Stacey (tin whistle, vocals), Jem Finer (banjo, guitar), Phil Chevron (guitar) and Andrew Ranken (drums). They breathed fresh, punky life into Irish music on the excellent albums *Rum, Sodomy And The Lash* (1985) and *If I Should Fall From Grace With God* (1988), and their big hit, 'Fairytale Of New York' (duet with Kirsty MacColl). MacGowan's wild lifestyle led to his departure, though band and singer reunited sporadically.

With 1988's Surfer Rosa, The Pixies *arguably became one of the most influential groups since The Beatles.*

THE PRETENDERS (VOCAL/INSTRUMENTAL GROUP, 1978–PRESENT)

Ohio-born Chrissie Hynde's tough, tuneful voice has established her as an iconic female rocker. Drawing on punk and 1960s pop, The Pretenders produced an exhilarating, melodic hybrid with broad appeal. 'Brass In Pocket' was a 1979 UK No. 1, and a hit in 1980 in her native US, where the band's self-titled debut reached the Top 10. Hynde and drummer Martin Chambers overcame the loss of original members James Honeyman-Scott (guitar, keyboards) and Pete Farndon (bass) to drugs in 1982 and 1983, and *Pretenders II* (1981) and *Learning To Crawl* (1984) also charted highly. In 1986, 'Don't Get Me Wrong' went Top 10. Further albums have been successful, if released at increasing intervals.

PUBLIC IMAGE LIMITED (VOCAL/INSTRUMENTAL GROUP, 1978–92)

Johnny Rotten reinvented himself after The Sex Pistols as John Lydon. He enlisted Keith Levene (guitar, drums), Jah Wobble (b. John Wardle, bass) and a variety of other transient contributors. The punky thunder of 'Public Image' stormed the UK Top 10 and a good self-titled debut album followed. Their second collection, 1979's *Metal Box 1* (*Second Edition* in the US, 1980) was extraordinary: a beguiling mix of dub, Krautrock and Eastern-inflected weirdness and Lydon's inspired, spooky rants. It amazingly made the UK Top 20. Two more masterpieces ensued before PIL's output got a little muddy. With PIL Lydon proved he was no one-trick pony but a major player and innovator.

RUN DMC (RAP GROUP, 1982–2002)

Pioneers of hip-hop, Run was born Joseph Simmons; DMC was Darryl McDaniel; Jam Master Jay (b. Jason Mizell) was on the decks. Their big, simple beats were heard on the eponymous debut (1983) and *King Of Rock* (1985), and as part of the first and best rock-rap crossover: 'Walk This Way' with Aerosmith. Run eventually translated his socially conscious raps into a Christian ministry. 'It's Like That' topped the UK chart in 1998, but their story ended in tragedy with the shooting of Jay in 2002.

John Lydon's post-Sex Pistols outfit, Public Image Limited, was an equally progressive group that took in rock and dance elements.

JOE SATRIANI (GUITAR, B. 1956)

Satriani was an influential teacher – students include Steve Vai, Kirk Hammett of Metallica and Primus's Larry LaLonde – before becoming a recording artist in his late 20s. He is not simply a stunt-guitarist, even though some of his playing on his debut *Surfing With The Alien* (1987) is jaw-dropping and inspired a generation of players. He mixes a plethora of styles from rock'n'roll workouts to lyrical ballads via jazz and funk odysseys. 1992's *The Extremist* went to a surprising No. 13 in the UK, after nu-metal guitarists started to sing his praises. After a short spell with Deep Purple, he released an entertaining live set with Vai and fellow axe-man Eric Johnson, entitled *G3 In Concert* (1997). Ever open-minded, he even experimented with electronica on *Engines Of Creation* (2001) and joined Chickenfoot with Sammy Hagar, Michael Anthony (ex-Van Halen) and Red Hot Chili Peppers drummer Chad Smith.

SIMPLE MINDS (VOCAL/INSTRUMENTAL GROUP, 1978–PRESENT)

Formerly known as Johnny and The Self-Abusers, Glaswegians Jim Kerr (vocals), Charlie Burchill (guitar), Derek Forbes (bass), Mick McNeil (keyboards) and Brian McGee (drums) took on board the experimentations of Krautrock and Eno for their second album *Real To Real Cacophony* (1979). They gently sloughed off their weirder tendencies over their next two albums, before 1982's *New Gold Dream (81-82-83-84)*, (with their first hits 'Promised You A Miracle' and 'Glittering Prize') chimed with the era's love of melodic, but mildly arty synth-pop. This led to success in America, which they exploited with 1984's *Sparkle In The Rain* and US chart-topper 'Don't You (Forget About Me)'. *Once Upon A Time* (1985) kept up the momentum, as they vied with U2 to be the world's No. 1 stadium rock band. After a decline in the 1990s, they have adapted their anthemic rock for smaller venues and continued to prosper.

THE SMITHS (VOCAL/INSTRUMENTAL GROUP, 1982–87)

The songwriting pair of former journalist Stephen Patrick Morrissey (vocals) and Johnny Marr (guitar) combined with Andy Rourke (bass) and Mike Joyce (drums) in Manchester to become the darlings of bedsit melancholics everywhere, exerting

The Smiths' lead singer Morrissey's lyrics were perfectly framed by the sensibilities of his bandmates, most notably guitarist Johnny Marr.

a huge influence on indie rock over the following decades. Their mesmerizing blend of 1960s beat music and new wave artiness was driven by Marr's ringing, inventive guitar, topped off by Morrissey's idiosyncratic wail and clever, often drily humorous lyrics. The shimmering power of 'How Soon Is Now' represents one of the best singles of the decade. Tensions grew and a split in 1987 became inevitable, but Morrissey and Marr went on to strong solo careers.

SONIC YOUTH (VOCAL/INSTRUMENTAL GROUP, 1981-2011)

Starting life as avant-garde noise merchants, Thurston Moore (vocals, guitar), his soon-to-be wife Kim Gordon (bass, vocals), Lee Ranaldo (guitar, vocals) and a variety of drummers, including Steve Shelley, have been influencing indie rock at the centre of New York's alternative music scene since the mid-80s. Highlights include the striking art rock of 1987's *Sister;* the almost conventional *Goo* (1990); a Madonna covers project, Ciccone Youth; and a genre-defying collaboration with Chuck D of Public Enemy. When Moore and Gordon separated in 2011, so did the band.

THE STYLE COUNCIL (VOCAL/INSTRUMENTAL GROUP, 1983-90)

After The Jam, Paul Weller sought a smoother sound; with Mick Talbot (keyboards), Steve White (drums) and Dee C. Lee (vocals) he came up with the modern soul of Top 5 UK hits such as 'Speak Like A Child'. *Café Bleu* (1984) was a fine showcase of his new direction, and classics 'Shout It To The Top' and *Our Favourite Shop* (1985) emerged before the band stagnated and Weller plotted anew.

TALKING HEADS (VOCAL/INSTRUMENTAL GROUP, 1975-91)

David Byrne (vocals), Tina Weymouth (vocals) and Chris Frantz (drums) formed Talking Heads at art school and were signed after performances at New York's famed CBGBs. Their 1977 debut album *Talking Heads '77* established their nervy, funky style, with Byrne's cryptic lyrics. Brian Eno became their producer with *More Songs About Buildings And Food* (1978). *Fear Of Music* (1979) broadened their palate with African sounds, while *Remain In Light* (1980) yielded the UK

Dissolving The Jam at the height of their early 1980s success, Paul Weller formed The Style Council as a way of exploring jazz and soul.

hit 'Once In A Lifetime'. Live album *Stop Making Sense* (1984), with its wonderful Jonathan Demme-directed film, set new standards in the field. After 1985's *Little Creatures*, the band was distracted by solo projects and the end was inevitable. Influential giants of new wave, they made art rock palatable to the mainstream.

TEARS FOR FEARS (VOCAL/INSTRUMENTAL GROUP, 1981–96, 2005–PRESENT)

Roland Orzabal (vocals, guitar, synthesizers) and Curt Smith (vocals, synthesizers, bass) began their chart-busting career in electro-pop mode with the sombre but enthralling 'Mad World' and 'Pale Shelter' from *The Hurting* (1983). But the release of 1985's *Songs From The Big Chair* saw a more expansive approach incorporating classic styles, while 'Everybody Wants To Rule The World' (1985) was positively jaunty. Though 'Sowing The Seeds Of Love' was a global smash, *The Seeds Of Love* (1989) was the band's last collaboration, as the duo argued over Smith's contribution. After a dip in fortunes, the pair were reunited for 2005's *Everybody Loves A Happy Ending* and have played together happily ever after.

TOTO (VOCAL/INSTRUMENTAL GROUP, 1977–2008)

Formed by crack US session musicians including keyboardist David Paich and drummer Jeff Porcaro, AOR supergroup Toto's most successful releases were 1978's self-titled debut LP with the single 'Hold The Line' and 1982's six time Grammy-winning *Toto IV*, including the US chart-topping 'Africa' and 'Rosanna'. The band released 18 albums and sold over 30 million records.

STEVE VAI (GUITAR, B. 1960)

After learning many of his chops from Joe Satriani, New Yorker Vai became Frank Zappa's 'stunt guitarist' on his mid-1980s albums. He was also a hired axe for John Lydon's PIL, Dave Lee Roth and Whitesnake, as well as playing 'The Devil's Guitar Player' in *Crossroads* (1986). His own work shows compositional maturity. On *Passion And Warfare* (1990), for example, he experiments and develops moods rather than just 'shredding'. His discography includes live DVDs.

More ambitious than many 1980s pop acts, Tears For Fears tried to meld jazz, pop, rock and psych.

VAN HALEN (VOCAL/INSTRUMENTAL GROUP, 1974-99, 2004, 2007-PRESENT)

Van Halen defined the US heavy metal scene for a decade, boasting a dashing, tuneful frontman, Dave Lee Roth (vocals), a wizard guitarist in Eddie Van Halen and poppy but rocking tunes, as 1978's debut *Van Halen I* proved. Eddie's brother Alex (drums) and Michael Anthony (bass) completed this golden gang. *Van Halen II* (1979) entered the US Top 10, and in 1983 Eddie provided the dazzling solo on Michael Jackson's 'Beat It'. But it was 1984's *1984* and its attendant pop metal smash 'Jump' that promoted the band to the superstar stratum. Ego battles between Roth and Eddie saw Sammy Hagar join as singer before a reunion tour with Roth in 2007 after Eddie's successful battle with cancer.

STEVIE RAY VAUGHAN (GUITAR, VOCALS, 1954-90)

Born in Dallas, Vaughan distilled Albert King, Jimi Hendrix and Lonnie Mack's blues and rock stylings on his superb US Top 40 album *Texas Flood* (1983). Tommy Shannon (bass) and Chris Layton (drums) formed his trusted Double Trouble back-up team. His ferocious but lyrical playing on *Couldn't Stand The Weather* (1984) and his live showmanship confirmed him as the new king of the blues guitar. After a 1990 show with Eric Clapton, Vaughan died in a helicopter crash, but SRV music lives on.

TOM WAITS (SINGER/SONGWRITER, B. 1949)

Born in Pomona, California, Waits has built a well-regarded career as a gravel-voiced documentarian of American low-life. The Eagles covered 'Ol' '55' from his jazzy debut *Closing Time* (1973); on *Blue Valentine* (1979) and on *Heartattack And Vine* (1980) he introduced a rockier sound; then came the trailblazing, percussive sounds of *Swordfishtrombones* (1983) and the UK Top 30 *Rain Dogs* (1985). Waits developed a career in soundtracks, including Francis Ford Coppola's *One From The Heart* (1981). His 1999 album *Mule Variations* was a US Top 30 and Rod Stewart made big hits of 'Downtown Train' and 'Tom Traubert's Blues'. He probably did not expect to be duetting with Mick Jagger onstage in 2013.

Tom Waits was one of the most consistently interesting artists of the century.

West-coast city Seattle was the unanticipated epicentre as grunge, the biggest 'back-to-basics' movement since punk, shook traditional American rock; Nirvana enjoyed iconic status for a spell until Kurt Cobain's death. The dance-rock of The Stone Roses, a holdover from the late 1980s, put Manchester briefly in the picture, but it was American bands like Metallica, Red Hot Chili Peppers and R.E.M., who had put in nearly a decade of hard graft apiece, whose influential but very different rock sounds gained commercial acceptance at last.

The now dominant influence of MTV made sure the emphasis remained on the visual, while the Britpop 'war' in the mid-1990s saw Blur and Oasis deliver a much-needed kiss of life to a British music business already in a torpor. After that excitement came The Spice Girls, whose Shangri-Las meets The Monkees act appealed to both sexes and proved you could still manufacture a pop phenomenon. They were, perhaps, the ultimate extension of the karaoke craze.

1990s acts were not known for their staying power, but the sheer variety of sounds and styles on offer reflected a society where diversity and tolerance were the buzzwords.

THE NINETIES

THE NINETIES: SOUNDS + SOURCES

The 1990s was a decade of rapid change – few of the names that dominated the early part of the decade would be conspicuous at its end. One such case was Sinead O'Connor, whose take on the Prince classic 'Nothing Compares 2U' was the UK chart-topper for the whole of February 1990 and, however briefly, one of the fastest-selling singles in worldwide chart history.

Equally, a pair of rap artists, one black (MC Hammer) and one white (Vanilla Ice) took the first year of the decade by storm only to subside as rapidly – no pun intended – as they had risen. Both 'U Can't Touch This' and 'Ice Ice Baby' (both 1990) purloined riffs – from Rick James and Queen respectively – for their hits, and sampling would now become an ever-growing ingredient of music due to advanced and ever more affordable studio technology.

KEEPING IT REAL

But technology was about to spawn a powerful rival to music in the affections of the younger generation. The first popular handheld console was launched by Nintendo in 1989, and computer games quickly became the status symbol for anyone under 20. New initiatives were necessary to prevent music from becoming just another teen lifestyle choice like Gameboys, Sega Megadrive and their ilk. These came in many shapes and from many sources. The Lollapalooza travelling festival kicked off in July 1991 and, staged annually thereafter, would launch many an alt-rocker's career – Nine Inch Nails the first beneficiary. Unusually, it was the idea of a musician, Perry Farrell of Jane's Addiction. MTV, keen to capture the 'mature' rock audience, kicked the *Unplugged* series into gear in January 1990, inviting established acts to bring their acoustic guitars and present their hits in stripped-down form. As well as a TV show, a best-selling album often

The Lollapalooza Festival became an annual highlight for alternative rock.

resulted (an unbelievable six Grammys were won by Eric Clapton's), but this 'exercise in creative recycling' eventually became a cliché itself. It took Bruce Springsteen – who insisted on performing plugged – to underline the fact.

OUT WITH THE OLD

At street level, grunge ruled, raucous Seattle three-piece Nirvana inspiring a host of soundalikes with their multi-platinum *Nevermind* and attendant anthemic single, 'Smells Like Teen Spirit' (both 1991). Eventually grunge met unplugged as Cobain and co. indulged MTV with one of their last shows before the troubled singer blew his brains out.

American bands tended to dominate the decade as a whole. Guns N' Roses, whose brand of bad-boy rock had hit big in the last years of the 1980s, were losing momentum, the tactic of releasing two albums simultaneously rebounding on them. 1992 saw them tour in partnership with Metallica, whose self-titled album had topped both the UK and US charts – the passing of the torch?

R.E.M., on the other hand, reaped the reward of continuity, which had seen them capitalize on a decade's apprenticeship away from the spotlight in the indie hinterland. They swept the board at MTV's Video Music Awards in 1991. The Red Hot Chili Peppers had similarly built gradually through the previous decade and, just like R.E.M., hit paydirt after pacting with the Warner Bros. label. Their fifth album, *Blood Sugar Sex Magik* (1991), went multi-platinum and contained the ballad 'Under The Bridge', which remains their signature track today. In both cases adding polish to a promising product reaped immense rewards, even if some originality was inevitably sacrificed. Elsewhere, the trend seemed to be updating previous decades' stereotypes for a new audience: shock-rocker Marilyn Manson was the 1990s' Alice Cooper, Hanson were a cross between The Osmonds and The Jackson Five; and white funk hope Jamiroquai was a Stevie Wonder soundalike.

MTV's Unplugged *shows attracted big names like Eric Clapton; the power of television created a huge demand for spare, unembellished music.*

THE ALT. SCENE

Country music was hitting the mainstream, in the US at least, with the likes of Garth Brooks selling in millions and leading a posse of 'hat acts' – Alan Jackson, Clint Black, Dwight Yoakam and Kenny Chesney among them – to multi-platinum glory. And young performers taking the pioneering spirit of The Byrds and The Flying Burrito Brothers, producing what became known as alt.country – Wilco, Son Volt, The Jayhawks and Whiskeytown among them – came up with exciting, if lesser-selling results.

The post-Nirvana alt.rock scene was increasingly attacked by British acts as the pendulum swung. The Manic Street Preachers, Primal Scream, Pulp and Supergrass were among those creating genuinely innovative music, while former Jam mainman Paul Weller was undergoing a creative renaissance. The Stone Roses bloomed briefly but influentially as a hangover from the 'Madchester' scene of the late 1980s, trading on the excellence of their 1989 debut album. The so-called Britpop war of 1995 that set Oasis and Blur against each other and made the national television news bulletins saw Blur's 'Country House' (with sales of 274,000) beat 'Roll With It' (a mere 216,000) to pole position. The Mancunians would have their revenge when their album *(What's The Story) Morning Glory* (1995) debuted at No. 1.

THE SHAPE OF THINGS TO COME

This stage-managed 'battle' was also, in retrospect, the last hurrah of the singles chart. It had long disappeared in the States, where rankings were now based more on radio airplay than sales, the result being that some hits never sold to the public, being offered to radio only. In Britain, sales would decline year on year until revived by the 2000s download-based charts. For now, it took 'oldies' acts Aerosmith and The Rolling Stones to cotton on to the potential of the internet. In 1994, Steven Tyler and friends released an unissued single for download, while The Stones authorized a 20-minute concert webcast. Few fans had access to the worldwide web then, but within a decade these things would be commonplace.

For a short period in the 1990s, Britpop made it respectable to accessorize with the Union Jack. Even in inflatable form.

In the States, the often-overlooked Hispanic population were coming into their own as record-buyers. Puerto Rico-born Ricky Martin emerged from their midst to top the chart in 1999 with his first English-language album. (Only Gloria Estefan had hitherto captured a significant slice of the pop market.) His success would open the door for Marc Anthony, Christina Aguilera, Enrique Iglesias and others, not to mention a revival for Carlos Santana. The foundation of the Latin Grammys in 2000 was soon to follow.

Hip-hop and rap were on the upswing, even if some of its practitioners seemed intent on destroying each other: Tupac Shakur and the Notorious BIG were among the stars to lose their lives in violent fashion. The Fugees were the first hip-hop supergroup, spawning Lauryn Hill, Pras Michel and Wyclef Jean as solo performers.

BOYS AND GIRLS

Solo acts Alanis Morissette, Robbie Williams, Björk, Beck and Sheryl Crow emerged to challenge the dominance of the groups – reinforced by the biggest crop of boy bands since The Osmonds and Jackson Five in the 1970s. Take That, Boyzone, Backstreet Boys, New Kids … all seemed more or less interchangeable. The same, however, could not be said of The Spice Girls, whose 'Girl Power' arrived in timely fashion to fill the tabloid newspaper gap created by Princess Diana's sad demise.

But pop's true princess was Kylie Minogue, the former soap star who became first a teenybop idol, then tried indie pop for size before wisely rejecting it and, as the decade ended, becoming a hot-panted, dance-music diva. Madame Tussauds, the legendary London waxworks, took the near-unprecedented step in 1998 of updating her mannequin to reflect the change. As the music business faced yet another bout of unwelcome challenges with the arrival of file-sharing on the internet (Napster launched in 1999), Kylie was somehow an unthreatening, much-loved constant.

Kylie Minogue, everybody's girl next door, was the perfect pop pixie for the 1990s.

THE NINETIES: KEY ARTISTS

METALLICA (VOCAL/INSTRUMENTAL GROUP, 1981–PRESENT)

Metallica was formed in California in 1981 by Lars Ulrich (drums) and James Hetfield (vocals, guitar), who shared a love of British new-wave heavy metal. Kirk Hammett (lead guitar) and Cliff Burton (bass) completed the line-up. The seminal debut *Kill 'Em All* (1983) laid the foundation stone of thrash metal, with fast interlocking instrumentals and brutal loud speed.

Hard touring and a second album, *Ride The Lightning* (1984), cemented a growing international cult status. After signing an eight-album deal with Elektra Records, they released *Master Of Puppets* (1986). Instrumental prowess on tracks like 'Orion' and 'Disposable Heroes' saw the album become Metallica's first fully fledged masterpiece. Tragedy struck that same year when Burton was killed when the band's bus turned over. Jason Newsted was later drafted in as a replacement. On the *Garage Days Re-Visited* EP (1987), tribute was loudly paid to influences like Diamond Head and Budgie. *...And Justice For All* (1988) showed trademark speed, hard riffing and quality control.

BLACK MASTERPIECE

Metallica cemented their status on 1991's *Metallica* (a.k.a. 'The Black Album') by adding orchestral backing and shorter, more melodic songs to the trademark hard-edged sound. It sold 15 million copies worldwide and spawned five hit singles, including 'Enter Sandman' and 'Nothing Else Matters'. *St. Anger* (2003) was the sound of a band trying to come to terms with fame, with new bassist Ron Trujillo (from Ozzy Osbourne). In 2011, they indulged themselves by teaming up with Lou Reed for *Lulu* before hunkering down to create the double *Hardwired... to Self Destruct* (2016).

The self-titled album Metallica *enabled the group to reach out to a wider audience, although they were criticized by some for selling out.*

NIRVANA (VOCAL/INSTRUMENTAL GROUP, 1987–94)

One of the most influential acts of the 1990s, Nirvana formed in Aberdeen, Washington, in 1987 with Kurt Cobain (guitar, vocals), Krist Novoselic (bass) and Chad Channing (drums) making the original line-up. Signed by Seattle's Sub Pop label, their first single was a cover version of Shocking Blue's 'Love Bug', with Cobain penning 'Big Cheese' on the B-side. The initial pressing was limited to 1,000 copies. On Nirvana's first Sub Pop album *Bleach* (1989) the bedrock of the Nirvana sound was evident, the melodic beauty of 'About A Girl' contrasting with the loud, aggressive punk metal of 'Swap Meet' and 'Paper Cuts'.

NEVERMIND

Nirvana's second Sub Pop single – 'Sliver'/'Dive' – was followed by the recruitment of drummer David Grohl. Now signed by Geffen, Nirvana recorded a second album. The initial pressing of 50,000 copies of *Nevermind* (1991) sold out in two days. By now, generational anthem 'Smells Like Teen Spirit' had given Nirvana their first Top 10 single in America and the UK. The follow-up 'Come As You Are' cemented Nirvana as the most celebrated band in the world, and the multi-platinum *Nevermind* became one of the most influential albums of the decade. *In Utero* continued the success and topped the charts on both sides of the Atlantic in 1993.

Away from music, Cobain married Hole singer Courtney Love in February 1992; she gave birth to their daughter Frances Bean six months later. By 1993, Cobain and Love were addicted to heroin, a chemical romance played out in public with state threats to remove the child from their care. Cobain's state of mind grew darker and, after failing with one suicide attempt in March 1994, he blew his brains out with a rifle at his Seattle home a month later. He left a wife, a daughter and a personal legacy that, today, has expanded into iconic proportions.

Nirvana's 'Smells Like Teen Spirit' of 1991 was voted by Rolling Stone *magazine 9th in its 500 Greatest Songs of All Time in 1994.*

RED HOT CHILI PEPPERS [VOCAL/INSTRUMENTAL GROUP, 1983–PRESENT]

Anthony Kiedis (vocals), Michael 'Flea' Balzary (bass), Jack Irons (drums) and Hillel Slovak (guitar) met at high school in Hollywood. They first played Los Angeles clubs under the Chili Peppers banner in 1983. Influenced by funk, rap, jazz and punk rock, their frenetic intensity soon won a local following. Signed by EMI America, only Flea and Kiedis appeared on the self-titled debut (1984) as Irons and Slovak were contractually tied to Mercury Records with another band. They were reunited on *Freaky Styley* (1985), but sales were low. The tide turned with *The Uplift Mofo Party Plan* (1987). Further momentum came with the *Abbey Road* EP (1988), featuring a cover showing them walking over the famed Abbey Road crossing, naked apart from their now-trademark socks. By now the Peppers had embraced the vices as well as the pleasures of the road and Slovak died of a heroin overdose in 1988. When Irons quit shortly afterwards, the end seemed nigh. But they regrouped with 18-year-old fan John Frusciante on guitar and Chad Smith on drums.

MUSICAL AND SPIRITUAL RENEWAL

Mother's Milk (1989) spawned their first US hit single, 'Knock Me Down'. Switching labels to Warner Bros., the Peppers produced familiar fare like 'Funky Monks' and 'Suck My Kiss', but also the ballad 'Under The Bridge'. The album *BloodSugarSexMagik* (1991) went multi-platinum and the band was now an international arena headliner, but the following year Frusciante left the band, citing stress. This triggered another period of uncertainty, with the remaining members often more interested in individual side projects, as replacement guitarists came and went. Frusciante's return in 1998 refocused the band and 1999's *Californication* spawned four hit singles. Sprawling double-disc *Stadium Arcadium* (2006) maintained a consistently high quality and when Frusciante quit a second time, his replacement, Josh Klinghoffer, was already waiting in the wings. 2011's *I'm with You* displayed a welcome professional maturity, confirmed on 2016's *The Getaway*

The phenomenal success of the Red Hot Chili Peppers' fifth album, 1991's BloodSugarSexMagik, launched the band into superstardom.

R.E.M. (VOCAL/INSTRUMENTAL GROUP, 1980–PRESENT)

Michael Stipe (vocals) met Peter Buck (guitar) in a record store in Athens, Georgia, in 1978. Two years later they met Bill Berry (drums) and Mike Mills (bass) at a party and Rapid Eye Movement – R.E.M. – was formed. A demo secured the release of 'Radio Free Europe'/'Sitting Still' on the Hib-Tone label, which, in turn, led to a deal with IRS. Mini-album *Chronic Town* (1982) was critically received. On their debut album *Murmur* (1983), Stipe's sometimes slurred, allusive vocals were background rather than foreground to the rich melodic music. By *Document* (1987) – their fifth album – R.E.M. were the biggest band on the American alternative college circuit. Having outgrown IRS, R.E.M. signed to Warner Bros. *Green* (1988) had artistic integrity, but retained the commercial edge on singles like 'Stand'. After a globe-trotting tour, the band took time out before returning with *Out Of Time* (1991). Addictive singles like 'Losing My Religion' and 'Shiny Happy People' became anthems at the height of the Nirvana-led grunge boom.

FINDING THE FORMULA

The eagerly awaited *Automatic For The People* (1992) was another classic, yielding five hit singles, including 'The Sidewinder Sleeps Tonight', 'Nightswimming', 'Everybody Hurts' and 'Man On The Moon'. The album went multi-platinum. *Monster* (1994) returned to the guitar-heavy early days and kicked off R.E.M.'s first international tour for five years. Recorded during stolen moments on a grinding 132-date schedule, *New Adventures In Hi-Fi* (1996) was a brave departure, although it did not yield the usual quota of hits. Berry left the band in October 1997 due to ill health.

The remaining members got experimental on *Up* (1998), before returning to the familiar on *Reveal* (2001) and *Around The Sun* (2004), but they had passed their peak in the US, although they retained their popularity in the rest of the world and particularly in Europe. After the expansive *Collapse into Now* in 2011, they came to an amicable conclusion.

R.E.M., touring in 1995, were at the peak of their success, with a string of Top 40 hits under their belt, including 'Losing My Religion'.

THE NINETIES: A-Z OF ARTISTS

BRYAN ADAMS (SINGER/SONGWRITER, B. 1959)

This Canadian singer/songwriter first found US success with his third album, *Cuts Like A Knife* (1984). With material ranging from pleasing orthodox rock to lung-sucking ballads, the rest of the 1980s were fertile soil, especially for rousing singles like 'Summer Of '69'. Adams began the 1990s with the theme song from *Robin Hood: Prince Of Thieves*, '(Everything I Do) I Do It For You', which topped the UK charts for a record 16 weeks in 1991. *Waking Up The Neighbours* (1991) and *So Far So Good* (1993) both went multi-platinum and spawned more singles, and *18 Till I Die* (1996) was a rousing collection of radio-friendly rock. Adams has spent much of the twenty-first century writing film songs and collaborating with other songwriters.

BECK (VOCALS, B. 1970)

By making music that incorporates eclectic influences from folk, hip-hop, rock, electronica and studio prowess, Beck Hansen has become one of the most influential American solo artists. Early EPs, albums and singles, like the classic 'Loser', were released on a variety of labels. When Beck signed to Geffen, *Odelay* (1996) delivered every promise. *Mutations* (1998) was more acoustic and *Midnite Vultures* (1999) equally assured. He got more personal on albums like *Sea Change* (2002), *Guero* (2005). *Modern Guilt* (2008) and *Morning Phase* (2014), which won three Grammys.

BJÖRK (VOCALS, B. 1965)

The vocalist in Icelandic band The Sugarcubes, Björk Guðmundsdóttir began her solo career after the group broke up in 1992. *Debut* was released in 1993, produced by Soul II Soul's Nellee Hooper, and Björk created an immediate impact with her avant-garde instincts and distinctive voice allied to pop and dance music. Staying true to her principles, every album she has released and every performance she has given since then has challenged her audience to follow her extraordinary talent.

Despite Bryan Adams' other successes, he will always be remembered for 'Everything I Do (I Do It For You)'.

THE BLACK CROWES (VOCAL/INSTRUMENTAL GROUP, 1984–2002, 2005–11, 2013–15)

Musically, The Crowes were a throwback to the classic rock swagger of The Rolling Stones. Formed in Atlanta, Chris Robinson (vocals), Richard Robinson (guitar), Jeff Cease (guitar), Johnny Colt (bass) and Steve Gorman (drums) combined hard touring and compelling albums like *Shake Your Money Maker* (1990) and *The Southern Harmony And Musical Companion* (1992). Success was interrupted by line-up changes and extended breaks, and when the Robinson brothers finally broke apart, so did the band.

BLUR (VOCAL/INSTRUMENTAL GROUP, 1989–2003, 2009–PRESENT)

Formed at London's Goldsmiths College, Damon Albarn (vocals), Graham Coxon (guitar), Alex James (bass) and Dave Rowntree (drums) tuned into the vibe generated by The Stone Roses with baggy anthems 'She's So High' and 'There's No Other Way'. Although *Leisure* (1991) showed a band adept at updating 1960s pop, *Modern Life Is Rubbish* (1993) revealed more depth. With the release of infectious electro single 'Boys And Girls' and the cockney swagger of 'Parklife', Blur found themselves the leaders of the 'Britpop' movement. Taking a louder and more experimental approach on *Blur* (1997) and *13* (1999) displayed greater musical maturity without losing sales or fans. Coxon departed for a solo career in 2002; Albarn had fun with the Gorillaz. They reconvened for shows in 2009 and a well-received album, *The Magic Whip*, in 2015. Another reunion 'is never not a possibility', according to Albarn.

JEFF BUCKLEY (GUITAR, SINGER/SONGWRITER, 1966–97)

Son of singer/songwriter Tim, Jeff Buckley possessed vocal range, emotional capacity and songwriting talent. His mini-album *Live At Sin-e* (1992) was the signpost to the classic debut *Grace* (1994), on which Buckley delivered the definitive cover of Leonard Cohen's 'Hallelujah'. Posthumous releases and acclaim followed Buckley's untimely drowning in 1997.

BUSH (VOCAL/INSTRUMENTAL GROUP, 1992–PRESENT)

Bush was formed in 1992 by Gavin Rossdale (guitar, vocals), Dave Parsons (bass), Nigel Pulsford (guitar) and Robin

Blur's massive success in the UK with Parklife *(1994) gave birth to a whole new Britpop scene.*

Goodridge (drums). The grunge-powered debut album *Sixteen Stones* (1994) received heavy rotation on American radio after the breakthrough 'Everything Zen'. Hard touring and the hard-sounding *Razorblade Suitcase* (1996) cemented their reputation – for a few years anyway.

THE CHARLATANS (VOCAL/INSTRUMENTAL GROUP, 1989–PRESENT)

Emerging out of the 'Madchester' scene, The Charlatans' initial organ-led groove music was soon embraced by the charts. Later, Tim Burgess et al matured into a rock band with a devoted fanbase. Keyboardist Rob Collins' death in 1996 was a massive blow, but subsequent albums like *Tellin' Stories* (1997) and *Up At The Lake* (2004) confirmed longevity. Burgess has released solo material.

THE CRANBERRIES (VOCAL/INSTRUMENTAL GROUP, 1991–2004, 2009–18)

Formed in Limerick in 1991, Dolores O'Riordan (vocals), Noel Hogan (guitar), Mike Hogan (bass) and Feargal Lawler (drums) soon became a chart staple. O'Riordan's unique keening vocal style made chiming melodic pop singles like 'Linger' and 'Dreams'. *Everybody Else Is Doing It, So Why Can't We?* (1993) and *No Need To Argue* (1994) best showcase their radio-friendly sound. They took a break in 2004, returning in 2009. They were midway through recording an album when O'Riordan was found drowned in her bath due to alcohol intoxication in 2018.

CREED (VOCAL/INSTRUMENTAL GROUP, 1995–2004)

Formed in Tallahassee, Florida, Creed is one of the biggest post-grunge rock acts. Debut album *My Own Prison* (1998) by Scott Stapps (vocals), Mark Tremonti (guitar, vocals), Brian Marshall (bass) and Scott Phillips (drums) boasts powerful rock tunes and genuinely spiritual lyrics, including US No. 1 singles 'One' and 'What's This Life For'. *Human Clay* (1999) and *Weathered* (2001) followed but troubled Stapps, and the band (now renamed Alter Bridge) went their separate ways in 2004, a 2009/10 reunion notwithstanding.

Bush's post-grunge sound was massively popular in the US, but received criticism in the UK.

THE DAVE MATTHEWS BAND (VOCAL/INSTRUMENTAL GROUP, 1991–PRESENT)

South African-born Matthews (guitar, vocals) formed his band in Virginia, recruiting Stefan Lessard (bass), Leroi Moore (saxophone), Boyd Tinsley (violin) and Carter Beauford (drums). Fusing elements of world music on to a sound that celebrated folk, funk and rock, they released their debut *Remember Two Things* in 1993. *Under The Table And Dreaming* (1994) and *Crash* (1996) greatly expanded their US following and led to chart albums. Then *Live At Red Rocks 8.15.95* (1997) showcased the band's compelling stage sound. *Before These Crowded Streets* (1998) was a chart topper, featuring hit single 'Don't Drink The Water'. Matthews' winning compositional ability and band interplay remain undimmed.

GARBAGE (VOCAL/INSTRUMENTAL GROUP, 1994–PRESENT)

Butch Vig, Steve Marker and Duke Erikson were already successful producers and musicians before they recruited Scottish singer Shirley Manson to form Garbage. Pristine intelligent rock of an eponymous solo album (1995) spawned the monster international single 'Stupid Girl'. Follow up *Version 2.0* (1998) was more electronic, but an equally compelling set. *Not Your Kind Of People* (2012) and *Strange Little Birds* (2016) have loosened the production grip without losing the band's originality.

THE GOO GOO DOLLS (VOCAL/INSTRUMENTAL GROUP, 1986–PRESENT)

Johnny Rzeznik (guitar, vocals), Robby Takec (bass, vocals) and George Tutuska (drums) formed The Goo Goo Dolls in Buffalo, New York, in 1986. Their first two albums took inspiration from the new wave although there were endless comparisons to the pop-punk sound of The Replacements. By *Superstar Car Wash* (1993) and *A Boy Named Goo* (1996) The Dolls had discovered their own melodic rock sound, which has continued to reap US chart rewards.

HOOTIE AND THE BLOWFISH (VOCAL/INSTRUMENTAL GROUP, 1989–PRESENT)

Formed in South Carolina, Darius Rucker (vocals), Mark Bryan (guitar), Dean Felber (bass) and Jim 'Soni' Sonefeld (drums) played pleasing blues rock with a hint of folk and a pop edge. A dedicated following helped sell initial self-financed EP,

Garbage lead singer Shirley Manson said: ['"Stupid Girl"'] became an anthem for a girl settling for less than what she wants or deserves.'

Kootchypop (1992). Debut album *Cracked Rear Mirror* (1994) was a sleeper until the US chart success of compulsive ecological single 'Hold My Hand' and 'Let Her Cry' turned the album into a multi-platinum success. *Fairweather Johnson* (1996) was another pleasing set. The band continued to tour, and showcased their feelgood style on albums like *Musical Chairs* (1998) and *Looking For Lucky* (2005). On hiatus from 2008–15, the band now stages an annual reunion.

JANE'S ADDICTION (VOCAL/INSTRUMENTAL GROUP, 1986-1991, 1997, 2002-04, 2008-PRESENT)

The charismatic Perry Farrell formed Jane's Addiction in Los Angeles in 1986, Dave Navarro (guitar), Eric Avery (bass) and Stephen Perkins (drums) completing the line-up. Their blend of punk, rock and elements of funk and jazz is best showcased on *Ritual De Lo Habitual* (1991). The band fractured just as they were hitting the big time in 1991; later reformations were followed by albums and tours.

LENNY KRAVITZ (MULTI-INSTRUMENTALIST, PRODUCER, SINGER/SONGWRITER, B. 1964)

Accused of being 'retro' when first emerging in 1989, Lenny Kravitz proved to be a trendsetter. Inspired by 1960s icons like Led Zeppelin, The Who and Jimi Hendrix, Kravitz developed a similarly warm, guitar-led sound that became hugely popular. *Mama Said* (1991) and *Are You Gonna Go My Way?* (1993) are prime examples. As well as his own resonant material, Kravitz wrote for other artists, including the sultry 'Justify My Love' for Madonna. He released his eleventh album, *Raise Vibration*, in 2018, followed by a tour.

MANIC STREET PREACHERS (VOCAL/INSTRUMENTAL GROUP, 1990-PRESENT)

When guitarist Richey Edwards disappeared/committed suicide in 1995 the end of the line seemed in sight for James Dean Bradfield (vocals, guitar), Nicky Wire (bass) and Sean Moore (drums), but they soldiered on, delivering *Everything Must Go* (1996). Retaining the artistic integrity of their punk-inspired principles, it yielded hit anthem after hit anthem. Subsequent albums were equally compelling.

Lenny Kravitz cut his musical teeth supporting the likes of Tom Petty, Bob Dylan and David Bowie .

MARILYN MANSON (VOCALS, B. 1969)

Setting out to shock everyone, Brian Warner certainly succeeded. After assuming the name Marilyn Manson, all members of his Florida-based band were required to adopt the names of female divas and serial killers. Industrially functional music grew increasingly melodic as time wore on, culminating in *Antichrist Superstar* (1996) and *continuing through Heaven Upside Down (2017)*. Manson is articulate in his own defence and is simply an updated version of the Kiss/Alice Cooper formula of character rock.

MORRISSEY (SINGER/SONGWRITER, B. 1959)

Morrissey's post-Smiths career has been nothing less than stellar. Writing mainly with guitarist Boz Boorer, Morrissey delivered a number of hit albums and singles. With North and Latin America eventually falling for him, he could even afford to lose his way on *Maladjusted* (1997). *You Are The Quarry* (2004) and *Ringleader Of The Tormentors* (2006) have returned him to form, but 2017's *Low in High School* slipped back into bad habits.

MUDHONEY (VOCAL/INSTRUMENTAL GROUP, 1988–PRESENT)

Mark Arm (vocals), Steve Turner (guitar), Matt Lukin (bass) and Dan Peters (drums) were the band that put the Seattle Sub Pop label on the map. Their grungy, guitar-driven rock was encapsulated by the 'Touch Me I'm Sick' single and *Superfuzz Bigmuff* mini-LP (both 1988). By the end of the century they looked to have shot their bolt, but have gained a new lease of life since.

OASIS (VOCAL/INSTRUMENTAL GROUP, 1993–2009)

The debut single 'Supersonic' (1994) from Mancunian brothers Liam (vocals) and Noel (guitar) Gallagher, Paul 'Bonehead' Arthurs (guitar), Paul 'Guigsy' McGuigan (bass) and Tony McCarroll (drums) was a melodic, guitar-driven tune over which Liam snarled out lyrics. By the end of the year another four instant classics had graced the charts.

Oasis' guitar-led, pop-rock sound heralded the Britpop movment of the mid-1990s.

Definitely Maybe (1994) spent 174 weeks in the charts due to Noel's perfectly constructed pop songs. *(What's The Story) Morning Glory?* (1995) went on to become the second biggest-selling UK album of all time and, although America never fell, *Be Here Now* (1997) kept the hits coming. After longrunning frictions, 2009 saw a very public split.

PEARL JAM (VOCAL/INSTRUMENTAL GROUP, 1990–PRESENT)

Emerging out of Mother Love Bone, Peal Jam's classic line-up consisted of Eddie Vedder (vocals), Stone Gossard (guitar), Mike McCready (guitar), Jeff Ament (bass) and Dave Abbruzzese (drums). The spiky hook-laden rock of *Ten* (1991) sold in large numbers after Nirvana made Seattle alternative bands popular. Touring with the Lollapalooza II circus cemented their position as major players and albums *Vs* (1993) and *Vitalogy* (1994) confirmed their position as one of the biggest bands in America. Subsequently Pearl Jam expanded their musical references to include folk and world music and by 2013's *Lightning Bolt* they could even count Pink Floyd among their influences.

PRIMAL SCREAM (VOCAL/INSTRUMENTAL GROUP, 1984–PRESENT)

Bobby Gillespie was the drummer in The Jesus And Mary Chain before forming Primal Scream. Early releases echoed The Byrds and Love before steering towards Cult-like rock territory on *Primal Scream* (1989). The acid-house scene was a revelation to the now stable line-up of Gillespie (vocals), Andrew Innes (guitar), Robert Young (guitar), Martin Duffy (keyboards), Henry Olsen (bass) and Philip 'Toby' Tomanov (drums), leading to club and chart anthems. *Screamadelica* (1991) was a compelling classic. They returned to rock with *Give Out, But Don't Give Up* (1994) and dub-like sounds on *Vanishing Point* (1997), moving on to the techno guitar fuzz of *XTRMTR* (2000); *Riot City Blues* (2006) was back to rock.

PULP (VOCAL/INSTRUMENTAL GROUP, 1981–99)

This Sheffield band secured their first John Peel session when still at school in 1981. Pulp then enjoyed/endured over a decade of cult success. Jarvis Cocker's droll observational lyrics fitted snugly over indie guitars that brushed occasional

Pearl Jam were one of the most popular and influential grunge bands of the time, creating five Top 10 albums during the 1990s.

electronica on tracks like 'My Legendary Girlfriend'. By the time of *His 'N' Hers* (1994), Russell Senior (guitar), Candida Doyle (keyboards), Steve Mackey (bass), Mark Webber (guitar) and Nick Banks (drums) had found the beginning of chart success. Replacing The Stone Roses at Glastonbury in 1995, Pulp's 'Common People' and 'Sorted For E's And Wizz' became anthems. *Different Class* (1995) was just that, spawning hits and turning Cocker into a media darling. *This is Hardcore* (1998) was a pretty soft farewell, however.

RAGE AGAINST THE MACHINE (VOCAL/INSTRUMENTAL GROUP, 1991–2000, 2007–PRESENT)

Formed in LA by Zack De La Rocha (vocals), Tom Morello (guitar), Tim Commerford (bass) and Brad Wilk (drums), RATM's left-wing lyrics were as polemical as their metallic rhythmic music, displayed on their 1992 eponymous debut album. La Rocha left in 2000, the others forming Audioslave, but they reformed in 2007 for gigs. In 2009 they had a UK Christmas No. 1 with 'Killing In The Name' after an anti-*X Factor* campaign, and have been inactive since 2011.

THE SMASHING PUMPKINS (VOCAL/INSTRUMENTAL GROUP, 1988–2000, 2005–PRESENT)

An important alternative band of the 1990s, Billy Corgan (guitar, vocals), James Iha (guitar), D'Arcy Wretzky (bass) and Jimmy Chamberlin (drums) fused metal, punk and melody over which Corgan delivered compelling lyrical narrative on essential albums such as *Mellon Collie And The Infinite Sadness* (1995). After a 2000 split, Corgan reformed the Pumpkins in 2005 and revived their career, occasionally featuring some – but never all – of the original members.

THE STEREOPHONICS (VOCAL/INSTRUMENTAL GROUP, 1996–PRESENT)

Friends Kelly Jones (guitar, vocals), Richard Jones (bass) and Stuart Cable (drums) formed their band in Cwmaman, Wales. Their obvious chemistry delivered passionate melodic rock, dominated by Jones's lyrics. *Word Gets Around* (1997) spawned UK chart hits like 'A Thousand Trees'; *Performance And Cocktails* (1999) provided further hits. By *Language. Sex. Violence. Other?* (2005) they were established rock stars. 2017's *Scream Above the Sounds* was their tenth album.

The Smashing Pumpkins have sold more than 40 million albums.

THE STONE ROSES (VOCAL/INSTRUMENTAL GROUP, 1985-96, 2011-PRESENT)

This Manchester band – Ian Brown (vocals), John Squire (guitar), Gary 'Mani' Mounfield (bass) and Alan 'Reni' Wren (drums) – announced their jangling guitar pop with single 'Sally Cinnamon'. An eponymous debut album (1989) fused the vibe of acid house on to hook-laden melodic pop. The funk groove of 'Fool's Gold' and the anthemic 'One Love' remain untouchable singles. *Second Coming* (1994) fell short of their debut. After splitting in 1996 they reformed in 2011, and have performed sporadically since.

SUEDE (VOCAL/INSTRUMENTAL GROUP, 1989-2003, 2010-PRESENT)

With lead singer Brett Anderson stating, 'I'm a bisexual who has never had a homosexual experience', Suede were one of the most exciting bands to emerge in the UK for years. After a startling eponymous debut (1993) and a masterful follow-up, *Dead Man Star* (1994), guitarist Bernard Butler departed. After recruiting drives, *Coming Up* (1996) and *Head Music* (1999) kept the faithful happy without ever fully delivering upon initial promise. On hiatus from 2003 to 2010 (with Butler and Anderson reuniting as The Tears in 2005), they resumed performing and eventually recording. 2018's *The Blue Hour* was their eighth album.

SUPERGRASS (VOCAL/INSTRUMENTAL GROUP, 1993-2010)

This Oxford group – Gary 'Gaz' Coombes (vocals, guitar), Mickey Quinn (bass) and Danny Goffey (drums) – delivered some of the finest and most chirpy pop to come out of the UK in the 1990s. Although 'Caught By The Fuzz' dealt with being busted for carrying cannabis, 'Alright', 'Going Out', 'Richard III', 'Pumping On Your Stereo' and 'Moving' were less controversial feel-good anthems. *I Should Coco* (1995) and *In It For The Money* (1997) remain essential albums. They split in 2010, citing 'a seventeen-year itch'.

The Stone Roses are often considered to be the founders of Britpop.

RICHARD THOMPSON (GUITAR, SINGER/SONGWRITER, B. 1949)

The career of this brilliant guitarist and songwriter began in the 1960s with Fairport Convention. Solo releases throughout the 1970s and 1980s – especially *I Want To See The Bright Lights Tonight* (1974), with then-wife Linda – cemented a reputation for an influential guitar style equally at home in folky acoustic and electric settings. During the 1990s, retrospectives like *Watching The Dark* (1993) and new albums like *Mirror Blue* (1994) more than kept him in the public eye. He has released some 40 albums in various guises.

THE VERVE (VOCAL/INSTRUMENTAL GROUP, 1989–99, 2007–09)

Founded in Wigan, Richard Ashcroft (vocals), Nick McCabe (guitar), Simon Jones (bass) and Peter Salisbury (drums) enjoyed critical indie success after the masterfully arranged *A Northern Soul* (1995). After a brief split they reformed for *Urban Hymns* (1997) which, propelled by 'Bittersweet Symphony', transformed them into international stars. Ashcroft's charisma and passion also turned 'The Drugs Don't Work' into an anthem. Ashcroft went solo before a one-album reunion produced 2008's *Forth*.

PAUL WELLER (GUITAR, SINGER/SONGWRITER, B. 1958)

'Modfather' Weller had already written himself into pop history with the feisty guitar pop of The Jam and soulfully commercial groove of The Style Council when he went solo in 1990. Musically and spiritually renewed by live work, *Paul Weller* (1992) laid strong acoustic foundations for the masterful *Wild Wood* (1994). This mature collection of songs showcased Weller's emotional depth and confirmed a songwriting genius not afraid to explore confessional and pastoral themes. Hit singles as diverse as the tender 'You Do Something To Me' and the rocky 'The Changingman' confirmed his appeal. Always a well-dressed style icon, albums like *Stanley Road* (1995), *Heavy Soul* (1997) and *Studio 150* (2004), on which he tackled a daring selection of cover versions, are essential. Since then he has picked a varied array of settings for his songs. His fourteenth studio album, the acoustic-led *True Meanings*, was released in 2018.

One of British music's major influences of the 1990s, Paul Weller became a somewhat reluctant leader of the mod revival.

By the advent of the new millennium, the music scene was unrecognizable from the one that had given birth to rock'n'roll in the 1950s. The means by which music is accessed had gone from vinyl records to CDs to downloads; two decades later, streaming is now the preferred way of listening to music.

Musically, the impact of rap was everywhere to be seen in the first years of the 21st century as artists across the spectrum looked to incorporate it into their style. A new breed of nu-metal bands sprang up, fusing their frenetic, heavy rock with rap vocals and groups like Limp Bizkit, Linkin Park and Slipknot found a huge following.

Art rockers like Radiohead and Coldplay flourished, as did a whole phalanx of rock dinosaurs who'd discovered that touring the world was an effective way to top up your pension plan. But the fact was that rock was gradually falling out of fashion and being superseded by pop.

The aura of political and social revolution that had surrounded rock music was long gone, replaced by fist-pumping clichés. There was still a smattering of punk outrage from the Libertines and (more successfully) Green Day, but the most successful rock bands like Foo Fighters concentrated on giving their audience a great night out. About the most rebellious thing you could do at a rock gig was light up a cigarette.

THE 21ST CENTURY: SOUNDS + SOURCES

If you wanted to buy a record in the 1950s, 1960s or 1970s, you had to go to a record shop, where you could buy a single or album – on 7-inch or 12-inch vinyl. The advent of the cassette in the 1970s offered a second format with portable possibilities that led to the Walkman revolution. Then along came the CD with its 'perfect' digital sound and that seemed to settle matters.

But technology had other ideas. The digital file encoded on to your CD could be downloaded on to your computer via the internet – legally or illegally. And record companies struggled to keep up. Fast forward two decades, however, and the wheel had spun again; by 2019, the majority of consumers were streaming their music via companies like Spotify. They were no longer choosing to own music; it had become so ubiquitous that it could be accessed on demand.

AS SEEN ON TV

The rise of reality TV shows at the beginning of the 21st century, in which the public got to vote for the winner, brought the manufactured pop act back to the fore. Hear'Say who won the 2001 *Popstars* show, went on to have a UK No. 1 album, but the follow-up failed to make the Top 20, thereby setting another trend. Girls Aloud, who won the 2002 series of *Popstars*, were the exception that proved the rule.

Pop Idol (UK) and *American Idol* boasted a better track record, with the 2002 *American Idol* winner Kelly Clarkson going on to have eight hit albums. And British contestant Will Young proved that you didn't have to win it to launch a successful career. *Pop Idol* was replaced by *The X Factor* in 2004, in which the judges mentored the contestants; the

Carlos Santana came back with a bang in the 2000s by combining sheer musical brilliance with modern marketing tools.

show was franchised around the world, and the show was frequently mired in controversy, and Noel Gallagher called it 'nothing to do with music and everything to do with television'. Nevertheless, some of the contestants made it work for them – like One Direction, Little Mix and Leona Lewis. Elsewhere, Australian band INXS even tried to replace their former lead singer Michael Hutchence via a US TV contest, although the winner lasted less than a year. An unexpected beneficiary of reality TV was Ozzy Osbourne, the befuddled former Black Sabbath singer whose household endured the MTV fly-on-the-wall treatment and emerged with superstar status – a kind of heavy metal Simpsons.

HEARING IT ALL OVER AGAIN

Musically, the new millennium had opened with a look back to the future – or so it seemed – with the Beatles' first bona fide greatest hits, *1*, selling 12 million worldwide in three weeks and becoming the fastest-selling album of all time. In addition, American duo Steely Dan returned with their first album in two decades and venerable guitarist Carlos Santana mopped up eight Grammys with *Supernatural*, courtesy of some smart collaborations with younger, hip names like Lauryn Hill, Eagle Eye Cherry and Rob Thomas from Matchbox 20.

NU DIRECTIONS

The last months of 2000 saw two of the leading nu-metal bands release best-selling albums. Linkin Park, who featured a singer, a rapper and a 'turntablist', issued *Hybrid Theory*, which would go on to be one of the following year's top sellers, while the more aggressive Limp Bizkit's *Chocolate Starfish And The Hot Dog Flavored Water* sold 12 million and spawned a UK No. 1 hit with 'Rollin''. They also expanded their fan base by linking up with WWE's wrestling franchise and eventually eclipsed Korn, the band that had originally discovered them. But nu-metal bands had to be careful not to get ensnared by the mainstream and lose their hardcore following.

Korn pioneered a new sub-genre of rock, nu-metal, by combining rap and hard rock.

Former Nirvana drummer Dave Grohl captured the post-grunge zeitgeist with his band, the Foo Fighters. His songs – each accompanied by a clever video that could be enjoyed at more than one level – demanded little yet gave instant gratification. They never disappointed live either, which ensured that they became an enduring festival attraction. They also steered clear of overt politics, which remained unfashionable despite the atrocity of 9/11, as American all-girl country band the Dixie Chicks discovered to their cost when they criticized President George W. Bush's 'war on terror' live on stage. Only artists whose reputations had become immortal could get away with that, as when Bruce Springsteen publically apologized for Donald Trump's election during his 2016 tour of America. It remains to be seen whether any bands will tackle the dramatic shift in the American political landscape head on.

THE VIDEO GENERATION

With the video revolution still evolving, teen magazine *Smash Hits*, that had helped a generation of bands to find fame for some two decades, closed in 2006. It was the same story with the BBC's *Top Of The Pops*, which ended its 42 year history, swamped by music on demand from innumerable TV channels – and the internet, which now offered 24-hour access to your favourite band. Unlike the internet, DVDs (Digital Versatile Discs) failed to make the impact that many had predicted. While concert films and collections of promo clips sold respectably, consumers seemed unwilling to pay the prices that were initially pitched. After all, music was getting cheaper. DVDs were often seen as a way of clawing back money from an expensive tour or to satisfy the demand for a now non-existent band.

SISTERS ARE DOING IT FOR THEMSELVES

Black music monopolized the US charts in the early 2000s, and in the 2001 singles charts, only nu-metallists Crazy Town and Canadians Nickelback registered a No. 1 outside the R&B/soul genre. And there was a definite female bias,

Hip-hop's move from street scene and underground to extravagant chart success was finally completed in early 2000.

with names like Janet Jackson, Destiny's Child, Alicia Keys and Mary J Blige among the most prominent. That bias was confirmed with Disney-raised pop stars Britney Spears and Christina Aguilera, and by the edgier P!nk, who mixed controversy and punk attitude into her songs. The female bias has continued with Taylor Swift, Beyoncé, Rihanna, Lady Gaga, Adele, Katy Perry, Selena Gomez and Ariana Grande, to name but a few.

FALLING IN AND OUT OF FASHION

2005's Live 8, 20 years on from Live Aid and garnering the same sort of attention, was probably the last great gathering of rock bands. Headliners Pink Floyd reformed especially for the occasion. The art-rock banner they'd flown for so long had been picked up by Radiohead, with Coldplay gathering steam on the back of relentless touring. But while rock bands were continuing to dominate the live scene, they were gradually falling from fashion as pop gained prominence. The new breed of pop stars were increasingly business savvy when it came to marketing their wares. There is 'Team Swift' adroitly spinning every professional and personal turn of Taylor. Ed Sheeran, meanwhile, carries around a country-by-country analysis of his album sales on his laptop.

As the second decade of the 21st century draws to a close, the last of the 1960s legends are still touring and commanding large audiences. The Rolling Stones were the biggest earning live band of 2018. Bob Dylan is continuing his 'Never-Ending Tour' and Paul McCartney gives an insight into the magic that was the Beatles. Even The Who are refusing to die before they get old (although there are only two of the original band left). But no-one is pretending that they are musical pioneers any more: people are flocking to see them because they can.

Rock has not lost its cutting edge, but it is no longer at the forefront of the music business. But as this book shows, popular music is cyclical and this may change.

2005's Live 8 was a headline-grabbing showcase for new and old acts to reaffirm their commitment to the 'Make Poverty History' movement.

THE 21ST CENTURY: KEY ARTISTS

COLDPLAY (VOCAL/INSTRUMENTAL GROUP, 1996-PRESENT)

Coldplay was formed in London in 1996 by Chris Martin (vocals), Jonny Buckland (guitar), Will Champion (drums) and Guy Berryman (bass). They began gigging in the Camden area of London and self-funded their first single. Only 500 copies of *Safety EP* (1998) were made, but fortuitously, some ended up in the hands of record company executives. After university, the band signed a five-album deal with UK label Parlophone. Smashes 'Yellow' and 'Trouble', from debut album *Parachutes* (2000), gained them worldwide exposure. Returning in 2002 with the impressive 'In My Place', their status had swelled enormously, largely as a result of the intense touring.

A RUSH OF SALES

A Rush Of Blood To The Head (2002) had much of the same balladry and musicianship as its predecessor. But Coldplay's musical direction was apparently shifting by 2003–04, as the band cited Kraftwerk and the more electronic side of Radiohead as influences. When *X&Y* was finally delivered in 2005, fans seemed pleased that the album was not, in fact, a techno record. The tours got bigger still, culminating in June 2005, when the band headlined the Glastonbury Festival and then duetted with their hero Richard Ashcroft at the London leg of Live 8. Released in June 2008, fourth album *Viva la Vida Or Death And All His Friends* topped the UK album chart after just three days' sales. Its title track became the band's first US No. 1. The band worked with Brian Eno on *Mylo Xyloto* (2011) and they had more producers than band members on 2014's *Ghost Stories*. For 2015's *A Head Full Of Dreams*, they brought in Noel Gallagher and Beyoncé, among others.

Chris Martin on stage in support of A Rush Of Blood To The Head – *Coldplay proved they were no one-album-wonders.*

EMINEM (RAPPER, B. 1972)

Marshall Bruce Mathers III was born in Detroit, Michigan, where his reputedly poverty-stricken upbringing provided ample subject matter for much of his lyrical material. A high school drop-out, Mathers found his talent in rapping and, taking the name Eminem (after his initials), he began performing at the age of 13. Rap entrepreneur/producer Dr. Dre somehow found Eminem's demo, *Infinite*, which he'd sold from the boot of his car. *Infinite* paved the way for Eminem's *Slim Shady LP* (1999). Slim Shady was an alias and a character who represented the more damaged side of the rapper. The album caused a storm of controversy but despite, or perhaps because of this, it sold triple platinum in its first year.

PERSONAL ISSUES

The Marshall Mathers LP (2000) sold three times as well as its predecessor. But later albums, although still selling extremely well, were perhaps too infused with Mathers' increasing mental instability to cross over as well as they had previously. Eminem's career ran out of steam after 2004's *Encore*. In 2008 he published the autobiography *The Way I Am* and returned to the musical fray in 2009 with *Relapse*; while it didn't manage to sell as well as previous efforts (some five million worldwide), it was named one of the top albums of the year. A follow-up, *Recovery*, was released in 2010. It debuted at No. 1 in the US, topping the chart for seven weeks.

He started working with other rock stars – Rihanna on the No. 1 single 'The Monster' from *The Marshall Mathers LP 2* (2013) and Gwen Stefani on the *Southpaw* soundtrack (2014). Three years later, *Revival* (2017) found him hooking up with Beyoncé ('Walk On Water'), Ed Sheeran ('River') and P!nk ('Need Me'). And then, almost without warning, he was back a year later with the angry and possibly appropriately titled *Kamikaze*. Regressing into juvenile attitudes, it seemed a strange move for the rapper to take.

Courting controversy from the start with a nothing-is-taboo lyrical content, Eminem has become one of the most successful rap artists ever.

KINGS OF LEON (VOCAL/INSTRUMENTAL GROUP, 1999-PRESENT)

Brothers Caleb (vocals and rhythm guitar), Jared (bass) and Nathan Followill (drums) and their cousin Matthew Followill (lead guitar) make up one of the world's most recognizable rock bands. Caleb and Nathan were initially signed to RCA before being joined by Jared and Matthew to make their first record, the *Holy Roller Novocaine* EP, in 2003. The provocatively titled record excited fans and critics alike, especially UK media, which dubbed them 'The Southern Strokes'. Their first album, *Youth And Young Manhood* (2003), was a great commercial triumph, peaking at No. 3 in the UK album charts. They stuck to their winning formula for *Aha Shake Heartbreak* (2004), which also reached No. 3 in the UK.

KINGS ON FIRE

The Kings Of Leon opened for U2 on the US leg of their Vertigo World Tour in 2005, helping them make a mark in their homeland. The Friday night headline slot at the 2008 Glastonbury Festival preceded their fourth album, *Only By The Night*. The success of lead single 'Sex On Fire' made Kings Of Leon the biggest band in the world at that moment. 'Sex On Fire' was named Best Rock Performance at the 2009 Grammys.

But behind the scenes were signs of strain: a punch-up between Caleb and Nathan left the former requiring surgery, and at T In The Park Festival in Scotland in 2009, Caleb irreparably smashed his beloved 37-year-old Gibson ES-325 guitar. But the hard-living and hard-drinking Followills had certainly made their mark on the Noughties, and their hard work paid off in 2010, when they were awarded three Grammys, including Best Rock Song for 'Use Somebody'. They eventually ground to a halt in 2011 after an inebriated Caleb walked offstage at a Texas gig. Taking some time to sort themselves out, they were back in 2013 with *Mechanical Bull*, finding a new equilibrium between their Southern roots and their big rock sound. *WALLS* (2016), recorded in LA, soaked up a little of the laid-back, West Coast vibe as they picked up where they had left off.

After a slow-burn start in their home nation, Kings Of Leon have become one of the biggest bands in the world.

RADIOHEAD (VOCAL/INSTRUMENTAL GROUP, 1986-PRESENT)

Radiohead are Thom Yorke (vocals, guitar, piano), Jonny Greenwood (lead guitar, effects), Ed O'Brien (guitar, vocals), Phil Selway (drums) and Colin Greenwood (bass). Formed at school in Oxford, they began jamming in 1986 as On A Friday, and gigged in their hometown after university. Bands such as Ride had already made quite a name for Oxford, spearheading a new 'shoegazing' movement in the early 1990s. EMI signed the band on a six-album deal, providing they change their name. Radiohead's debut album, *Pablo Honey* (1993) included the song 'Creep'. A second release of the song in the US caught a wider audience's attention. Their second album, *The Bends* (1995), achieved high worldwide sales, though was arguably more formulaic. *OK Computer* (1997) marked a progression and was lauded as the greatest album of the year in many publications.

UNDER THE INFLUENCE

Radiohead, ever forward-thinking, introduced new sounds and influences in *Kid A* (2000) and *Amnesiac* (2001). 2003 brought the release of *Hail To The Thief*, a provocatively titled collection that almost saw a return to the rock of the mid-1990s. In 2007, having fulfilled their EMI contract, Radiohead caused headlines by issuing *In Rainbows* on the internet, inviting fans to pay what they thought the album was worth. It later appeared in physical form to critical acclaim and chart success, debuting at No. 1 both in the UK and in the US. Having loosened the traditional bonds between band and record company, Radiohead took advantage by following their own timetable, releasing music, playing shows and indulging in side projects as and when it suited them. Their next album, *King of Limbs* (2011) eschewed conventional rock instrumentation in favour of sampling and loops and required an additional drummer to perform it live. *A Moon Shaped Pool* (2016) was accompanied by singles and promo videos, musically fusing strings and guitars with electronic beats. It was followed by two years of touring.

Singer Thom Yorke has become one of the most singular minds in music, consistently pushing boundaries without losing Radiohead's fanbase.

ED SHEERAN (SINGER/SONGWRITER, B. 1991)

Quite possibly the perfect pop star for the 21st century, Ed Sheeran subconsciously draws on any musical style that suits his purpose – from folk to hip hop – to create music that is distinctively his own with a broad appeal and, without seeming to try, has become one of the most successful artists on the planet while remaining natural and unassuming.

Of course he did try. Very hard and very astutely. He began writing songs when he was barely into his teens and recorded a self-made album aged 13. He played gigs all over his native Suffolk before leaving school at 16 and moving to London, working as a guitar tech and continuing to gig wherever possible. He released two more independent EPs and posted clips of his shows on YouTube.

BREAKTHROUGH

In 2010 he flew to Los Angeles for a show on the strength of a single contact and hung around looking for more gigs, playing his songs to anyone who would listen. At the end of that year he signed to Asylum after sleeping on the A&R guy's floor, unaware of who he was. His first single, 'The A Team', entered the UK charts in 2011 at No. 3, shortly followed by his debut album, +, winning him the British Breakthrough award at the 2012 Brit Awards. His US breakthrough came after supporting Snow Patrol that year and Taylor Swift on her Red tour in 2013.

His second album, x, in 2014, debuted at No. 1 in the UK and US and became the second-biggest-selling album of 2015 as he toured the world in support. His third album, ÷, in 2017, topped the charts in 20 countries and featured his epic paean to Suffolk, 'Castle On The Hill'. He has consolidated his ubiquity by writing for other acts, including Justin Bieber, as he married his childhood sweetheart.

Ed Sheeran has a pitch-perfect sound for the 2010s, eclectic yet appealing, collaborating with a diverse range of artists from pop to hip-hop.

THE 21ST CENTURY: A-Z OF ARTISTS

ADELE (SINGER/SONGWRITER, B. 1988)

From Tottenham via the BRIT School for Performing Arts, Adele hit the zeitgeist with her second album, *21*, in 2011. A break-up album conveyed by a voice of unadulterated honesty and feeling, the album won six Grammys and has sold an astonishing 31 million copies to date, breaking chart records like Twiglets. Despite the extraordinary hype, she remained unaffected and down-to-earth. Her fans had to wait four years for the follow-up, *25*, but Adele achieved the highest first week sale ever after becoming the first artist to sell a million downloads of her 'Hello' single. Another five Grammys duly followed. Her fourth album was released in 2019.

ALABAMA SHAKES (VOCAL/INSTRUMENTAL GROUP 2011-PRESENT)

Their gritty mix of blues-rock and Southern soul rocked the Athens, Georgia, quartet's 2012 debut album, *Boys & Girls*, up to No. 6 in the US charts. The band, led by irrepressible frontwoman Brittany Howard on vocals and guitar, took their time over the follow-up, carefully exaggerating their unique characteristics, and were rewarded when *Sound & Color* shot straight to No. 1 in the US in 2015. They seem to be in no hurry to put out a third album just yet.

ARCADE FIRE (VOCAL/INSTRUMENTAL GROUP, 2003-PRESENT)

A combination of thoughtful indie music and energetic live shows propelled Canada-based Arcade Fire into becoming one of the new millennium's most successful bands. Critical acclaim began with their debut, *Funeral*, in 2004, and they spread the word with intensive touring. 2007's *Neon Bible* expanded their style and content, and they topped the US charts with reflective, Grammy-winning *The Suburbs* in 2010. The only way was up with ambitious double album, *Reflektor* (2013), followed by a world tour. Critical doubts came with 2017's *Everything Now* but by then they were too big to care.

Arcade Fire's anthemic indie rock has transformed them from underground favourites to chart-topping sensation.

ARCTIC MONKEYS (VOCAL/INSTRUMENTAL GROUP, 2005-PRESENT)

After fans shared their demos online, Sheffield's Arctic Monkeys – Alex Turner (vocals), Jamie Turner (guitar), Matt Helders (drums) and Andy Nicholson (bass) – saw their wryly accurate take on northern English life consumed by the public. Their debut album *Whatever People Say I Am, That's What I'm Not* was released in January 2006 and became the fastest-selling album ever in the country. They spent the next decade craftily meshing their very British pop songs with their heavy metal attitude.

AWOLNATION (VOCAL/INSTRUMENTAL GROUP, 2009-PRESENT)

AWOLNATION started as a side project by Los Angeles-born Aaron Bruno for songs that didn't fit his band Under The Influence of Giants. The band's electro pop 'Sail', taken from debut album *Megalithic Symphony*, was a worldwide hit in 2011. 2015's *Run* and 2018's *Here Come the Runts*, have developed his gentle, genre-breaking style and built up a loyal following.

THE BLACK KEYS (VOCAL/INSTRUMENTAL DUO, 2001-PRESENT)

It took six albums and selling an earlier song for a Japanese car commercial for the tough, blues-based guitar/drums duo from Akron, Ohio, Dan Auerbach and Patrick Carney, to make the breakthrough. 2010's *Brothers* brought a grander texture to their gritty sound (courtesy of Danger Mouse) and produced three hits and three Grammys. Albums *El Camino* (2011) and *Turn Blue* (2014) consolidated their success as their songwriting flourished without deserting or diluting their roots.

BIFFY CLYRO (VOCAL/INSTRUMENTAL GROUP, 1995-PRESENT)

Scottish rock trio Biffy Clyro – Simon Neil (vocals and guitar), James Johnston (bass) and twin brother Ben (drums) – issued breakthrough UK No. 2 album *Puzzle* in 2007 after their first three LPs failed to reach the Top 40. Follow-up

Arctic Monkeys' 'I Bet You Look Good On The Dancefloor' was a hit out of nowhere, thanks to online support.

Only Revolutions (2009) also hit the Top 10, ensuring their guitar-laden alt-rock permeated the airwaves, and 2013's *Opposites* proved they can stretch out without losing their immediacy.

THE DARKNESS (VOCAL/INSTRUMENTAL GROUP, 2000–06, 2011–PRESENT)

The Darkness – Justin Hawkins (vocals), Dan Hawkins (guitar), Ed Graham (drums) and Richie Edwards (bass) – are the most unlikely rock stars. Good looks and credibility take second place to stadiums full of fans and steely rock riffs transplanted straight from their heroes, Queen. Debut album *Permission To Land* (2003) sold well. The group split after a water-treading second album, but reformed to release *Hot Cakes* (2012), *Last Of Our Kind* (2015) and *Pinewood Smile* (2017), while going through more drummers than Spinal Tap.

DEERHUNTER (VOCAL/INSTRUMENTAL GROUP, 2001–PRESENT)

Experimental rockers Deerhunter from Atlanta, Georgia, led by gangly, effervescent singer Bradford Cox and solemn guitarist Lockett Pundt, teetered on the edge of their own avant garde stylings before they found a way to let their melodies shine through the sonic haze on their third album, *Microcastle*, in 2008. They established a fan base that has willingly followed the band through the twists and turns of 2010's *Halcyon Digest*, 2013's *Monomania* and 2015's *Fading Frontier*. 2019 saw the release of their eighth album, *Why Hasn't Everything Already Disappeared?*.

FALL OUT BOY (VOCAL/INSTRUMENTAL GROUP, 2001–PRESENT)

Riding the pop-punk/emo genre tightrope and the swirling social media currents, Chicago-based Fall Out Boy have defiantly survived and prospered amid the fast-moving vagaries of fashion. Formed by extrovert bassist Pete Wentz with drummer-turned-singer Patrick Stump, they released three increasingly successful albums until problems recording the fourth led to a hiatus after its release in 2008. Reuniting triumphantly five years later, they are still going strong after three more albums.

Frontman Justin Hawkins and The Darkness resurrected the sounds and attitudes of late-1970s hard rock for a new generation.

FEEDER (VOCAL/INSTRUMENTAL GROUP, 1992–2012, 2015–PRESENT)

Feeder – Grant Nicholas (guitar, vocals), Taka Hirose (bass) and Mark Richardson (drums, left 2009) – are a Welsh/Japanese/English hybrid. It was not until third album *Echo Park* (2001) that their brand of bombastic, yelping, yet highly singalong rock was noticed by the masses. The suicide of first drummer Jon Lee in early 2002 cast a grim light on subsequent material, but by 2005's *Pushing The Senses,* the group was selling more records than ever. They lost momentum for a couple of albums, but regained their ambition on *Generation Freakshow* (2012) and *All Bright Electric* (2016).

FLORENCE + THE MACHINE (VOCAL/INSTRUMENTAL GROUP, 2007–PRESENT)

Launching her debut album on the back of appearances at Glastonbury and London's Hyde Park in 2009 showed the great expectations that surrounded 22-year-old south Londoner Florence Welch and her band. *Lungs* revealed all the pleasures of her quaint gothic pop, her poised, distinctive vocals with Celtic tinges and her lyrical charm. Unfazed by the critical excitement, her career has proceeded at her own unhurried pace ever since, with three more albums expanding her magical musical tapestry.

FOALS (VOCAL/INSTRUMENTAL GROUP, 2005–PRESENT)

Cutting a swathe through the indie rock scene with their 2008 debut, the jerky pop-influenced *Antidotes*, Oxford-based Foals, fronted by Greek island-born Yannis Philippakis, justified the hype that had preceded the album. Their songs were both clever and infectious. 2010's *Total Life Forever* loosened up without losing interest and by 2013's *Holy Fire* they were ready to move into the mainstream, becoming more expansive without compromising their style. 2015's *What Went Down* took them there.

FOO FIGHTERS (VOCAL/INSTRUMENTAL GROUP, 1995–PRESENT)

Foo Fighters, the post-Nirvana project of Dave Grohl, with Taylor Hawkins (drums), Nate Mendel (bass) and Chris Shiflett

Dave Grohl took the spotlight for what was, initially, a solo project. Foo Fighters are now one of the most popular bands in rock.

(guitar), saw the drummer-turned-singer storm the charts again and again with an honest, workaday approach to rock that was, more often that not, humorously handled. Thankfully too, Grohl could write a melody, and this meant his new band made countless radio hits. Their 1995 self-titled debut consisted of Grohl's homemade solo recordings, but on *The Colour and the Shape* (1997) and *There Is Nothing Left to Lose* (1999) they embodied the spirit of post-grunge modern rock. *In Your Honor* (2005) was divided into a rock CD and an acoustic CD to reinvigorate their sound, while *Echoes, Silence, Patience & Grace* merged rock and acoustic elements and won a couple of Grammys. The songwriting on 2011's *Wasting Light* earned them five more Grammys, and 2017's *Concrete and Gold* saw them stretching out, Seventies style.

FRANZ FERDINAND (VOCAL/INSTRUMENTAL GROUP, 2001–PRESENT)

Glasgow's Franz Ferdinand – Alex Kapranos (vocals), Robert Hardy (bass), Nicholas McCarthy (guitar) and Paul Thomson (drums) – formed from the scene around the city's art college. Their tightly suggestive brand of 'art rock' and winning melodies brought mainstream acclaim, their eponymous debut winning the Mercury Music Prize in 2004. They stuck to their stylish sound for *You Could Have It So Much Better* (2005), branching out into dance and pop for *Tonight: Franz Ferdinand* (2009). They got back to what they were best at on *Right Thoughts, Right Words, Right Action* (2013). After line-up changes, they gave their dance inclinations another roll of the dice on 2018's *Always Ascending*.

GREEN DAY (VOCAL/INSTRUMENTAL GROUP, 1986–PRESENT)

Californian rock trio Billie Joe Armstrong (vocals, guitar), Mike Dirnt (bass, vocals) and Tré Cool (drums) enjoyed global success with 1993's *Dookie*. They were unashamed punk-rock throwbacks and made entertaining music videos. They turned to producing more carefully crafted pop fare, but could not recapture their popularity until 2004's *American Idiot* hit a nerve by lampooning George W. Bush's America. They pushed themselves to the limit, clearing out their song cupboard with three albums, ¡Uno!, ¡Dos! and ¡Tré! in 2012, after which Armstrong had a meltdown and went into rehab. But 2016's *Revolution Radio* showed they can't be written off.

Since the 1990s Green Day have evolved from slightly mindless punkers to one of the most influential bands of their generation.

HAIM (VOCAL GROUP, 2006–PRESENT)

Growing up to the soundtrack of the 1980s in sun-kissed California, the three Rockinhaim sisters also listened to their parents' 1970s record collection. They distilled the whole experience on their *Days Are Gone* debut album in 2013, revelling in the close harmonies while toughening up the beats. Their second album, *Something to Tell You* in 2017, proved they still had plenty left to mine.

P.J. HARVEY (VOCALS, B. 1969)

Dorset-born and raised, PJ Harvey is now eleven albums into an extraordinarily diverse career that has seen her veer from the highly charged indie rock of *Dry* (1992) to the 'aggressive eroticism' of *Rid of Me* (1993), the 'towering goth version of grunge' on *To Bring You My Love* (1995), the rock-pop of Mercury Music Prize-winning *Stories from the City, Stories from the Sea* (2000), the piano ballads of *White Chalk* (2007) and the war-infected *Let England Shake* (2011). Along the way, she has collaborated with Radiohead's Thom Yorke, Nick Cave and Tricky. She has also been an influence on many female singer-songwriters.

IMAGINE DRAGONS (VOCAL/INSTRUMENTAL GROUP, 2009–PRESENT)

Springing out fully-formed, ready to rock an arena near you, Las Vegas quartet Imagine Dragons were hard to avoid in 2012, as the singles from their slick, big-sounding debut album, *Night Visions*, swept across the radio airwaves. Some critics were sceptical but the public were not, making 'Radioactive' a colossal worldwide hit and a Grammy winner. 2015's *Smoke + Mirrors* and 2017's *Evolve* did not stop the critics' scepticism or the band's increasing success; *Origins*, a 'sister' to *Evolve*, was released in 2018.

INCUBUS (VOCAL/INSTRUMENTAL GROUP, 1991–PRESENT)

Formed in 1991 by singer Brandon Boyd with schoolmates Mike Einziger and Jose Pasillas, Californian quintet Incubus found mainstream success by altering their initially experimental sound. 2001's more commercial *Morning View* hit No.

Imagine Dragons have honed their sound over the years, and are now best known for stadium-shattering anthems.

2 on the *Billboard* 200. *A Crow Left Of The Murder* landed in the same spot three years later. In 2006 they scored their first US No. 1 LP with *Light Grenades* before taking a hiatus. They've been moodier since their return in 2011.

THE KAISER CHIEFS (VOCAL/INSTRUMENTAL GROUP, 2003-PRESENT)

Leeds' Kaiser Chiefs – Ricky Wilson (vocals), Andrew White (guitar), Simon Rix (bass), Nick Hodgson (drums) and Nick Baines (keyboards) – plough the same indie furrow that fellow Brit-poppers Blur did during their *Parklife* era. Wilson elicits playful singalong choruses from unexpected places while his band churn out building, shuddering riffs on singles such as 'I Predict A Riot' and 'Oh My God'. They let their fans choose their own tracklisting for 2011's *The Future Is Medieval* and showed no signs of complacency on 2016's *Stay Together*.

KASABIAN (VOCAL/INSTRUMENTAL GROUP, 1999-PRESENT)

From the same school as proletariat rockers Oasis, Kasabian – Tom Meighan (vocals), Serge Pizzorno (guitar), Chris Karloff (guitar) and Christopher Edwards (bass) – hail from Leicester. Not a simple rock template, much of the band's sound is augmented by multiple vocal sections and a chatter of electronica evoking Primal Scream's mid-period albums. They have amassed a loyal following over six albums.

KEANE (VOCAL/INSTRUMENTAL GROUP, 1997-2013)

Ever since guitarist Dominic Scott left the band in 1999, Keane – Tom Chaplin (vocals), Tom Rice-Oxley (piano, bass) and Richard Hughes (drums) – have taken the unusual route of not replacing him, supplementing their sound instead with piano. The move proved to be a wise one, as the comparatively unique sound they created has found success. Formed, like many indie bands, as friends in their home town (Battle, Sussex), the best example of their work is 'Everybody's Changing', a chiming slice of whimsy that reached No. 4 on its UK re-release in 2004. Third album *Perfect Symmetry* (2008) reached UK No. 1 but they have been largely inactive since 2013.

Inspired by the punk rock of the 1970s, The Kaiser Chiefs' debut album Employment *was an international hit.*

THE KILLERS (VOCAL/INSTRUMENTAL GROUP, 2002-PRESENT)

Vegas's Killers – Brandon Flowers (vocals), Dave Keuning (guitar), Mark August Stoermer (bass) and Ronnie Vannucci Jr. (drums) – were formed from a variety of wanted adverts after Flowers was thrown out of his first band. Influenced by the mass singalongs of Oasis, the technological edge of New Order and the introspection of The Smiths and The Cure, the band found mass acclaim in 2004 with their *Hot Fuss* album. All five of their albums – including 2017's *Wonderful Wonderful* – have topped the British charts and, despite line-up changes, there is more to come from the Killers.

THE LIBERTINES (VOCAL/INSTRUMENTAL GROUP, 2001-04, 2010, 2014-PRESENT)

The Libertines – Pete Doherty (vocals, guitar), Carl Barat (vocals, guitar), John Hassall (bass) and Gary Powell (drums) – hailed from the east end of London. Across their short lifespan they made two albums (*Up The Bracket*, 2002 and *The Libertines*, 2004) of exceptionally idiosyncratic indie symbolizing the post-millennial post-punk chaos. In Doherty and Barat lay a raucous and compelling songwriting team. The band eventually spluttered out in 2004 (with Doherty sacked for his drug problems, later forming Babyshambles; Barat would form Dirty Pretty Things), but they reunited for headlining festival appearances in 2010 and again in 2014, this time with a third album, appropriately titled *Anthems For Doomed Youth*.

LIMP BIZKIT (VOCAL/INSTRUMENTAL GROUP, 1994-PRESENT)

Limp Bizkit – Fred Durst (vocals), Wes Borland (guitar), DJ Lethal (turntables), Sam Rivers (bass) and John Otto (drums) – are something of a global phenomenon, and the benchmark against which all nu-metal and rapcore bands are judged. Their fusion of the direct vocal delivery of rap with the sledgehammer riffing of metal has found a fan base with disaffected youths the world over. Second album *Significant Other* (1999) broke them on a small scale; 'Break Stuff' remains a fan favourite. The sentiments behind third album *Chocolate Starfish And The Hotdog Flavored Water* (2000) were as unpleasant as the title, although it sold a record-breaking million copies in its first week. But Borland left, and without him Limp Bizkit struggled. Since his return progress has been stilted and the follow-up to 2011's *Gold Cobra* remains unreleased.

The fashion for rap-metal crossover is usually only successful when embarked upon by the rap artist, but Limp Bizkit bucked that trend.

LINKIN PARK (VOCAL/INSTRUMENTAL GROUP, 1996–PRESENT)

Other bands in the genre may be more acclaimed, and some more stylistically diverse, but Linkin Park – Chester Bennington (vocals), Mike Shinoda (MC), Brad Delson (guitar), Dave Farrell (bass), Joseph Hahn (DJ) and Rob Bourdon (drums) – are certainly the most successful in the nu-metal sphere. The band incorporate hip-hop approaches to music into their heavy rock sound – and the formula works well. Each of their four studio albums since 2000 has reached the Top 3 in the US, and their collaboration with rapper Jay-Z, *Collision Course* (2004), topped the chart. Their restless nature means the band are always ready to experiment. They tried growing up on 2012's *Living Things*, went back to basics on *The Hunting Party* (2014) and got poppier on *One More Light* (2017).

MUMFORD + SONS (VOCAL/INSTRUMENTAL GROUP, 2007–PRESENT)

Emerging from the London folk revival, Mumford & Sons blew a blast of fresh air through the UK rock scene with their 2009 debut, *Sigh No More*. There were banjos, mandolins, accordions and a double bass, but the sound was big enough to compete with their electric contemporaries. 2012's *Babel* spread the word to America, winning a Grammy, while 2015's *Wilder Mind* turned down the folk and turned up the rock. In late 2018 they unveiled the latest episode of their journey, *Delta*.

MUSE (VOCAL/INSTRUMENTAL GROUP, 1997–PRESENT)

Matthew Bellamy (vocals), Chris Wolstenholme (bass) and Dominic Howard (drums) provide such an enlivening take on the classic power trio formation in rock that it is sometimes easy to forget they are just a trio. Formed in Devon, but building their sound through American influences such as Soundgarden and Nirvana rather than the British ones, Muse were very much outsiders from the start. Albums *Showbiz* (1999) and *Origin Of Symmetry* (2001) saw them stretch rock's confines further, and 2006's UK chart-topping *Black Holes And Revelations* was outrageous, bombastic in its scope and blatant in its nods to rock's past. Their fifth studio album, *The Resistance* (2009), topped the charts in 19 countries. Critics

Muse's prog-metal ambitions, and slight self-obsession of lead Bellamy, has given them a crossover appeal within a mainstream youth market.

praised its ambition, classical-music influences and the 13-minute, three-part 'Exogenesis: Symphony'. Muse have continued to test boundaries, pushing the electronica button on *The 2nd Law* (2012), creating their own version of *The Wall on Drones* (2015) and deliberately stripping back their sound on *Simulation Theory* (2018).

MY CHEMICAL ROMANCE (VOCAL/INSTRUMENTAL GROUP, 2001–13)

This melodic yet heavy emo-rock band from New Jersey, led by singer Gerald Way, found success and controversy in equal measure. The quintet reached the US/UK Top 40 with their second album, 2004's *Three Cheers For Sweet Revenge*. Their third LP, *The Black Parade*, hit No. 2 in the US and UK, with the band's gothic image claimed by a British newspaper to glamourize suicide. This only increased album sales. After swapping emo for heavy power pop on *Danger Days: The True Lives of the Fabulous Killjoys* (2010) the band decided to quit while they were still ahead.

NEON TREES (VOCAL/INSTRUMENTAL GROUP, 2005–PRESENT)

Utah quartet Neon Trees nailed down their catchy pop rock so firmly on 2010's *Habits* it was hard to see where they could go from there. The addition of 1980s synth-pop to their palate on 2012's *Picture Show* gave them the wriggle room they needed, and 2014's *Pop Psychology* got distinctly more personal without sacrificing their increasingly electronic pop. Singer Tyler Glenn's solo album in 2016 fuelled rumours of a break-up but the band insist they are just refocussing.

NICKELBACK (VOCAL/INSTRUMENTAL GROUP, 1995–PRESENT)

Benefitting from a rule that Canadian radio had to play more homegrown talent, post grunge outfit Nickelback – Chad Kroeger (vocals), Ryan Peake (guitar), Mike Kroeger (bass) and Daniel Adair (drums) – had their 2001 national hit, 'How You Remind Me' from their third album, *Silver Side Up*, picked up by US radio. It set up an international career that the band have elongated by adding power pop to their range, notably on *Here and Now* (2011) and *No Fixed Address* (2014).

With 'How You Remind Me', Nickelback became only the second Canadian band to simultaneously top the US and Canadian charts.

NINE INCH NAILS (VOCAL/INSTRUMENTAL GROUP, 1988–PRESENT)

Nine Inch Nails – Trent Reznor (vocals), Aaron North (guitar), Jeordie White (bass), Alessandro Cortini (keyboards) and Josh Freese (drums) – are the latest line-up of Reznor's ever-popular band. Somehow walking the thin line between electro and metal, mainstream yet eternally credible, they are one of America's least deified rock bands, but a five-album, double Grammy-winning career shows they are not totally forgotten. Largely a showcase for Reznor's prodigious multi-instrumental talent, NIN (as it is often abbreviated) found their music reaching the most unexpected of ears when a certain Johnny Cash recorded their 'Hurt' epic in 2004 on the fourth of his hugely appreciated American Recordings albums. The death of the country giant less than a year later, and the emotionally draining video, brought legions of new appreciators of Reznor's work, which now spans nine albums.

OF MONSTERS AND MEN (VOCAL/INSTRUMENTAL GROUP, 2010–PRESENT)

The delicate, catchy indie-folk charm of Icelandic band Of Monsters and Men's first single, 'Little Talks' was such a worldwide success in 2012 that it threatened to brand them a one hit wonder until their album, *My Head Is an Animal*, revealed the full range of their acoustically driven grand, romantic songs with detailed arrangements and a distinctive dual-vocal style. 2015's *Beneath the Skin* finessed the format successfully and they started work on their third album during 2017.

OUTKAST (RAP DUO, 1991–PRESENT)

Cutting a swathe through the rap rivalries between the East and West Coasts with their Southern hip hop, Atlanta-based OutKast, featuring André and Big Boi, racked up a series of platinum albums in the mid- to late-1990s after their 1993 breakthrough hit 'Players Ball'. *Southernplayalisticadillacmuzik* (1994), *ATLiens* (1996), *Aquemini* (1998) and *Stankonia* (2000) used funk, psychedelia and jazz as a musical backdrop, and the double *Speakerboxxx/The Love Below* (2003) won a Grammy. After a break for solo projects, they returned in 2014. They have sold over 25 million albums.

OutKast's melodic, lyrical rap has taken the duo to commercial and critical heights.

PANIC! AT THE DISCO (VOCAL/INSTRUMENTAL GROUP, 2004–PRESENT)

Las Vegas emo pop band Panic! At The Disco barged to the fore with their hyperactive, compelling songs on 2005's *A Fever You Can't Sweat Out*. They briefly went psychedelic for *Pretty. Odd* in 2008, going through line-up changes before the big-hitting *Vices & Virtues* in 2011 and 2013's dance-infused *Too Weird To Live, Too Rare To Die!*. By now, singer Brendon Urie was the only original member, but the band still topped the US charts with 2015's *Death of a Batchelor*. *Pray for the Wicked* was released in 2018, debuting at No. 1 in the US charts.

PARAMORE (VOCAL/INSTRUMENTAL GROUP, 2004–PRESENT)

Formed by Tennessee teen singer Hayley Williams, Paramore struck a chord with the emo crowd on their 2005 *All We Know Is Falling* debut that turned into a hardcore following on 2007's platinum *Riot!*. *Brand New Eyes* in 2009 featured their biggest hit, 'The Only Exception', but the band was fraying at the seams, and a messy split left Williams bloodied but unbowed. 2013's pop-oriented eponymous album went platinum, and 2017's *After Laughter* continued in the same direction.

QUEENS OF THE STONE AGE (VOCAL/INSTRUMENTAL GROUP, 1997–PRESENT)

Godfathers of the Californian desert rock scene, heavy QOTSA – Troy van Leeuwen (guitar), Joey Castillo (drums), Alain Johannes (bass) and Natasha Schneider (keyboards) – were formed from the ashes of Kyuss by Josh Homme (vocals, guitar). Their breakthrough came with 2000's *Rated 'R'*, which featured the sarcastic anthem 'Feel Good Hit Of The Summer' , and they have maintained a high standard across their eight albums.

RAZORLIGHT (VOCAL/INSTRUMENTAL GROUP, 2002–PRESENT)

Very much a vehicle for precociously talented singer Johnny Borrell, Razorlight – with Bjorn Agren (guitar), Carl Dalemo (bass) and Andy Burrows (drums) – trade in modern indie rock so appealing that their performance at Live 8 in 2005 saw sales of their debut album *Up All Night* (2004) rocket. The eponymous follow-up (2006) looked to have carved out

a sharp distinctive style to exploit, but 2008's *Slipway Fires* unaccountably veered into the mainstream. Within two years, Borrell was the only original member. A decade later *Olympus Sleeping* (2018) sounded dated.

RIHANNA (SINGER/SONGWRITER, B. 1988)

Barbados-born Robyn Rihanna Fenty had already won talent and beauty contests before she was spotted by vacationing NSYNC/Christina Aguilera producer Evan Rogers, aged 15. She signed with Jay Z's Def Jam label in 2005 and her first single, 'Pon De Replay' in 2005, started an extraordinary continuous hit career that has so far notched up 11 No. 1s (including 'Umbrella' and 'Only Girl (In The World)') and eight multi-platinum albums (notably 2007's *Good Girl Gone Bad*, 2009's *Rated R* and 2016's *Anti*) and numerous collaborations, innovatively mixing pop, dancehall, R&B and EDM with dynamic results. She has become a global brand for the twenty-first century.

SLIPKNOT (VOCAL/INSTRUMENTAL GROUP, 1995–PRESENT)

Iowa-based nu-metallers Slipknot – Corey Taylor (vocals), James Root (guitar), Nathan Jordison (drums), Sean Crahan, Chris Fehn (both percussion), Sid Wilson (DJ), Mick Thompson (guitar), Paul Gray (bass) and Craig Jones (samples) – are literally unrecognizable. They hide behind masks and boiler suits, giving them a menacing anonymity. Word-of-mouth saw debut album *Slipknot* (1996, widely considered their best) sell close to a million copies. Four years and two albums later, 2008's *All Hope Is Gone* debuted at the top of the *Billboard* 200. But Gray's death brought turmoil that was not resolved until 2014's *.5: The Gray Chapter*. Their sixth studio album came out in 2019.

SNOW PATROL (VOCAL/INSTRUMENTAL GROUP, 1994–PRESENT)

Formed around Irish-born/Scotland-based singer Gary Lightbody, alt-rockers Snow Patrol broke through with their third album, *Final Straw* (2004), by which time Lightbody was the only original member. The album followed by *Eyes Open* (2006). They took a break after *Fallen Empires* (2011) but returned strongly in 2018 with *Wildness*.

Snow Patrol used to be known as Polar Bear, a name referenced in the title of their 1998 debut Songs for Polarbears.

THE STROKES (VOCAL/INSTRUMENTAL GROUP, 2001–PRESENT)

The Strokes – Julian Casablancas (vocals), Nick Valensi, Albert Hammond Jr. (both guitar), Nikolai Fraiture (bass) and Fabrizio Moretti (drums) – signify the mass appeal revivalist bands from the US can achieve. Their 2001 debut, *This It?*, was a short burst of well-trimmed songs and lean riffs. They've come back strongly from one hiatus, but 2013's *Comedown Machine* is their most recent album, although they still play shows.

TAYLOR SWIFT (SINGER/SONGWRITER, B. 1989)

Pennsylvania-born Shania Twain fan Taylor Swift was being courted by record companies aged 14. She had a writing credit on every track of her self-titled country-pop debut in 2006 and the breakthrough follow-up, *Fearless*, in 2008 that featured the eight-million selling global hit 'Love Song'. Pop took precedence over country on 2010's *Speak Now* as Swift went global with a world-conquering tour. Same again with *Red* (2012). Amid celebrity collaborations, perfumes and high-profile dalliances Swift and the formidable 'Team Swift' have moved relentlessly onward. *1989* in 2014 was totally pop and the production-heavy, moodier feel of 2017's *Reputation* headed towards a new era.

30 SECONDS TO MARS (INSTRUMENTAL/VOCAL GROUP, 1998–PRESENT)

Formed in Los Angeles by guitarist/vocalist Jared Leto and his brother, drummer Shannon, progressive rockers 30 Seconds To Mars released their eponymous conceptual debut album in 2002. The band added alternative rock to their style for 2005's *A Beautiful Lie* and played their first headlining tour of the US the following year. The tours expanded as the band's popularity grew with *This Is War* (2009), *Love, Lust, Faith and Dreams* (2013) and *America* (2018).

KANYE WEST (RAPPER/PRODUCER, B. 1977)

Aspiring rapper Kanye Omari West's career took off when his production work and beatmaking style on Jay Z's *The Blueprint* (2001) and other collaborations set him up for a solo career. His 2004 debut, *The College Dropout*, won a

Since her 2008 breakthrough, Taylor Swift has shed her country roots to reach stratospheric pop superstardom.

Grammy, as did 2005's *Late Registration*. Since then he's released another ten albums, notably *Graduation* (2007), *My Beautiful Dark Twisted Fantasy* (2010) *Yeezus* (2013) and *Kids See Ghosts* (2018). He's also continued a wide-ranging stream of collaborations, run a fashion line, married Kim Kardashian and frequently adopted a controversially high profile that has included invading the stage at the Grammys and expressing unpopular political views.

THE WHITE STRIPES (VOCAL/INSTRUMENTAL DUO, 1997–2011)

Divorcées Jack (vocals, guitar) and Meg White (percussion) formed The White Stripes with the mission statement of keeping a childlike simplicity in their music and imagery. Playing a thrilling version of blues and rock (owing as much to Led Zeppelin as pioneers like Son House), the pair found mass acclaim with third album *White Blood Cells* (2001), which married Jack's jackhammer riffing with a more tender, acoustic side. Next album *Elephant* (2003) explored multi-tracked vocals, and follow-up *Get Behind Me Satan* (2005) saw a darker approach. After 2007's *Icky Thump*, Meg got cold feet and they eventually disbanded.

JAY-Z (RAPPER/PRODUCER, B. 1969)

Achieving extraordinary success both as a rapper and a businessman, Shawn Corey Carter – Jay-Z – combined both talents from the start of his career in the mid-1990s when he formed his own company to release his records. Born and raised in a rough neighbourhood of Brooklyn, New York, Jay-Z initially funded his rapping career by drug dealing but the success of his *Reasonable Doubt* (1995) and *In My Lifetime, Vol. 1* (1997) gave him the breakthrough he quickly capitalized on with the Grammy-winning *Vol. 2… Hard Knock Life* (1999) and *The Black Album* (2003). He has had a dozen No. 1 albums and achieved mainstream success with artists as diverse as Rihanna, Linkin Park and Alicia Keys. As well as heading his own Roc-A-Fella, Roc Nation and Def Jam label Jay Z also owns the NBA Brooklyn Nets team, and the Tidal music streaming service. He is married to Beyoncé and their combined net worth is estimated at more than $1.6 billion.

The White Stripes were one of the most influential group to have come out of the early 2000s garage explosion.

NEARLY MADE-ITS

WHO TO INCLUDE?

In a book like this, it is necessary to make difficult choices about which artists to include that represent the sound of their particular eras. Some seem important at the time, but then as the years go by, their reputation and influence fades, and the reason for their inclusion in rock's story is unclear, while others' stars remain bright and shiny, even when their musical days are over. We regularly re-visit our list, and assess every artists' worthiness to remain as cheerleaders for their decade. Sadly, some do not make the cut, as we have to make way for new faces in this ever-evolving narrative. However, we don't want to be rid of them entirely, forever, so here are the names of the Nearly Made-Its. Gone, but not forgotten.

THE EARLY YEARS

Joe Brown
Bobby Darin
Ricky Nelson
Conway Twitty
The Ventures
T-Bone Walker
Marty Wilde

THE SIXTIES

Badfinger
Mike Bloomfield
Gary 'Us' Bonds
The Bonzo Dog Doo-Dah Band
The Crazy World of Arthur Brown
The Creation
Dick Dale
Donovan
Georgie Fame
Family
Wayne Fontana and the Mindbenders
The Fugs
Billy Fury
Moby Grape

The Graham Bond Organization
Richie Havens
The Herd
Herman's Hermits
Love
Marmalade
MC5
The Nice
P.J. Proby
Tim Rose
Screaming Lord Sutch
The Seeds
The Soft Machine

Spirit
The Swinging Blue Jeans
The Tornados
The Tremeloes
The Turtles

THE SEVENTIES

The Adverts
America
Atomic Rooster
Bachman-Turner Overdrive
Bauhaus

Can

Cheap Trick

Cockney Rebel

Devo

Dr Feelgood

Echo and The Bunnymen

Davd Edmunds

Peter Frampton

The Gang of Four

Generation X

Humble Pie

Jefferson Starship

John Martyn

The Mekons

Nazareth

Ted Nugent

The Rezillos

Tom Robinson

The Runaways

Boz Scaggs

Sham 69

Squeeze

Stiff Little Fingers

Teardrop Explodes

Ten Years After

Joe Walsh

Bill Withers

THE EIGHTIES

Big Audio Dynamite

Big Country

Cabaret Voltaire

The Cars

China Crisis

Dexy's Midnight Runners

The Go-Betweens

Joe Jackson

Judas Priest

Living Colour

John (Cougar)
Mellencamp

Men At Work

The Mission

New Model Army

The Replacements

The Sugarcubes

Saxon

Slayer

Spear of Destiny

The Stray Cats

Talk Talk

The Waterboys

THE NINETIES

Ash

The Boo Radleys

Steve Earl

Hole

Kula Shaker

Lush

Alanis Morissette

Napalm Death

Phish

Ride

Soundgarden

The Spin Doctors

Super Furry Animals

THE 21ST
CENTURY

Audioslave

Babyshambles

Justin Bieber

Bloc Party

Joe Bonamassa

Lana Del Ray

Disturbed

Drake

Editors

Five Finger Death
Punch

Gym Class Heroes

Norah Jones

Klaxons

The Kooks

The Lumineers

Orson

Maximo Park

Passion Pit

Katy Perry

The Raconteurs

Stormzy

Swans

Vampire Weekend

White Lies

Amy Winehouse

ACKNOWLEDGEMENTS

AUTHOR BIOGRAPHIES

MICHAEL HEATLEY (General Editor)

Michael Heatley edited the acclaimed *History of Rock* partwork (1981–84). He is the author of over 50 music biographies, ranging from Bon Jovi to Dave Grohl, as well as books on sport and TV. He has penned liner notes to more than 100 CD reissues, and written for magazines including *Music Week*, *Billboard*, *Goldmine*, *Radio Times* and the *Mail on Sunday* colour supplement.

RICHARD BUSKIN (Author)

Richard Buskin is the *New York Times* best-selling author of more than a dozen books on subjects ranging from record production, The Beatles and Sheryl Crow to Princess Diana, Phyllis Diller and Marilyn Monroe. His articles have appeared in newspapers such as the *New York Post*, *The Sydney Morning Herald*, *The Observer* and *The Independent*, and he also writes features and reviews for music magazines around the world. A native of London, England, he lives in Chicago.

ALAN CLAYSON (Author)

Musician and composer Alan Clayson has written over 30 books on musical subjects. These include the best-sellers *Backbeat: Stuart Sutcliffe - The Lost Beatle* (subject of a major film), *The Yardbirds* and *The Beatles* boxes. Moreover, as well as leading the legendary Clayson and The Argonauts, who reformed recently, his solo stage act also defies succinct description. For further information, please investigate www.alanclayson.com.

JOE CUSHLEY (Author)

Joe Cushley has written extensively for *Mojo*, *Q* and *Uncut* and contributed to several books on music, including *The Rough Guide To The Beatles* and *The Mojo Collection*. He compiles albums for Union Square Music, including the acclaimed *Balling The Jack*, *Beyond Mississippi* and *Definitive Story of CBGB* collections. He is a respected DJ and presents a regular show on London's Resonance FM. Joe is currently Theatre and Books Editor of *What's On In London* magazine.

RUSTY CUTCHIN (Author)

Rusty Cutchin has been a musician, recording engineer, producer, and journalist for over 25 years. He began his journalism career in New York as editor of *Cashbox*, the music-business trade magazine. Cutchin has been Technical Editor of *Guitar One* magazine, Associate Editor of *Electronic Musician* magazine, and Editor in Chief of *Home Recording Magazine*. As a recording engineer he has worked on records by artists such as Mariah Carey, Richie Sambora, Yoko Ono, C&C Music Factory and Queen Latifah. He has been a consulting editor and contributor to several books on home recording, guitar and music history.

HUGH FIELDER (Author; 2019 text updates)

Hugh Fielder can remember the 1960s even though he was there. He can remember the 1970s and 1980s because he was at *Sounds* magazine (RIP) and the 1990s because he was editor of Tower Records' *TOP* magazine. He has shared a spliff with Bob Marley, a glass of wine with David Gilmour, a pint with Robert Plant, a cup of tea with Keith Richards and a frosty stare with Axl Rose. He has watched Mike Oldfield strip naked in front of him and Bobby Womack fall asleep while he was interviewing him.

MIKE GENT (Author)

Nurturing an obsession with pop music which dates back to first hearing Slade's 'Gudbuy T'Jane' in 1972, Mike Gent remains fixated, despite failing to master any musical instrument, with the possible exception of the recorder. A freelance writer since 2001, he has contributed to *Writers' Forum*, *Book and Magazine Collector*, *Record Buyer*, *When Saturday Comes*, *Inside David Bowie and the Spiders* (DVD), *The Beatles 1962–1970* (DVD), Green Umbrella's *Decades* and *The Little Book of the World Cup*. Fascinated by the decade that gave the world glam, prog and punk rock, he is working on a novel set in the Seventies.

DREW HEATLEY (Author)

A writer for the *Nottingham Evening Post*, Drew Heatley was co-author of *Michael Jackson: Life Of A Legend 1958–2009* and *Kings Of Leon: Sex On Fire*, both published in 2009. He has also written books on football, including *Lost League Grounds* and *European Football Stadiums*.

JAKE KENNEDY (Author)

Jake Kennedy is a music journalist from west London. He worked at *Record Collector* for seven years, where he was Reviews Editor. He is the author of *Joy Division & The Making Of Unknown Pleasures*. He writes for numerous magazines and fanzines, and has been a correspondent for Radio 1, BBC 6 and *NME*. He has contributed to Colin Larkin's *Encyclopedia of Popular Music* and the *1001 Albums You Must Hear Before You Die* volume. He is married but never wants kids.

COLIN SALTER (Author)

Since he bought his first single – 'Reach Out I'll Be There' by The Four Tops in 1966 – Colin Salter has spent a life in music as composer, performer, promoter and researcher. His first performance, as a panto dame singing ABBA and Supertramp hits in 1975, was succeeded by stints in a Glasgow punk band, a Humberside jazz-folk group and a Kendal jam collective. He worked in theatre for 15 years as a sound engineer and writer of ambient soundtracks. Since 2003 he has been developing a live music network in rural Cumbria. He moonlights as a golden-oldies mobile DJ.

IAN SHIRLEY (Author)

Ian Shirley lived and pogoed his way through British punk rock and has been buying records and watching bands ever since. He is an experienced music journalist whose feature work and reviews appear in respected magazines like *Record Collector* and *Mojo*. He was written the biographies of Bauhaus and The Residents, as well as two science-fiction novels. He has also written the definitive tome on the links between comics and music: *Can Rock And Roll Save The World*. He is currently the editor of *Record Collector's Rare Record Price Guide* and has a collection of over 2,000 vinyl albums and 5,000 CDs.

JOHN TOBLER (Author)

John Tobler has been writing about popular music since the late 1960s, during which time he has written books on ABBA, The Beach Boys, The Beatles, Elton John, Elvis Presley, Cliff Richard and several generic titles. He has written for numerous magazines including *ZigZag*, *Billboard*, *Music Week*, *Melody Maker*, *NME*, *Sounds*, *Country Music People* and *Folk Roots*. He has written literally thousands of sleeve notes.

PiCTURE CREDiTS

FURTHER READING

Asbjornsen, D.E., *Scented Gardens of the Mind: A Comprehensive Guide to the Golden Era of Progressive Rock: 1968–1980*, Borderline Productions, New York, 2001

Billboard Guide to American Rock and Roll, Billboard Books, New York, 1997

Bogdanov, V. (ed.), et al, *All Music Guide to Rock*, Backbeat, London, 2002

Brend, M., *American Troubadors: Groundbreaking Singer-Songwriters of the 60s*, Backbeat Books, San Francisco, 2001

Byworth, T. (ed.), *The Illustrated Encyclopedia of Country Music*, Flame Tree Publishing, London, 2006

Carr, R. and Farren, M., *Elvis: The Complete Illustrated Record*, Eel Pie, London, 1982

Christe, I., *The Sound of the Beast: The Complete Headbanging History of Heavy Metal*, William Morrow, New York, 2003

Cohn, N., *Awopbopaloobopalopbamboom: The Golden Age of Rock*, Grove Press, New York, 2003

Draper, J., *Led Zeppelin Revealed*, Flame Tree Publishing, London, 2008

Draper, J., *The Rolling Stones Revealed*, Flame Tree Publishing, London, 2007

Du Noyer, P. (ed.), *The Illustrated Encyclopedia of Music*, Flame Tree Publishing, London, 2003

Ellinham, M., *The Rough Guide to Rock*, Rough Guides, London, 1996

Escott, C. with Hawkins, M., *Good Rockin' Tonight: Sun Records and the Birth of Rock 'n' Roll*, St. Martin's Press, New York, 1992

Fielder, H., *The Beatles Revealed*, Flame Tree Publishing, London, 2010

Fong-Torres, B., *The Hits Just Keep On Coming: The History of Top 40 Radio*, Backbeat Books, San Francisco, 2001

George-Warren, H. et al, *The Rolling Stone Encyclopedia of Rock & Roll*, Fireside, New York, 2001

Graff, G. and Durchholz, D., *MusicHound Rock: The Essential Album Guide*, Gale, 1998

Gray, M., *Song and Dance Man III: The Art of Bob Dylan*, Continuum International Publishing Group, New York, 1999

Harrison, H., *Kurt Cobain, Beyond Nirvana: The Legacy of Kurt Cobain*, The Archives Press, 1994

Heatley, M. (ed.), *Rock & Pop: The Complete Story*, Flame Tree Publishing, London, 2006

Ingham, C., *The Book Of Metal*, Carlton Books, London, 2002

Jeffries, N. (ed.), *The "Kerrang!" Direktory of Heavy Metal: The Indispensable Guide to Rock Warriors and Headbangin' Heroes*, Virgin Books, London, 1993

Juno, A., *Angry Women In Rock*, Juno Books, 2003

Kent, M., *The Who Revealed*, Flame Tree Publishing, London, 2010

Larkin, C., *Encyclopedia of Popular Music*, Virgin Publishing, London, 2002

Larkin, C., *The Guinness Who's Who of Sixties Music*, Guinness Publishing, London, 1992

Larkin, C., *The Virgin Encyclopedia of Heavy Rock*, Virgin Books, London, 1999

Larkin, C., *The Virgin Illustrated Encyclopedia of Rock*, Virgin Books, London, 1999

Logan, N. and Woffinden, B. (eds.), *The Illustrated New Musical Express Encyclopedia of Rock*, Hamlyn, London, 1976

Mandel, H. (ed.), *The Illustrated Encyclopedia of Jazz & Blues*, Flame Tree Publishing, London, 2005

Marcus, G., *Mystery Train: Images of America in Rock'n'Roll Music*, E P Dutton, 1975

McIver, J., *Nu-Metal: The Next Generation Of Rock And Punk*, Omnibus Press, London, 2002

McNeil, L. and McCain, G. (eds.), *Please Kill Me: The Uncensored Oral History of Punk*, Penguin USA, New York, 1997

McStravick, S. and Roos, J. (eds.), *Blues-rock Explosion: From The Allman Brothers To The Yardbirds*, Old Goat Publishing, California, 2002

Mulholland, G., *This Is Uncool: The 500 Greatest Singles Since Punk and Disco*, Cassell, London, 2002

Pascall, J., *The Golden Years of Rock & Roll*, Phoebus Publishing, New York, 1974

Porter, D., *Rapcore: The Nu-Metal Rap Fusion*, Plexus Publishing, New Jersey, 2002

Reynolds, S., *The Sex Revolts: Gender, Rebellion and Rock'n'roll*, Harvard University Press, Harvard, 1995

Shirley, I., *Pink Floyd Revealed*, Flame Tree Publishing, London, 2009

Smith, J., *Off the Record: An Oral History of Popular Music*, Warner Books, 1988

Spicer, A., *The Rough Guide to Rock (100 Essential CDs)*, Rough Guides, London, 1999

Strong, M.C., *The Great Metal Discography*, Mojo Books, London, 2002

Strong, M.C., *The Great Rock Discography*, Canongate Publications, Edinburgh, 2002

Swern, P. and Greenfield, S., *30 Years of Number Ones*, BBC Books, London, 1990

Thompson, D., *Pop*, Collectors Guide Publishing, 2000

Unterberger, R., *The Rough Guide to Music USA*, Rough Guides, London, 1999

Unterberger, R., *Turn! Turn! Turn!: The 60s Folk-Rock Revolution*, Backbeat UK, London, 2002

Wall, G. and Hinton, B., *Ashley Jennings: The Guv'nor & The Rise of Folk Rock*, Helter Skelter Publishing, London, 2002

Whitburn, J., *Billboard Top 1000 Singles 1955–2000*, Hal Leonard Publishing, Milwaukee, 2001

White, C., *The Life and Times of Little Richard*, Harmony Books, 1984

INDEX

Page references in *italics* represent illustrations; page references in **bold** identify major articles on the subject. All band members are not always separately indexed, but can be found in the major band article; all are referred to by their stage names.